CHAKRAS,
REIKI HEALING
AND
BUDDHISM
FOR BEGINNERS

Balance Yourself and Learn Practical
Teachings for Healing the Ailments of
the Soul to Awaken Your Body's
Energies and Transform Anxiety &
Stress

Sarah Allen

This extends to creating a secondary or tertiary copy of the work or a recorded copy and is only allowed with the express written consent from the Publisher. All additional right reserved.

The information in the following pages is broadly considered a truthful and accurate account of facts and as such, any inattention, use, or misuse of the information in question by the reader will render any resulting actions solely under their purview. There are no scenarios in which the publisher or the original author of this work can be in any fashion deemed liable for any hardship or damages that may befall them after undertaking information described herein.

Additionally, the information in the following pages is intended only for informational purposes and should thus be thought of as universal. As befitting its nature, it is presented without assurance regarding its prolonged validity or interim quality. Trademarks that are mentioned are done without written consent and can in no way be considered an endorsement from the trademark holder.

TABLE OF CONTENTS

Chakras Healing for Beginners

CHAPTER 1 11

WHAT ARE THEY AND WHAT ARE THEY FOR? 11

WHAT ARE THE CHAKRAS, AND HOW DO THEY WORK? 11

CHAPTER 2 16

7 WONDERFUL ENERGY CENTERS 16

CHAPTER 3 26

THE CHAKRAS, ENERGY POINTS THAT YOU MUST
ACTIVATE 26

CHAPTER 4 32

THE MISSION AND FUNCTIONING OF THE CHAKRAS
....32

CYCLES OF HUMAN EVOLUTION IN LIGHT OF CHAKRA
THEORY 41

CHAPTER 5 46

THE ORIGIN OF BLOCKAGES IN CHAKRAS 46

CHAPTER 6 60

THE DISSOLUTION OF THE BLOCKAGES 60

CHAPTER 7 74

HOW WE CAN DETECT THE CHAKRAS WE HAVE
BLOCKED 74

KINESIOLOGICAL MUSCLE TEST 79

CHAPTER 8 88

SEXUALITY AND CHAKRAS 88

MISSION AND OPERATION OF THE FIRST CHAKRA 95

POSSIBILITIES OF PURIFICATION AND ACTIVATION OF THE
FIRST CHAKRA 100

MISSION AND OPERATION OF THE SECOND CHAKRA 106

POSSIBILITIES OF PURIFICATION AND ACTIVATION OF THE
SECOND CHAKRA 110

MISSION AND OPERATION OF THE THIRD CHAKRA 115

POSSIBILITIES OF PURIFICATION AND ACTIVATION OF THE
THIRD CHAKRA 121

CHAPTER 9 128

MISSION AND OPERATION OF THE FOURTH CHAKRA
....128
POSSIBILITIES OF PURIFICATION AND ACTIVATION OF THE
FOURTH CHAKRA...134
POSSIBILITIES OF PURIFICATION AND ACTIVATION OF THE
FIFTH CHAKRA 148
MISSION AND OPERATION OF THE SIXTH CHAKRA...........154
POSSIBILITIES OF PURIFICATION AND ACTIVATION OF THE
SIXTH CHAKRA 161
CONCLUSION **167**

TABLE OF CONTENTS
Reiki Healing for Beginners

INTRODUCTION **171**
CHAPTER 1 173
EVERYTHING YOU NEED TO KNOW ABOUT REIKI173
CHAPTER 2.. 180
THE UNIVERSE IS ENERGY 180
CHAPTER 3.. 187
THE HUMAN ENERGY BODY FROM A BUDDHIST
POINT OF VIEW...187
CHAPTER 4.. 194
PRACTICE REIKI DAILY - FOR A LIFETIME 194
CHAPTER 5.. 202
THE PATH TO HAPPINESS AND WELL-BEING 202
CHAPTER 6 212
THE INAUGURATION IN REIKI...212
CHAPTER 7 219
FEELING COMFORTABLE MEANS BEING AT HOME
....219
CHAPTER 8.. 228
THE TEACHING CONTENT OF REIKI 228
CHAPTER 9.. 234
REIKI IS PEACE AND SILENCE 234
CHAPTER 10 243
PRACTICE DAILY FOR A BETTER WORLD 243

CHAPTER 11..**249**
REIKI IN THE PRESENT DAY, REIKI FOR THE
EXHAUSTED SELF 249
CHAPTER 12 ....**255**
WIRELESSLY HAPPY? REIKI SHOWS US HOW...............255
CHAPTER 13 ....**263**
THE REIKI-GRADE...263
CHAPTER 14 ....**275**
REIKI LIFE RULES..275
CHAPTER 15 ....**282**
ON MOUNT KURAMA NEAR KYOTO................................282

TABLE OF CONTENTS

Buddhism for Beginners

INTRODUCTION 302
CHAPTER 1..306
KNOWING YOUR MIND 306
FIXED MINDSET VS GROWTH MINDSET 312
GROWTH MINDSET 316
ANGER MANAGEMENT...334
DON'T LET FEAR CONTROL YOUR LIFE 340
BEST STRATEGIES TO HEALING YOURSELF...............358
CHAPTER 2..377
WHAT IS BUDDHISM? 377
ORIGINS OF BUDDHISM 377
THE STORY OF SIDDHARTHA GAUTAMA.....................378
BUDDHISM 101 380
THE BASICS OF BUDDHISM...381
CHAPTER 3..397
THE TEACHING OF BUDDHISM.....................................397
THE NOBLE EIGHTFOLD PATH...398
DHARMA - THE PATH TO PERFECT
ENLIGHTENMENT 400
SUFFERING AND NEUROSIS 401
POSTURES OF BUDDHA 407
CHAPTER 4..410
BUDDHISM NUMBERS 3 410

THE 3 JEWELS OF REFUGE 410
THE 3 UNIVERSAL TRUTHS 412
THE 3 POISONS 415
THE DIFFERENT SCHOOLS OF BUDDHISM 416
BUDDHIST PHILOSOPHY 101 417
THE 4 NOBLE TRUTHS 418
THE 4 DHARMA SEALS 419
THE 5 SKANDHAS 419
THE 6 PERFECTIONS OF MAHAYANA BUDDHISM 422
CHAPTER 5...423
MINDFULNESS MEDITATION...423
BENEFITS OF MINDFULNESS 423
TRAINING THE MIND 425
CLASSIC MINDFULNESS MEDITATION STEP-BY-STEP
....426
DIFFERENT BUDDHIST RITUALS 427
CHAPTER 6...429
JAPANESE BUDDHISM 429
BUDDHISM IN THIS ERA 429
CREATING A MEDITATION SPACE IN YOUR HOME 432
5 STEPS TO START BUDDHIST MEDITATION 433
BUDDHISM FOR CHILDREN 438
CHAPTER 7...442

CHAKRAS HEALING FOR BEGINNERS

Discovering the Secrets to Detect and Dissolve Energy Blockages - Balance and Awaken your full Potential through Yoga, Meditation and Mindfulness

Sarah Allen

CHAPTER 1

WHAT ARE THEY AND WHAT ARE THEY FOR?

The chakras are points of energy that, when in balance, enhance our vital energy. In turn, that energy assures us of greater well-being both physically and mentally. In recent years, a wide variety of complementary therapies of oriental origin have become popular in the West, recognized for their ability to promote well-being. While the evidence on their safety and efficacy is limited, the testimonies of those who have tried them have aroused the interest of many patients. This time, we want to talk a little more about the chakras and their uses.

According to sources such as Wikipedia, the chakras come from Hinduism and refer to centers of immeasurable energy located in the body, specifically from the perineum to the area of the aura that is above the crown. There are seven, according to the Hindu tradition, and each one has a determined, energetic vibration that is associated with aspects of life and health. Let's see more about this.

What are the chakras, and how do they work?

The term chakra comes from Sanskrit and means "circle" or "disk." According to Hinduism, the chakras are 7 energy centers that are located in different parts of the human body. They function as "valves," regulating the flow of energy and, depending on their location, vary in their vibratory force and speed.

In India, it is believed that inhaled air (known as prana energy) runs through the body giving strength to the energy centers. The chakras receive, accumulate and distribute prana to optimize the functions of various parts of our body.

Therefore, since ancient times, they have been used as a resource in energy medicine, suggesting that they can contribute to treating certain medical conditions and problems.

However, although studies have been carried out in this regard, such as a study published recently in Global Advances in Health and Medicine, there is insufficient evidence to ensure that they are useful against diseases.

According to this research, the chakra system is related to the endocrine system of the body. In addition, as we have already mentioned, it has 7 vital energy centers, which mainly focus on the spine.

Being producers of energy vortices, the chakras, when healthy, provide energy information through which the body's systems create a global information system, which will be the one that affects well-being.

However, more research is required to determine if these types of therapies really help to fight diseases through the subtle energy generated at these points.

What feelings are the chakras associated with?

Despite the lack of evidence, chakras continue to stand out in alternative medicine as an adjunct against problems related to the mentioned glands. In addition, following the Hindu and Buddhist texts that speak about it, they are also associated with certain feelings.

1) Muladhara the Root Chakra

- It is located between the anus and the genitals.
- The color that identifies it is red.
- Its element is the earth.
- It is blocked by fear. Therefore, let the fears be clearly displayed to free them.

2) Svadhisthana or Chakra Sacro

- It is found in the sacrum.
- It is associated with the color orange.
- Its assigned element is water.
- Guilt blocks it. Hence, we have to get rid of this. And, for this, it is necessary to know how to forgive.

13

3) Manipura or solar plexus chakra

- It is located two fingers above the navel.
- Its color is yellow.
- Fire is its element.
- It is blocked by shame.

4) Anahata or Heart Chakra

- It is located in the heart region.
- Its color is green.
- Its assigned element is air.
- It is blocked by pain.
- It is related to the feelings of the heart.

5) Vishuddha or Chakra de la Garganta

- It is located in the throat region.
- It corresponds to the color blue.
- Its element is ether.
- It is related to communication.

6) Ajna or Third Eye Chakra

- It is located between the two eyes.
- Its color is violet.
- It is associated with intuition and taste.
- It is blocked by illusion.

7) Sahasrara or Crown Chakra

- It is in the crown.
- It corresponds to the color violet or indigo.
- It is blocked by worldly ties.

The chakras are another resource that give us oriental medicine as a supplement to promote wellness. However, given the lack of evidence, it is important to consider it a therapeutic option and not a first-line treatment against diseases.

To learn more about its benefits and practice, it is convenient to seek the guidance of an expert. It is often combined with other health therapies, such as yoga, quartz baths, and deep breathing exercises.

CHAPTER 2

7 WONDERFUL ENERGY CENTERS

The chakras are energy centers located in the human body that have been identified by oriental culture. In these points, biological and psychological aspects of our way of relating are integrated, so that through its balance we can achieve well-being.

According to Hinduism, the balance of the chakras is achieved based on how we interact with ourselves, with other people, with nature, and with the divine. Being unbalanced is when some personal and social dysfunctions manifest.

It is important to know that each of the chakras is related to a color, a location in the body, and a sound, which promotes their balance and activation when meditating. Here we tell you about each of these wonderful energy centers.

"Nothing leaves our life until it teaches us what we need to learn."

-Pema Chödrön-

First Chakra: Root Chakra

Name: Muladhara

Color: Red

Associated element: Earth

Location: The base of the column

Sound: LAM

This chakra is related to biological, psychological, and relational support. In this way, this center has to do with group strength and roots. The associated parts of our body are the legs, the feet, the immune system, the spine, and the bones.

In addition, this energy center is the first one we develop and is the one that sustains everyone else. Through this, we develop in relationships with nature, with others and with ourselves. In addition, it is strongly connected with the energy of our ancestors, which can help us in the most difficult moments.

However, on a psychological level, it has to do with security, defense and the ability to provide needs. These aspects foster support, as they have to do with the strength, protection, learning and beliefs of our groups.

When this chakra is not in equilibrium, it could be associated with dysfunctions from a lack of support. For example, immune system conditions, back pain, and leg pain. And on a psychological level, it can be related to mood disorders such as depression and anxiety.

To keep it in balance, we must be aware of the way we relate to our roots, for example, the way we are with our families and the beliefs we have learned. In addition, we can be in balance through meditation.

«Your beliefs are not made of realities. It is your reality that is made of beliefs».

-Richard Bandler-

Second Chakra: The Wonderful Way In Which We Interact!

Name: Svadhisthana

Color: Orange

Associated element: Water

Location: From the lower abdomen to the navel area

Sound: VAM

It's about the dynamics we have with others, with nature and with ourselves. Therefore, it has to do with the vision we have of the world. Thus, it is linked to creativity, money management, ethics and sexuality. In other words, it relates to the way we link and interact.

Now, in our body, it is mainly in: the sexual organs, the intestine, the bladder and the vertebrae. Thus, dysfunctions are associated with problems in these places. On a psychological level, the imbalance reflects aspects such as: attachment, pressure, lack of satisfaction, impulsivity, and a feeling that the world is flat.

To keep it in balance we can be attentive to our creative selves, the way we manage money, the ability to put ourselves in the place of others and the way in which we communicate. To activate it, meditation is useful.

Third Chakra: Personal Power!

Name: Manipuraka

Color: Yellow

Associated item: Fire

Location: Solar plexus

Sound: RAM

It is the chakra of self-esteem; it is related to intention, coordination and control. This chakra has to do with our self and with our personality.

The associated organs are: the stomach, the liver, the kidneys, the pancreas, the adrenal glands, and the central part of the spine. When not in balance, they manifest: fear, intimidation, anorexia, bulimia, arthritis and chronic or acute indigestion, among others.

As for the emotional manifestations, this is one of the chakras that is linked to: trust, self-care, and others, and responsibility when making decisions. When it is in imbalance we have problems in these aspects. To balance it, meditation is useful, to connect with our inner strength and visualize what we truly want.

> *"The measure of what we are is what we do with what we have."*

> *-Vince Lombardi-*

Fourth Chakra: The Incredible Power Of Emotions

Name: Anahata

Color: Green

Associated item: Air

Location: Chest center

Sound: Yam

This is the energy center of unconditional love. It is related to understanding, love and forgiveness. On an organic level it has to do with: the heart, lungs, shoulders, arms, circulatory system and diaphragm. Then, physical dysfunctions reflect: circulatory system failures, asthma, breast cancer, and pneumonia.

Its emotional manifestations are: love and hate, self-centeredness, loneliness, commitment, hope, forgiveness, compassion and trust.

Thus, emotional dysfunctions have to do with: dependence, confusion, not believing, lack of trust, and inability to forgive and commit.

> *"Love unconditionally, don't ask for anything in return. You will receive a lot without asking - you will make it something else - but don't be a beggar. In love to be an emperor. Just give and wait, what happens: you will receive a thousand times more."*

> *-Osho-*

Fifth Chakra: The Will

Name: Vishudda

Color: Blue

Associated Element: Ether

Location: Throat

Sound: Ham

Chakra 5 is that of will and self-expression. The organs involved in this energy center are: the throat, the thyroid, the trachea, the cervical vertebrae, the mouth, the hypothalamus, the teeth, and the gums, among others. Physical dysfunctions have to do with conditions in these parts, for example: hoarseness or thyroid disorders.

Emotionally it is related to: choice, expression, faith, knowledge, judgment, criticism, addiction and following goals. Then, it is linked to the ability to express what we feel, make decisions and follow motivations. When it is unbalanced it has to do with the way of judging and the difficulty in communicating and deciding.

"Who has will has strength."

-Menandro-

Sixth Chakra: The Power Of Our Mind

Name: Ajna

Color: Violet

Associated item: Light

Location: The center of the forehead

Sound: Om

This wonderful center of energy is the one that connects with wisdom, intuition and perception. On a physical level it is related to: the nervous system, eyes, ears and nose. In imbalance there may be dysfunctions such as: neurological disorders, blindness, deafness and learning problems.

Now, it is manifested psychologically in: the way to evaluate ourselves, the truth, emotional intelligence and tolerance when listening to other people's ideas. In other words, it is the power we have to evaluate our own beliefs and attitudes, introspection and the capacity for judgment. If it is in imbalance, we show problems in these aspects.

> "Rejoice because every place is
> here and every moment is now."

-Buddha-

Seventh Chakra: The Spiritual Connection

Name: Sahasrara

Color: White

Associated item: Cosmic sound

Location: Crown

Sound: Silence

This is the energy center of the spiritual, of the transcendent, the force chakra between mind, body and spirit. So, it is related to: the ability we have to trust life, generosity, global vision, faith, inspiration, and devotion. When it is not balanced, energy disorders and extreme sensitivity to environmental factors can occur.

> *"The secret of human freedom is to act well, without attachment to the results."*
>
> *-Bhagavad Gita-*

Now, as you have seen, to revitalize our chakras we could meditate and thus enter into a deep connection. Also, to facilitate the practice and balance of the chakras, we can focus on the colors, sounds, elements and places of the body of each chakra. In addition, it will also help us visualize the balance we want to reach into our lives and perform healthy practices emotionally and physically.

Furthermore, we can listen to our body and mind to know which chakras are in imbalance, and try to reach a state of fullness. It's about being attentive to the problems we have and trying to solve them. Meditation could help us connect and find a way out.

According to the oriental culture, peace is achieved through the care of this energy flow. It is a way that allows personal growth and from which you can learn step by step to reach harmony, through deep connection. In addition, being attentive to our chakras is a source of self-knowledge. Learn from yourself and your environment by seeking energy balance because, as Caroline Myers said, "the healing of the body comes through the healing of the soul."

Myss, C. (1996). Anatomy of the Spirit: The healing of the body comes through the soul. Pocket Zeta, Spain.

CHAPTER 3

THE CHAKRAS, ENERGY POINTS THAT YOU MUST ACTIVATE

Here we discuss how you can optimize the chakras in different ways: gems, aromas, music, massages, etc.

The chakras are 7 energy points that are strategically distributed in our body. They regulate our health. In addition, they can influence us emotionally and spiritually.

For this reason, if we do not lead a coherent, kind and beneficial lifestyle, we cannot find balance. We could even get blocked.

Next we will discuss how you can improve the functioning of the chakras. For this, we can resort to some natural methods such as music, aromas, gems, colors or massages.

So if you want to improve your day-to-day life and enjoy well-being, do not hesitate to give them a chance. Rest assured, it will be worth it.

As mentioned earlier, the chakras are 7 energy points that are found along our spine and head.

They follow a straight line right in the center of our body and regulate the different functions of the body, as well as our abilities and emotions. They are the following:

- **Root Chakra:** Is located at the base of the spine. It is linked to trust.

- **Sacral Chakra:** It is found in the sacrum bone, above the genitals. It is related to sexuality and creativity.

- **Solar Plexus Chakra:** The third chakra is two fingers above the navel. It is linked with wisdom.

- **Heart Chakra:** It is in the center of the chest. Thus, this chakra is related to love and healing.

- **Throat Chakra:** This chakra corresponds to the throat and, therefore, also to the thyroid. Work communication.

- **Eyebrow Chakra:** In the eyebrows we find the famous third eye, related to consciousness and knowledge.

- **Chakra of the Crown:** In the crown is the seventh and last chakra. It is the energetic center of spirituality, which connects our body with the highest.

1. Musical notes

27

To begin, we must know that the chakras correspond to the 7 musical notes. It is not a coincidence, since everything in nature has its harmony.

Therefore, music can also help us physically and spiritually. And we will start, for example, singing the note of the chakra that we want to help balance. Thus, each chakra corresponds to its note:

- **Root: Do**
- **Sacral: Re**
- **Solar Plexus: Mi**
- **Heart: Fa**
- **Throat: Sun**
- **Entree: The**
- **Crown: Yes**

2. Essential oils

Aromatherapy can offer us a pleasant and delicious therapy by means of essential oils. Thus, it can help us improve our physical, spiritual and emotional wellbeing. In this way, each chakra has its specific aromas:

- **Root: Cedar and clove**
- **Sacral: Ylang-ylang and sandalwood**

- **Solar plexus: Lavender, rosemary and bergamot**

- **Heart: Rose, mint and musk**
- **Throat: Sage and eucalyptus**
- **Entree: Mint and jasmine**
- **Crown: Olive and lotus**

First, we can use the essential oils to massage the corresponding points.

However, we must ensure that they are of the highest quality, since there are many chemical essences on the market. These only work to give a scent, but not to cure.

3. Colors

The chakras are related to different types of vibrations which, in turn, correspond to colors.

In this sense, the chromotherapy or healing through color can help us in finding balance.

Therefore, the chakras correspond to the following colors:

- **Root: Red**
- **Sacral: Orange**
- **Solar Plexus: Yellow**

- **Heart: Green**
- **Throat: Blue**

- **Entrecejo: Indigo**
- **Crown: Violet**

The colors that surround us can influence our quality of life.

Actually, when choosing clothes or accessories, painting the house or putting certain pictures, we are promoting one aspect or the other.

For this reason, it is recommended that you choose them conscientiously. In addition, you can also use chromotherapy lamps.

4. Gems

Gemmotherapy is a curative therapy according to which each gem or stone would have medicinal properties.

Also, each chakra has its own. In this way, we can put it on that part of the body through accessories or while we are resting. In this sense, the corresponding gems are the following:

- **Root: Ruby and Garnet**
- **Sacral: amber and topaz**

- **Solar Plexus: Agate**

- **Heart: rose quartz and malachite**

- **Throat: aquamarine, turquoise and lapis lazuli**

- **Entrecejo: amethyst and moonstone**

- **Crown: white quartz and diamond**

5. Massages

Finally, massages can also contribute to improving the functioning of our body's energy points.

Thus, there are different therapies such as yoga or reiki that work with this type of energy. However, we must perform them in appropriate places and with certified professionals.

In addition, we can combine massages with the other techniques to multiply their effects.

Some examples are massages with essential oils and gems, set with colored light and with the appropriate musical accompaniment. An experience for all the senses and levels of the individual!

CHAPTER 4

THE MISSION AND FUNCTIONING OF THE CHAKRAS

In this chapter, we will look at the most fundamental information on the functioning of the chakras. The theoretical understanding of these relationships is the basis on which practical knowledge about each of the individual chakras described in this book is based.

The writings that tradition has bequeathed to us mention a large number of chakras: 88,000. This means that in the human body there is hardly any point other than a sensitive organ for the reception, transformation and retransmission of energies. However, most of these chakras are very small and play a subordinate role in the energy system. There are approximately 40 secondary chakras that are assigned greater importance. The most important of these are in the area of the spleen, in the nape of the neck, in the palms of the hands and on the soles of the feet. The seven main chakras, located along a vertical axis next to the anterior half of the body, are so decisive for the functioning of the most fundamental and essential areas of the body, spirit and soul of man, that a chapter has been dedicated to each of them. In these chapters you will be able to see what specific mood-spiritual qualities are related to each of the chakras, which body areas are subject to their influence, how the blockages of each of the chakras affect, and many other things.

Here, let's describe the characteristics that are common to the seven main chakras. They truly settle in man's etheric body. They resemble funnel-shaped floral calyxes and a varied number of petals. Therefore, in the cultural sphere of the East they are often also called parrot flowers. The subdivisions of the flowers into independent petals represent the nadis or energy channels through which energies flow and penetrate the chakras and through which energy is relayed from the chakras to the non-material bodies. Its number varies from four channels in the radical center to almost a thousand energy channels in the center of the crown.

The chakras are in a permanent circular motion. To this quality they owe the name "chakra," which in Sanskrit means "wheel." The rotating movement of these wheels causes the energy to be drawn into the chakras. If the direction of rotation changes, the energy is radiated from the chakras.

The chakras can rotate to the right or to the left. Here one can recognize a contrasting principle in man and woman, or complementation in the expression of the energies of different "species" since the same chakras that in man turn to the right

33

(clockwise), in the woman turn left, and vice versa. Every right turn has as its peculiarity a predominance of the male quality, an accentuation of the yang according to Chinese doctrine; that is, it represents will and activity, and in its negative form of manifestation, also aggression and violence. Every left turn has a predominance of yin and represents sensitivity and agreement, and in its negative aspect, weakness.

The direction of rotation changes from one chakra to another. Thus, the basal chakra of man turns to the right, and more actively expresses the qualities of this center: in the sense of conquest and dominance in the material and sexual realm. On the other hand, the woman's first chakra has a sense of rotation to the left, which makes her more sensitive to the earth's life-giving and spawning force, which flows through the radical center. In the second chakra the signs are reversed: the direction of rotation to the right in the woman indicates greater active energy in the expression of feelings; man's sense of rotation to the left can preferably be interpreted here as the receptive, often even as a passive attitude. And so on.

Sense of spin of chakras in women

The continuous line that rises undulating symbolizes Pingala, solar energy, and the dotted line represents Ida, the lunar force.

Knowing the direction of rotation of the chakras allows them to be incorporated into some forms of therapy. For example, in aromatherapy you can apply the aromas with a circular movement in the corresponding direction, or also a plot with the precious stones turns in the same sense that the energy centers have.

Most people's chakras have an average length of approximately 10 centimeters. In each of the energy centers there are all the chromatic vibrations, although it always masters a certain color, which coincides with the main function of the corresponding chakra. In a superior development of man, the chakras continue to spread and increase their vibration frequency. Also, their colors become lighter and more radiant.

The size and number of vibrations (frequency) of the chakras determine the quantity and quality of the energies they absorb from the most varied sources. These are energies that come to us from the cosmos, the stars, nature, the radiation of all things and all the people of our environment, our different non-material bodies, and also from the original unmanifested reason of all beings. These energies reach the chakras, in part, through the nadis, and, in part, flow into them directly. The two most important and fundamental forms of energy are absorbed through the radical center and the coronal center. Between these two chakras runs the

Sushumna, to which all the energy centers are attached through their "petioles" and which feeds all of them with life force. It is the channel through which the so-called Kundalini energy rises, which rests, "rolled like a snake", at the lower end of the spine, and whose gateway is the radical center. Kundalini energy represents the cosmic energy of creation, which in Indian wisdom is also called Shakti or the female manifestation of God. This active aspect of the divine being provokes all manifestations of creation. Its opposite pole is the pure, amorphous and self-inherent aspect of the divine being, in which we will have a closer look later.

In most people, Kundalini energy only flows through Sushumna in scant proportion. As he wakes up from a growing development of consciousness, he ascends through the spinal canal in an ever-increasing flow and activating the different chakras. This activation results in an extension of the energy centers and an acceleration of their frequencies. Kundalini energy feeds chakras with the energy vibration that empowers men to gradually open up in the course of their evolution all the faculties and energies that act in the different energy planes and materials of creation, with the intention to integrate these energies into your life.

During its ascent, Kundalini energy is transformed into a different vibration in each chakra, corresponding to the functions of the respective chakra. This vibration is minimal in the radical center and finds its maximum expression in the coronal center. Transformed vibrations are relayed to different non-material bodies or to the physical body, and perceived as feelings, ideas and physical sensations.

The degree to which a person allows the action of Kundalini energy depends on the degree of consciousness he has in the different spheres of life represented by the chakras, and the extent to which stress and unprocessed experiences have caused blockages in the chakras. The more conscious a person is, the more open and active their chakras are, so that Kundalini energy can flow to them more intensely; and the more intense this flow of energy, the more active the chakras become, which in turn awakens greater awareness. In this way a permanent cycle of mutual influence arises, as soon as we begin to eliminate our blockages and to walk a path of the development of consciousness.

In addition to Kundalini energy, there is another force flowing into each of the chakras through the Sushumna canal of the spine. It is the energy of the pure divine being, of the unmanifested aspect of God. It enters through the coronal chakra and makes man know in all planes of life the amorphous existential aspect of God as the original, immutable and penetrating reason of that manifestation. This energy is particularly suitable for removing chakra blockages. In Indian wisdom it is called Shiva, the divinity, which is the great destroyer of ignorance and which, with its mere presence, unleashes a transformation towards the divine.

This representation of chakras from Nepal is approximately 350 years old. The seven main chakras, represented by parrot flowers, can be recognized. Each of these chakra flowers represents a plane of consciousness, starting with the lower ones and ending with the upper ones at the top. The main energy channels, Sushumna, Ida and Pingala, can also be recognized.

Thus, Shiva and Shakti work hand in hand in the integral development of the person, which we have integrated into our lives both the divine and all the planes of the relative being.

Alongside Sushumna, there are two other energy channels that play a particularly important role in the energy system: in Sanskrit they are called Ida and Pingala. Pingala doubles as a carrier of solar energy, full of burning and motor force. This channel starts to the right of the radical chakra and ends at the top of the right nostril. Ida is the carrier of the cooling and serene lunar energy. This channel begins to the left of the radical chakra and ends in the left nostril. On their way from the radical center to the nose, both nadis sink around Sushumna.

Ida and Pingala have the ability to absorb prana directly from the air by breathing, and to expel poisonous substances into the exhalation. Together with Sushumna, they constitute the three main channels of the energy system. In addition, there are a large number of other nadis that provide chakras with energies from secondary chakras and non-material bodies, and that relay that energy to neighboring energy bodies.

But chakras also directly absorb vibrations from the environment, vibrations that correspond to their frequencies. Thus, through their different forms of operation, they unite us with the events of our environment, nature and the universe, serving as antennas for the full range of energy vibrations. We can also call chakras non-material sensory organs. Our physical body, together with its senses, is a vehicle adapted to the laws of life of our planet. And with whose help we manage in the external realm of life, but with which we can simultaneously realize our values on earth, and know internal processes. The chakras serve as receptors for all the energy vibrations and information that come from the physical realm. They are the openings that unite us with the unlimited world of the most subtle energies.

The chakras also radiate energy directly into the environment, thus modifying the atmosphere around us. Through the chakras we can emit healing vibrations and messages, conscious and unconscious, influencing both positively and negatively on people, situations and even matter.

To experience an inner fulness, and the energy, creativity, knowledge, love and blessing associated with it, all chakras must be open and work in mutual harmony. However, this circumstance occurs in very few people. In general, different chakras have a different degree of activation. And many times only the lower two chakras are activated. In people who hold an outstanding social position, or who in some way exert a great influence, it is common that, in addition, the solar plexus chakra is disproportionately active. Any combination of open, blocked or marked chakras may exist in a particular sense. In addition, these degrees oscillate throughout a lifetime, since at different times different topics may become important.

Therefore, the knowledge of the chakras can provide you with invaluable help for self-knowledge, and guide you on your way to discover all the innate faculties, giving you a life of maximum fullness and joy.

Cycles of human evolution in light of chakra theory

In our universe, everything is subject to clearly specific rhythms and cycles. These begin on the atomic plane and extend to all forms of existence of the entire creation. In a heartbeat and in our breathing, in the rhythmic succession of days and nights, in the seasons, and even in the predictable displacement of the stars, we detect the rhythmic regularities described. Also in the evolution of living beings we can detect periodic cycles. Thus, for example, in the plants, we observe how the germ first appears, then the leaves, the bud, the flower, and finally the fruit. A certain sequence of evolutionary phases is always respected, which are not freely interchangeable with each other: it is quite evident that man, as being intelligent in a material body, has also evolved according to periodic laws. Not only do they get older every day and their abilities and experiences increase, but their evolution is consumed in very special mental and spiritual evolutionary cycles. Not all the issues are of the same importance in all times of life, and if we look at this fact more closely we realize that "Mother Nature" gives us very specific tasks in specific times, tasks that must be solved at that exact time. While these tasks can be presented with different 'clothes,' it can generally be said that a given evolution can only be optimally summed up at a certain time in life. For example, it is very

41

difficult to recover at 25 years of age, an evolution that we omitted when we were between 5 and 12 years old. And so it happens that the vital building of some people is supported for a lifetime on wobbly foundations, because in the years of youth certain experiences were not made or only certain capacities were insufficiently formed.

The knowledge of the cycles of life is not new: in any case we could say that it has been lost again. Various intellectual schools, however, continue to imply this knowledge today with the total evolution of man. In anthroposophical circles, and within them Waldorf's pedagogy is fundamentally known, these relationships are well known. Learning plans were reasonably developed to adapt them to a correct human evolution based on evolutionary cycles of children's natural and internal processes. The founder of the anthroposophical movement, Rudolf Steiner, left us an immense legacy on this subject (for example, the book Vom Lebenslauf des Menschen "The Curriculum of Man"). In anthroposophical anthropology we recognize a vital path that takes place in clearly articulated rhythmic phases, divided into "seven-year cycles." It is quite clear that time hides in itself different qualities, or that at certain times in his life man is differently "open" to certain influences and experiences, and therefore "mature" for totally specific evolutionary progress.

It is interesting that this knowledge is seamlessly integrated into the knowledge of the functioning and functions of our chakra system. Thus, starting from the basal center, we move every seven years to a different chakra, whose qualities constitute a fundamental theme of our life during that time. Simultaneously, this period is divided into seven additional main themes, each of them lasting one year, and they also begin in the basal chakra, to travel year after year one of the following seven chakras.

Then begins a new cycle of another seven years, but this time with the fundamental pattern of the second chakra. Thus, year after year we go through one more evolutionary stage, which consists of the fundamental theme of the septenary and seven main themes of a year. After 5 x 7 years we have reached about half of our life. After 7 x 7 years of life we have finished a full cycle of 49 years. So as we enter the fiftieth year of life, a whole new stage begins, we effectively have the opportunity to start again from the beginning, but this time in a "top octave" of evolution. Also after the age of 50, totally special learning stages await us, which must be summed up. Thus, some people end at the age of 98, the second great journey through human evolutionary cycles.

Every year that passes brings us a new main theme, and every seven years a new fundamental theme; in this process the topics are always complimented in the most optimal way. The knowledge of the meaning and function of each chakra shows us the way to optimally take advantage of each particular year for the benefit of our evolution. In addition, it allows us to understand in greater depth the evolution of our children and always give them the right kind of dedication and stimuli that will be most valuable to them in a given time.

Also, in the material plane, a transformation is consuming with a cyclical rhythm of seven years. You may have already heard the existence of the biological proof that our bodies are completely renewed every seven years. At seven years old, all body cells have been replaced by new ones, and we are completely new people from a physical point of view. If, on the other hand, on the psychic plane it seems as if in those seven years nothing has actually changed, it is because our emotional body is loaded with patterns similar to those of the beginning of this period of time. But it can also happen that after a long time you meet again with a person who has taken a violent evolutionary step. A fundamental change is absolutely possible in seven years.

In the following pages we will try to convey an overview about the experiences that man must broadly navigate in each of his years of life, and the influences to which he is particularly sensitive. In the next chapter we will explain in more detail some examples.

CHAPTER 5

THE ORIGIN OF BLOCKAGES IN CHAKRAS

By our true nature, we are one with that strength that manifests itself in the vibrations and regular laws infinitely varied, in the colors and shapes, in the aromas and sounds of all creation. We're not separated from anything. The most intimate core of our being lives in inseparable communion with the absolute, immutable, omnipresent being that we call God and which has produced and penetrates all areas of relative existence. This pure, unlimited existence is by nature the glory.

As soon as the silent and calm ocean of the divine being is curled in waves of joy, the dance of creation begins, of which we too are a form of manifestation and in which we can participate, in all its planes, through our bodies, not necessarily the physical body.

However, we lose consciousness of unity at the moment when we begin to rely exclusively on the information that comes to us through the physical senses and rational understanding, forgetting our origin and our divine base. We lost the feeling of inner fullness and safety in life and began to look for it in the outdoor field. But in that quest the coffering of full consummation was let down over and over again. This experience raised anguish over a new disappointment. We also forget that we can never be extinguished, since death only means a variation of the external form.

Anguish always causes a contraction and, therefore, a grip or blockage, which in turn intensifies the feeling of separation and allows the anguish to continue to grow. Breaking this vicious cycle and regaining lost unity is the declared goal of almost all the spiritual pathways of East and West.

Chakras are those connection points in man's energy system in which blockages conditioned by distress are preferably established. There may also be other locks along the nadis. When these contractions become permanent, they cause vital energies not to flow freely and feed our various bodies with everything they need to reflect and maintain the awareness of unity. When the experience of separation, abandonment, inner emptiness and fear of death prompts us to seek in the outside world what we can only find in the most intimate of our being, we become dependent on the love and recognition of other people of the sensory arrivals, success and material possession. Instead of enriching our lives, these things become peremptory needs with which we try to fill the void. If we lose them, we suddenly find ourselves at nothingness, and the slight sense of anguish that accompanies almost everyone is presented to us again as real. And, of course, it is the others who take from us what we so evidently need for our realization and satisfaction. We forget that all of us have our common origin in divine existence and that we are mutually united on this plane. Instead of loving our fellow citizens, we begin to consider them as competitors or even enemies. Finally, we think that we have to protect ourselves, without letting certain people, situations or information come to us or enter us. We retract our receiving antennas so that we do not have to face challenges, and with this we cause a new contraction and the blocking of our chakras.

However, the need for recognition by our congeners or by a group to which we feel to belong is so intense that we are willing to guide our lives in broad areas according to the ideas of certain people close to us or according to generally accepted social rules, and to suppress our spontaneous feelings as soon as they cease to match expectations or conventions. This is only possible if we contract our chakras to such an extent that no controlled emotion can pass the filter. It then produces energy congestion in the affected chakra. Because energies can no longer radiate in their original form, they are distorted, break down the barrier and discharged inappropriately, in the form of intense and often negative emotions or an over-thetop activity boost.

This corresponds to a reaction to the blockage marked by the yang. But as if there is an expression of energies, into the chakra new energies can flow, which will be discharged in the same inappropriate way.

A reaction to the blockage of the chakras marked by the yin manifests itself in an almost absolute containment of energies, with which the energy flow practically paralyzes, since no space is created for the energies that flow later. The consequence is the undernourishment of vital energy and weakness in the manifestation of the affected chakra. The repercussions of similar hypofunction, as well as an overload of the corresponding chakras, can be found in the corresponding chapters of the chakras. There we will give some general guidelines that, in some points, may differ from your individual reactions, since they are ultimately determined by the experiences that have caused the blockage and that are stored in the emotional body and, in less measure, also in the mental body.

These stored experiences are not left behind by us with physical death. We drag them from one incarnation to the next, until we have polished them in the course of our evolution. They largely determine the circumstances in which we are reborn and the experiences we unconsciously attract in our new life through the irradiation of our emotional body.

However, in each life we have the possibility to dissolve very quickly, from childhood itself, our emotional structures. In a new-born, the entire energy system is still completely open and permeable. This means that in principle every born-again soul receives a new opportunity to lead a fulfilling life. But it also means that it is open to all vibrations and experiences, and with it also to all kinds of the imprint.

A new-born cannot yet consciously participate in the configuration of his life, nor can he relativize his experiences. Therefore, it is totally dependent on the goodwill and care of adults. Here lies for parents a great opportunity, and also a great task.

In the following pages we will describe what influences a child's needs in the first years of life to be able to develop optimally, to avoid new blockages and to dissolve old structures.

In our day, many highly evolved souls await suitable parents in which to incarnate without accumulating unnecessary blockages that could hinder the fulfillment of their mission on this earth. Other souls would like to be reincarnated in this time of ours of change, for they will hardly offer the self a similar opportunity to learn and grow again.

Knowing this can help prospective parents give a childlike soul the best starting possibilities for the way of life. But it can also help each of us better understand our own "history of blockages" and manage it more easily on this basis.

Already in the mother's womb, blockages in the energy system can begin when the incipient life is rejected, or when the mother lives in a permanent situation of stress, since a fetus lives and feels the world largely through the mother. A loving dedication to the little being found in the womb will provide your energy system with vibrations that will make you feel absolutely well and protected. When the mother lives the months of pregnancy happily, she is creating the optimal conditions for her child's life, in which she can fully discover her potential for happiness and creativity.

An important milestone in every person's life is the moment of birth. In certain circumstances, the experience of birth can mark us throughout a lifetime, and can be decisive for us to perceive the world as a friendly and pleasant place or as something hard, devoid of love and cold. With childbirth, the child abandons the complete physical security. During his first nine months of existence on earth, he has lived in a blissful state of timelessness and weightlessness, that provided him with food and protection. But the little being is ready for birth and curious about the world.

Therefore, a natural birth, in which neither the mother nor the child is weakened by medicines, means great work and effort, but at the same time does not constitute a shock to the child. For which, however, it is not prepared at all for the separation of the mother immediately after birth. As long as the baby continues to feel the mother's body along with her familiar vibrations and sits cradled in the usual energetic vibrations of the mother's aura, she is ready to open herself with full confidence to new experiences.

In addition, body contact with the mother immediately after birth implies a deep bond between the mother and the child, which in specialized circles is called bonding. A flow of loving feelings, with positive emotional energy, flows automatically and without conscious participation from the mother to her new-born, and is not interrupted as long as the child feels the mother's body or stays at least within her emotional aura. This energy fills the little soul with confidence and joy. An interesting fact is that parents also develop more intimate contact with their babies and a more intuitive understanding when they have been present at birth and have been able to touch and caress the child.

Conversely, if the new-born is removed from the mother just after birth, he or she experiences deep pain from separation and loneliness. As long as the mother continues to consciously send her feelings and loving thoughts to the new-born during a separation, a contact will still be maintained, and the child will not be completely insulated from the mother's energetic supply. However, if she devotes her attention to other things or is tired or numb due to medications, this contact will also be broken.

The little creature senses its derelicts in an unknown and cold world in which it feels completely abandoned without the warm and protective presence of the mother. This experience is so violent that, in general, the child's energy system is not in a position to process terrible feelings, and experiences a profound impression, which results in the first blockage of energies. The blockage is preferably shown in the radical chakra area.

In the first year of life, when the child accumulates experiences predominantly through the physical body, the child needs first and foremost body contact with the mother, and sometimes also with the father or with other trusted people.

At this age the child does not yet have a concept of time. When she cries out of loneliness or hunger, she doesn't know if this state will end, and she easily despairs. On the other hand, if her demand is immediately met, the confidence that this earth provides children with everything they need to maintain their bodies and meet their physical needs is formed in her. The child can be opened, both physically and on the non-material plane, to the nourishing and protective energies available to us by our mother planet.

Practically, all primitive people have an intuitive knowledge of these relationships. They continually carry their babies wrapped in cloth by the body until they start crawling, and do not even abandon it when the continuous swinging has cradled and numbed the little creature. When the child starts crawling, they always lift him up as soon as the child wants it. At night the children stay with the mother in bed, and whenever they feel hungry, the mother's breast is at their service. The radiant eyes and satisfied faces of these happy little creatures speak for themselves. Children in these villages cry very rarely and are willing from an early age to take on social responsibility.

If in our society a mother also had this dedication during her child's first year of life and left her own needs in the background, she would have provided the creature with the best potential for her life. This investment is really worth it. The automatic flow of love and joy that is triggered in the mother through permanent body contact with the child is a broad compensation for all the little things he may not be able to do at that time.

If a child loses the original feelings of trust, safety, satisfaction, and protection, growing up, he will continue to look for them in the external and material realm. He will establish relationships with things rather than establishing them with people. It all starts with pets, which are used as a substitute for human closeness and heat. He then obtains more and more new toys and baubles, in an unconscious search for something to which he is driven by the slightly corrosive feeling of emptiness. And as adults, beautiful dresses, cars, furniture and perhaps a house of your own, as well as professional or social standing, are the things to which most men make their hearts more expensive, hoping to recover with them the feeling of security and abandoned childhood satisfaction. Our consumer society could not exist without that insatiable need for the vast majority of its members.

But the number of people who have realized that the experience of internal security and satisfaction cannot be achieved through material goods is also increasing. They set off for an inner quest, and here in fact lies the only chance to rediscover the lost paradise that most of us have abandoned with birth.

In the second year of life, the fundamental theme of the radical chakra, which extends over the first seven years of life, is joined by a new main theme of a single year. The growing child comes into contact with the energies of the second chakra. Delicate contact, caresses and pampering are now becoming more important, along with mere body contact. The child begins to discover his sensuality and to experience and express his sensations and emotions more consciously. From this moment the contents of the emotional body also begin to appear gradually, brought from the previous life. In his second year of life the child lives the most fundamental emotional structures in the first place.

It is now very important that parents do not try to impose a certain attitude on the child, because in that case he will start to retract emotions and suppress them in any way. If, on the other hand, the child learns to simply live his emotions, to accept the existence of them and to treat them playfully, he could dissolve in a short time all the negative emotional imprints.

Parents should understand that a child of that age does not express any negativity. If it gets choleric, it's only because a natural need has been disappointed. The raging cries and the legs release the blockage produced, and thus release the child. However, most parents find it difficult to accept their child as he is with his emotional expression, since they themselves do not have very clear things. They love their child when they do this or leave that, and with it they convey the following message: "Being like this you are not good enough."

The child assumes the attitude of the judgment of the parents, and because he does not want to lose his love, he relegates the parts of himself that are not dear. This results in a profound energy effect. If, in addition, sensory stimulation is lacking, a lack of original confidence arises in the emotional field and the sacral chakra is blocked.

Then the adult will find it difficult to accept and express his or her natural emotions. In order to feel something, you need a crude sensory stimulant, and you develop a tendency to observe others as objects that serve your own satisfaction.

The third year of life puts the little creature in contact with the energies of the solar plexus chakra. Emotional expression becomes more differentiated, and the explanations we have given regarding the second year of life only apply within certain limits. Now the child wants to prove himself as an independent personality, learns to know his influence and always says "no," to see what happens in that case.

When there is a power struggle between parents and the child because parents think that they can only educate the child by imposing their will on them, such a struggle culminates in the third year of life. If the child then does not feel loved and accepted in his growing personality, the energies of the solar plexus chakra are blocked. When you want to learn, you will lack the confidence and courage to live your individual personality, to configure your existence according to your own ideas and to learn from negative experiences. Instead, he will adapt or try to control his world.

Thus continues the journey of the little creature along with the energies of the different chakras. But let us leave these examples for now. With the help of the list of life cycles and with the description of each of the chakras, you will find it easy to complete the rest of the way yourself.

In all these explanations we should always bear in mind that it is us who have chosen the circumstances of our rebirth. We have embodied ourselves in a given couple to be properly polished, to gather experiences that our soul needs to develop towards perfection.

The fewer of us may have gone to parents who had such a deep understanding and a love so selfless that among their loving and expert hands, they melted, until the last restrictive structures of the emotional body disappeared. This means only the following: that in this life our mission and destiny are to develop the sympathetic love for ourselves that will dissolve the blockages and save the unwanted and imposed parts of our soul. Without being aware of this, our parents are the first teachers who, with their behavior, refer to our weaknesses, so that, based on pain and feelings of lack, we end up looking for ways to regain inner integrity. Then we take other people on this task and vital situations that we unconsciously attract, and that serves as a mirror for the anemic parts of us that we have repressed in the grim area of our psyche.

In the next chapter we will see the possibilities that exist to dissolve the chakra locks and rediscover the experience of inner unity.

CHAPTER 6

THE DISSOLUTION OF THE BLOCKAGES

There are essentially two ways to act on our chakras with a liberating and harmonizing effect. The first way is to expose the chakras to energetic vibrations that approach the frequencies with which a chakra naturally vibrates without blockages, and that works harmoniously. These energetic vibrations can be found, for example, in pure luminous colors, in precious stones, in sounds and essential oils, and also in the elements and multiple forms of manifestation of nature.

As soon as our chakras flow at frequencies that are higher and purer than those corresponding to their current state, they begin to vibrate more quickly, and the slower frequencies of the blockages gradually dissolve. Energy centers can absorb new vital energies and relay them unhindered to non-material bodies. It's as if, through our energy system, a cool breeze blows. The flowing prana charges the etheric body, which in turn transmits energy to the physical body. It also flows into the emotional body and the mental body, where blockages also begin to dissolve, as their vibrations are slower than those of the energy flowing into it. Finally, the pulse of vital energy affects the nadis of the entire energy system, and the body, spirit and soul begin to vibrate more highly, and radiate health and joy.

When stagnant energies are released in this process of purification and clarification, their contents appear once again in our consciousness. With this we can again live the same sensations that caused the blockage: our anxieties, our anger and our pain. Body diseases may come out for the last time before being completely cleaned. During these processes we probably feel uneasy, excited or even very tired. As soon as the energies have an expeditious way, they return to us deep joy, serenity and clarity.

However, many people do not have the courage to go through the necessary clarification processes. Often, they simply have no knowledge of them, and the experiences presented interpret them as a step backward in their evolution.

In fact, the blockages of our energy system are purified only to the extent that, since our complete evolution, we are willing to look to the face of the unwanted and repressed part of ourselves, and to redeem it through our love. And with this we come to the second way, which we mentioned at the beginning of this chapter. This route should permanently accompany the first path of direct activation and purification of chakras, but at the same time it is itself an independent possibility to harmonize our internal energy system and free it from blockages.

This path is the inner attitude of unconditional acceptance, which leads to complete détente. Tension implies the opposite, the remedy against tension, against contraction, and against blocking. As long as we consciously or unconsciously reject any scope of ourselves, as long as we prosecute ourselves, and therefore count and reject parts of ourselves, a tension will remain that prevents complete bloating and, therefore, both, the dissolution of the blockages.

We've all met more than once with people who say they can't relax. These people permanently need distraction or activity, even in their free time or on vacation, and when they ever do nothing there is always inner dialogue. As soon as they reach peace externally they feel an inner unease. In these people the self-healing mechanism is so active that the blockages begin to dissolve immediately as soon as some peace of mind is established in the energy system. However, because the people affected do not understand this mechanism, they flee again and again to the activity, thus suppressing the processing and purification of blocked energies.

Other people encapsulate their mental bodies to circumvent confrontation with the contents of their emotional body. For these people, all experiences take place through understanding. They analyze, interpret and categorize, but never get into an experience with their whole being.

We also sometimes encounter people who have tried to force the opening of the chakras by practicing disproportionately and without being guided by anyone. For example, certain exercises of Kundalini yoga, and they end up flooded with the contents unconscious of the corresponding chakra. Attempts to reject these contents can sometimes lead to deeper blockages. It is also not uncommon for someone who has started a spiritual path to only activate their upper chakras and unconsciously maintain the blockages of the lower chakras, since they do not want to identify with the contents that are released. One of these may have access to wonderful experiences from the realms of his upper chakras, and yet he may feel deep inside him a lack or void. Unconditional joy, the feeling of complete life joy and safety in life can only arise if all chakras are uniformly open and their frequencies vibrate on the highest possible plane.

However, the attitude of unconditional acceptance demands a great deal of honesty and courage. Honesty means in this context the willingness to see ourselves with all our weaknesses and negativity, and not as we would like to see ourselves. Value is the willingness to accept the observed. It's the value of saying yes to everything without excluding anything.

We have assumed in us the judgments of our parents to win their love. We have suppressed certain emotions and desires of ours to meet the expectations of society, a group or an image of ourselves. Abandoning this means orienting ourselves inwardly and absolutely, and losing the love and recognition of others. But it is only the act of rejection, of denial, that allows our energies to adopt negative manifestations. Repressed emotions only become "bad" because we reject them, rather than face them with love and understanding. The more violently they are rejected, both "worse" and mortifying will they be, until at some point we release them from prison through our love.

Behind all sentimental stimulus is, ultimately, the drive to regain the original paradisiac state of unity. However, as soon as we adapt to the prevailing worldview and only accept as real the external plane of reality that can be perceived through our physical senses and rational understanding, this desire for communion, of unification with life, becomes a will to possess. Our eagerness to possess a person, a position, love and recognition and material goods, however, is disappointed again and again, or in the long run is not satisfied as expected, since such satisfaction can only be achieved through an inner union.

For fear of a new disappointment we suppress our energies: our energy system is blocked. The energies that subsequently flow are distorted by the blockage and manifest themselves as negative emotions, which in turn we try, once again, to repress and retain so as not to lose the sympathy of our fellow citizens.

We can interrupt this circle if we devote all our attention to our emotions. At that very moment they begin to transform, for finally, we recognize that they are simply energies that have arisen from the desire for unity, and that were blocked in their original manifestation. Now they become a force that helps us continue on the path to totality.

There is a simple analogy that can clarify these relationships. If you're afraid of a person and you shun them, you'll never know them in their entire being. If, on the other hand, you devote your attention to them and make them feel your unconditional love, they will open to you gradually. You will know that after their negative behaviours, which you have condemned, there is nothing but the longing for disappointed satisfaction. Your understanding will help you walk the path to real satisfaction. In this analogy, your emotions happen the same as that person.

The written attitude of acceptance without prejudice corresponds to the position of our higher self. As we consciously assume it for ourselves, we open ourselves to the vibration plane of the inner guidance in us and entrust it with the mission of guiding us to a whole and healthy existence.

The higher self is that part of the soul that binds us to divine existence. It's unlimited in space and time. For this reason, it has access at all times to the integral knowledge that affects both life in the universe and our personal life. If we entrust ourselves to our guide, it will lead us to the straightest and most direct way towards the inner unit, and the existing blockages in our energy system will dissolve as smoothly as possible.

If we understand these relationships, we can make the forms of therapy described in this book effective. Always admit all the experiences that appear during the performance of therapy, even (and more if possible) when they appear at an unpleasant or negative time; give them your neutral attention and your love and give them the healing power of your higher self.

There are forms of meditation that can help you practice this attitude of acceptance, dissolve blockages, and admit the self-healing energies of your higher self. One of these meditation techniques, is transcendental meditation, also known by its abbreviation, MT. Here, consciousness is guided without any effort or concentration of any kind by the most direct way towards the experience of the pure being. This process is accompanied by a growing relaxation in which the blocked energies dissolve on their own. The liberated thoughts and emotions are not rejected, but are continually replaced by the experience of increasing relaxation and joy. With this meditation, you have in your hands a wonderful and highly effective instrument that, used correctly, represents by itself a way to activate your chakras harmoniously, to purify your energy system from all blockage and to explore all your intellectual and mood potential. However, this form of meditation can only be learned through a qualified teacher.

There are also other forms of meditation that can help you on your way. Keep in mind that in the meditation you choose, your thoughts and feelings are not prosecuted and rejected, but integrated as part of the necessary cleansing process. Even in the most effective and natural forms of meditation, it can happen that, due to habit, there is always some judgment. Even experiences resulting from the dissolution of blockages can often be unconsciously suppressed, as they have felt unpleasant. This can cause you to lose impartiality, and the effectiveness of meditation will suffer. An experienced teacher can help you find the original meditation experience again.

As soon as you have learned to love and accept yourself entirely, as you are, you will radiate these vibrations through your aura, and attract the corresponding experiences in the outside world. This means that only then will you really gain the love and recognition of others, whose loss you may have feared before. They begin to value you as you are in your true essence, and admire you for your true value of being yourself. Authentic love and communion are only possible under this premise.

Here's one last point in relation to the subject of this chapter. On your way to an integral evolution, there can be phases in which your chakras are relatively open without all the blockages being dissolved. So you are very sensitive to the energies that fall within the scope of your aura, but you still do not radiate enough luminous energy to attract only profitable energies to be able to neutralize negative energies in your environment.

If you remain now in a tense atmosphere where vibrations of dissatisfaction, hostility or aggressiveness prevail, your chakras can be loaded with negative energies, or contracted to protect themselves from such influxes. In both cases, the consequence is a positive vital energy underfeeding.

As soon as the energy fields of two people touch or overlap, there is an immediate exchange and mutual influence of energies. We unconsciously perceive the other energetically, whether we want to or not. When a person is spontaneously sympathetic or unfriendly to us, it is largely due to the energetic vibrations we experience in their aura. If we feel fear, dissatisfaction or anger, these vibrations not only influence the image we have of it, but also our own energy system. When, for no apparent reason, you feel tense or uncomfortable in the presence of a person; and you even get the feeling that everything contracts within you, the reason is in the irradiation of your aura. If, on the contrary, in a person's aura you feel joy, love and serenity, in their presence you will feel particularly well, even if you do not exchange any words with them. In a group of people who have gathered for a particular purpose, the collective aura that arises can have such an intense effect that all the members of the group are reached by it. Suffice it to think of the contagious environment that occurs so often among the viewers of a football match.

On the other hand, when a group meets for devotion or common meditation, the individual can rise to planes of consciousness far higher than those corresponding to their normal state of evolution.

Places also have their own irradiation, since matter can store vibrations. This happens especially in enclosed spaces.

We believe that when dealing with young children it is particularly important to understand these relationships. The energy system of these small beings is not yet completely sensitive to all kinds of energy vibrations. It reacts in a particularly sensitive way to every loving thought and to any feeling of joy, but also to aggressions or quarrels and to the aggressiveness of its environment. Here the body closeness to a parent or a reference person with whom you are familiar represents valuable protection: for example, when the child is exposed to vibrations of others when going shopping. The adult's aura acts as a bumper that captures and absorbs vibrations. For this reason, it is better to carry a child than to leave him/her in a baby stroller.

We adults can also contribute a lot to making our own chakras and our children's chakras remain relaxed and open. When we fundamentally attract those vibrations and situations that correspond to our own energy radiation, we also have a certain space of action to consciously shape our life in the exterior aspect. For example, we can participate in activities in which an atmosphere of joy and love is generated, we can visit places that radiate positive and uplifting energy, and we can even create the enchantment of a similar place in our own home. Stimulating colors, flowers, aromas and soothing music contribute a lot to a harmonious and flattering atmosphere of life. By choosing the TV shows, conversations and activities we develop within our four walls, we can put certain accents and create an atmosphere in which the energy system of all the people present recovers from negative influences.

Also, internally, you can do something to protect yourself especially from unwanted influencers from the environment. We recommend that you pay special attention to therapy to open the heart chakra, since the love that radiates outward is able to neutralize or transform all negative vibrations. Here is a special challenge to develop your love together with other faculties.

In addition, when you develop your heart chakra, you will know and evaluate more and more the positive sides of other people, and you will automatically let into you only those vibrations. Through your assessment, these qualities will be enhanced and activated at the same time on your opponent. Thus, each encounter can become an enrichment for both parties.

Active outward irradiation in all cases represents good protection. As soon as you have learned to accept yourself as you are and openly radiate your energies, the external negative vibrations will not be able to penetrate the crown of lightning that emerged from you. If you remain inwardly relaxed and completely calm, the tensions of the atmosphere will not find any echo essential in you and will not be able to settle inside you or influence you negatively.

Of course, we are aware that these capabilities presuppose a truly advanced evolution. That's why we want to mention some more simple possibilities with which you can protect yourself from unwanted influences and keep negative energies away.

When you want to protect yourself in a situation or intensify your own influence, imagine that you introduce light into your body through your coronal chakra, and let that light radiate from your solar plexus chakra again, wrapping your body in a controller luminous protector that will dissolve all dark influences. You can also imagine the luminous radiation coming from the solar plexus chakra as if it were a shower or a spotlight or a projector that eliminates all negative vibrations in its path.

Another very effective protection is that offered by essential oils; you should apply these directly to the chakras. They fill your aura with pure irradiation and neutralize un-harmonic tensions and influences, from the outside to your aura.

Carrying a rock crystal with you will enhance the luminous quality and protective irradiation force of your aura. Its effect complements very well with the influence of essential oils.

Silk underwear is also energy protection, and is especially recommended for infants and young children. If you ever get too tight due to a sudden scare, shock or anger, here's a very effective possibility that will allow you to immediately eliminate stagnant energies. Sit with your legs slightly outstretched and for a few seconds tighten as many muscles as possible. If you're alone, shout as loud as you want; otherwise, just expel air from your lungs with intense pressure. Repeat this exercise until you feel better. It serves to dissolve the blockages that have arisen because your energy system could not process the sudden experience. If you've done well, then you can stretch hard, as you do after a deep, restful sleep. It is interesting that in some people the phenomenon of muscle tension appears spontaneously in meditation, and precisely in those regions of the body where blockages want to be dissolved. This is a clear sign of the usefulness and effectiveness of this exercise.

CHAPTER 7

HOW WE CAN DETECT THE CHAKRAS WE HAVE BLOCKED

As in this book, we offer several possibilities to harmonize and balance your chakras, of course, it is of great interest to know if your chakras are unbalanced or blocked, and which of them are. If you don't know, you could harmonize all the chakras with the possible therapies on offer, and we highly recommend this method of comprehensive treatment. But if, for example, you have detected that there are two chakras that prefer to need therapy, you can dedicate yourself predominantly to those two energy centers.

In addition, the knowledge of dissonant chakras hides a great opportunity for self-knowledge, which can be fully opened to those who are interested. This is always, first, about ourselves, and only secondly to others, to whom, of course, we can tell our experiences. However, the goal is not to convert others, but to know and save oneself, and then to be able to lovingly lead others on the same path of selfknowledge.

For the diagnosis of chakras, we are offered several different possibilities. So using one of those opportunities will be enough to perform a selfdiagnosis or effective diagnosis of the chakra system.

1. In this book, when describing each of the chakras, we give clear characteristics for recognition, in which you can measure which of your chakras are dissonant, harmonized or functioning defectively. With the help of these criteria, anyone can know their problem areas quickly. We have tried very clearly, sometimes even in an exaggerated way, to outline the repercussions of a dysfunction of the chakras, to clarify certain trends quickly and unequivocally. When reading further, you should also consider that not all the repercussions described apply to anyone. However, it may happen that you feel very affected by certain passages of text or feel that they don't affect you at all. That's not our goal. However, we want to get you to recognize yourself clearly and unequivocally, and that when some of the descriptions are correct in your particular case, they make you feel involved. Please do not value this as a reproach of ours directed against you, for the goal is not to hurt you, but to help you gain knowledge. However, self-knowledge is not always pleasant; also, sometimes our gloomy sides must be illuminated, for only in this way can they be released. So this way for knowledge will be worth it, without a doubt, since at the same time it puts in your hands a whole series of possibilities for the self-treatment of chakras and the self-harmonization of them.

2. Another possibility to analyze our chakra system is to carefully observe which chakras react strikingly in situations of extraordinary stress or shock. It could be that, in certain difficult life situations, you will always be assaulted by the same ailments: for example, if the radical chakra is hyperfunctioning, in a strong situation of effort you can have the feeling of "losing foot," which may even give you diarrhea. In the case of hyperfunction of the first chakra, it is easy to be assaulted by anger and aggressive outbursts. If in your second chakra there is a lack of functioning, in the face of extraordinary tensions there is a blockage of feelings; with an exaggerated function, you will in all likelihood break down in tears or react with uncontrolled emotionality. In the case of hypofunction in the third chakra, in the face of great efforts, a feeling of impotence, a feeling of incapacity, or an uncomfortable sensation in the stomach or a stubborn nervousness will be established. An overload in this chakra is characterized by nerve excitability and the attempt to control the situation through hyperactivity. If you get the feeling that "your heart stops," you have to blame it on a hypofunction of the coronal chakra. When your heart is broken in the face of stress, it's an indication of a generalized dysfunction of the fourth chakra. In the case of hypofunction of the neck chakra, you get a lump in your throat, you will probably start to stutter or your head will shake

uncontrollably; in the event of dissonant hyperfunction, you will try to take the situation firmly by means of an avalanche of unripe words. If in situations of stress or shock you cannot have clear ideas, it means a hypofunction of the frontal chakra and an overload would often be expressed with headaches.

Such reactions always occur only in the weaknesses of our energy system. An interesting observation can open our eyes to these cases.

3. Now we can continue to use body language. For the first time it is possible to determine, by the external form and by the external qualities of a person's body, whether any area is energetically in dissonance. At the end of the day, our body is a perfect mirror image of non-material energy structures. Whenever bodily abnormalities occur, whether spasms, swellings, tensions, weaknesses or the like, we can assign them to the corresponding chakra depending on where they occur. We all know the differences in bodily appearances that we can use to form a clear image of the particular person; often, spontaneously and without reflection. Frequently, this image can be easily transferred to the chakras. Thus, we find people who obviously have all their energy oriented upwards, and who in the lower part of the body have absolutely weak characteristics. In others, the exact opposite is true; and there are also others that

seem to be composed only of weaknesses or strengths. Observe yourself sometimes, consciously, in the mirror or in photographs. Voice is often an important criterion for prosecuting the state of the neck chakra.

If you also take into account the organic weaknesses or even the symptoms of the disease, you have one of the most transparent reference points on what is the area of the chakra system where deficiencies exist, to effectively apply the therapy.

4. As a fourth possibility, we put in your hand a special test with which many therapists work, in addition to a large number of laypeople. For this, you usually need two people, placed face to face. This is a kinesiological test, which was developed in the course of the Touch for Health method.

In practice, it proceeds as follows: place your right hand on a chakra and simultaneously laterally extend the left arm to the right angle with the body. The other person doing the test with you gives the order to "oppose resistance," and while you try to keep your arm in the right position, she tries to push her arm down, exerting pressure at about wrist height. If the chakra is harmonized and balanced in its operation, the extended arm offers a clear and intense resistance; if, on the other hand, the chakra being tested is blocked, it can be easily noticed that the arm does not oppose this resistance, and the person performing the test will be able to push it down with very little force.

Kinesiological Muscle Test

Through this test method we can go through the seven chakras, from the radical chakra to the coronal chakra; which allows us to get a clear picture of the energetic state of the chakras. When there are disorders in the chakra, in the test, the arm always reacts with weakness. We can then repeat this same test to find that there are changes. With a disorders chakra system, the arm test should give the "strong" result seven times: that is, the down pushed arm should offer sensitive resistance seven times. You can pause briefly between tests of the different chakras to prevent possible phenomena of arm fatigue.

Measurements made with a special kinesiometer have shown the result that a similar test resists approximately 20-kilogram pressure, if the test result is 'strong'; Otherwise, the arm will no longer offer resistance with approximately 8 kilograms of pressure. Of course, account must be taken of the individual physical constitution of the person subject to the test. However, the difference between 'strong' and 'weak' will be clearly perceived both by the person undergoing the test and by the person administering the test.

Another variant of this test is to hold down the thumb against the index finger of the right hand, and with the left hand cover the chakra object of the test. Our companion in the test will try, when the relevant order is given, to separate the fingers that we hold firmly tight against each other. If the fingers offer great resistance, the chakra under test is in good condition. If, on the contrary, the resistance is reduced, the chakra tested is disrupted and needs therapy.

However, we have often found people who perform this test with themselves. To do this they press the index finger against the thumb of one hand, and try to separate them with the thumb and index finger of the other. In doing so they are mentally concentrated in a given chakra. Also here it is clearly shown by the feeling of "weakness" or "strength," which chakra is deranged. If the fingers that are pressed against each other can be released by the other hand ("weak"), the chakra being tested is deranged. If the fingers remain firmly united ("strong"), the chakra is in good condition. It is true that for these kinesiological tests we need some practice if we are to achieve safe results. However, this method works excellently, and serves to recognize well in which of the chakras we should work to harmonize it.

5. We will call "internal vision" another possibility that we have to prosecute our chakras. For many

people it is the easiest and fastest way to get in touch with your energy system.

To do this, we go into a meditative state of silence for a few minutes and try to form an idea of the state of each of the chakras through our "inner eyes." In doing so, we systematically and slowly traverse the chakras, from the bottom to the top. Many people can clearly recognize the status of their chakras based on chromatic changes. Other people tend to see shapes. If this is your case, look at whether they are round and have a harmonic balance, or if they have intussusceptions or show other variations. And, in turn, there are other people who recognize the harmonic state of the chakras by their size and power of irradiation. A combination of these different elements is often perceived. All these possibilities and valuation criteria are, however, based on a certain self-experience, and need to be trained often, if we want to come up with unequivocal and clear results.

6. More and more people are able to feel with their hands the energetic situation of the chakras. It feels a certain resistance when it is impacted with the energy envelope of your own etheric body, in which the chakras settle, or with the energy envelope of another person. This resistance feels similar to what happens when moving in water. You may be able to detect certain roughness, holes, or excrement. We can practice it by slowly bringing

hands closer to our own body, to another person's body or even to animals and plants, and trying to sensory-perceive the changes that are being operated on. Also, in this case, the experience born of the frequent application of the technique itself is essential for clear divination. A workshop in this regard would be advisable.

7. The most direct path we may well consider to be 'providence,' even if only a relatively small number of people possess this gift. Through this power the "seer" has direct access to the energy situations and processes that are consumed in himself and in other people. It is possible to know and value both the bodily references and the intellectual ones. If you count on the blessing of these media faculties, it is of great importance to interpret correctly what is observed and for this it takes a lot of training, experience and a gift of observation.

If you are not completely sure whether or not you have these faculties, you can do the following tests: sit in a completely dark room, for example, in a basement, a sauna or even a scot-in closet, where the slightest light does not penetrate. Stay in it silently for several minutes. As objects for testing, some rock crystal tips placed at a certain distance or held in the hands are sufficient at first. If you are able to perceive certain subtle energy radiations at the tips of rock crystals, especially when moving with swing motion, it is indicative of a tendency to clairvoyance. Don't give in to the first, because sometimes this ability has to be trained. First of all, this exercise should be done completely stress-free. If you want to detect the energetic body around a person, a predominantly black background should be preferred, to which the person being tested sits or stands. From a few meters away, looking in the direction of the person, or better through it, since that is where the energetic crown, the aura, is located. The best results will be obtained in a certain meditative state.

Take your time for it. Presumably, in this exercise you will first detect the etheric body, which envelops the physical body as a radiant energy envelope. With some practice you will also be able to distinguish the colors and shapes of the emotional body. Don't expect any fixed or rigid color image, since non-material energies are in continuous motion and have predominantly translucent intense gloss qualities. Basically, it can be said that the harmonic colors and shapes in this energetic image allow the existence of a harmonious person to be concluded; unsharp colors and undefined shapes point to that person's problematic areas.

If you want to try to detect your own aura, you can stand in front of a wall mirror and carry out the corresponding studies. Most people find it easier to achieve this by first looking at someone else's energy radiation.

In addition, there are special glasses for auras, which have dark violet glasses with a wrap that makes them airtight and opaque around. These glasses should be classified as auxiliary means; they don't automatically open access to non-material plans to all users, but they can really help us move up to them.

More and more people are in a position to judge and evaluate the energetic body, and in particular the system of other people's chakras, even at great distances, several hundred or even thousands of kilometers. In general, this is done through a photo of the consultant, or also through the phone.

If it causes you trouble recognizing or understanding such extraordinary phenomena, think about all that is possible today, for example, thanks to radio and television. Also, here, images and sounds are sent and captured invisibly through the ether in the form of waves. Almost all of our technical developments previously existed as natural phenomena, as did wireless transmission.

And, of course, it is up to your free will to reject the methods and possibilities that you find difficult for you, since a whole series of different possibilities of analysis referring to chakras have previously been shown.

Another way to detect the functioning of someone else's chakras is the medial ability to perceive in our own chakras exactly what our consultant experiences and feels. To do this, the therapist first goes into resonance with the patient's energetic body. There are some therapists who work like this and make clear diagnoses. However, not a few of them feel bad after the appointment, suffering the same symptom as the consultant. Hence, preference should be given to other procedures.

Some traditional Asian texts mention different characteristics of a dominant foundation of specific chakras. In this regard it is particularly interesting to analyze our sleep habits.

When a person lives, above all, through his first chakra, in general he will have quite large sleep needs, ranging from 10 to 12 hours, and will prefer to sleep upside down. People who need approximately 8 to 10 hours of sleep, and preferably sleep in the fetal position, live predominantly through the second chakra. When life is first and foremost configured by the third chakra, they preferably sleep on their back, and natural sleep needs range from 7 to 8 hours. A man whose fourth chakra is widely developed usually lies on the left side, and needs approximately 5 or 6 hours of sleep per night. If the fifth chakra is open and it is the one that sets the pattern, he only falls asleep 4 to 5 hours per night, alternating between the right or left side position. When in a person the sixth chakra is open, active and dominant, he will only spend approximately 4 hours between sleep and wakefulness. Watchful sleep is a state in which inner consciousness is maintained while the body sleeps. This form of rest is what you would expect with a seventh open and dominant chakra. The fully enlightened, therefore, does not sleep in the usual sense of the term; in any case, if you give your body a resting phase.

So, through these features, we are able to check the functioning of our chakras.

Alongside the possibilities shown there are some other technical means of support from the para scientific sector. These include the pendulum and magic wand, as well as The Kirlian photograph, which some therapists resort to performing the analysis of the chakras. Among the magic wands, one of the most suitable is the so-called zahorí pendulum, which is also called a biosensor. With this device, the state of the chakras can be known with relative ease, as with a pendulum: a stable chakra will manifest itself by the large circles it produces in the pendulum or wand, and an altered chakra, by minor circles or even because the pendulum or wand are rested. Of course, here it is also necessary to practice a little to be able to clearly differentiate the results.

Kirlian photography is a special technical procedure that allows us to obtain photographs of energy radiation, for example, of our body, and to represent them in colors. Recently a really interesting diagnostic possibility has been developed from this method. The diagnosis of energy terminal points by healer, Peter Mandel, is currently of great interest. Meanwhile, a large number of doctors and healers already work through this bioenergy diagnostic method.

Sophisticated electronic systems are already being used in Japan to arrive at the corresponding diagnostics in the field of non-material. But since we are more confident in our own interior possibilities, we only mention in passing these technical auxiliary means.

At the end of the day, so that only one of the methods presented here to check the chakras will be useful to you, it can be more than enough. It is often better to properly master one thing than several half-hearted things. So we wish you to be able to apply this knowledge sensibly.

CHAPTER 8

SEXUALITY AND CHAKRAS

Human sexuality is a form of manifestation and a mirror of the perpetual act of creation that is consumed uninterruptedly on all the planes of the da in the universe. When at the moment of creation multiplicity emerged from unity, the amorphous being was first divided into two fundamental forms of energy: a male fertilizer and a spawning female force. A few thousand years ago, the Chinese gave these original forces the denomination of yin and yang. From the game of these energies comes creation. The female yin is continuously fertilized by the male seed of yang and engenders life in its infinitely varied forms.

On a physical level of man, this game of forces manifests itself as sexuality. Through it, man is united in its entirety with the perpetual act of creating life, and the ecstasy he can experience in it reflects the blessing of creation.

The forces of yin and yang manifest the most universe as polarity. In order to exist, everything has an opposite pole. Each of the poles exists only by the other pole; if one polarity disappears, so does the other. This fundamental rule can apply to everything. For example, we can only breathe out if we also breathe in; if we leave one of them, we are also deprived of the other; the interior conditions the outside; day conditions the night; light conditions the shadow; birth, death; women, men, etc., with both polarities being mutually interchangeable. Each pole needs to be complemented by the opposite.

Yin and yang very intuitively symbolize the rhythmic movement of a lifetime. The yin represents the face of the whole, the feminine, extensive, intuitive, passive and unconscious; the yang represents the male, concentrator, intellectual, active and conscious. However, no assessment is included here in the sense of "having more value than the other."

The balance that exists in the universe around us is the result of the relationships between opposing couples. As in this universe everything is in a perpetual flow of motion, both yin and yang are already present latently at the corresponding opposite pole. This is symbolized by the white dot inside the dark yin, and by the dark point inside the white yang. Each of the two poles conceals the opposite pole in the form of seed, and it is only a matter of time when one of the polarities will be transformed into the corresponding other. In some areas, this investment is consumed in fractions of a second, such as at the atomic level. In humans, this change of polarity, from male to female, or vice versa, is only possible through various incarnations.

Day and night need on average twelve hours to make such a change, and inspiration and exhalation only a few seconds.

Reversing Polarities

All things come and go, as well as move and change due to the exchange and interaction of these two fundamental forces of the universe. But only both cycles result in the entire unit.

Love and sexuality are also founded by this regular law. Two poles merge into the unit, attracting each other like the different poles of a magnet. If a union of the opposing forces occurs, they are exchanged with each other. Women and men have opposite polarization in all their fundamental features. This different polarization also exists on the energy plane. Wherever the man presents a positive pole, the woman is endowed with a negative pole, and vice versa. As already explained in the introductory chapter, this phenomenon also occurs in the direction of rotation of chakras (in homosexuality, for example, there is an energy polarization opposite to the norm).

Thus, between the woman and the man there is an attraction and complementation in all the planes represented by the chakras, which can lead to complete intimate fusion. To achieve it, however, chakras must be as free from blockages as possible.

In sexual union, the energetic flow along the main channel, Sushumna, is strongly aroused and intensified. The energy flow of the second chakra increases greatly and, when there are no blockages in the chakra system, it is energy-intensive and loads all other chakras. Here sexual energy, which represents a certain form of prana, is transformed into the frequencies of the remaining chakras. From the chakras, and through the nadis, it radiates in the physical body and towards the energetic body, and fills them with multiplied life force. At the climax of this union there is a violent mutual discharge of energy through the seven chakras and fusion in all planes, represented by the chakras. Both partners feel enlivened to the depths of their being and at the same time totally relaxed; they feel an intimate union and a love that goes beyond the personal will to possess. The relationship is consummated without relying on the external things.

Such a satisfactory sexual union can only be lived in this dimension when the partners give each other completely and free the self from any anguish that could hinder the free flow in the energy system. It is sufficient that a single chakra is blocked in one of the components of the couple so that the union cannot be experienced in all its completeness. The blocked chakra also causes an alteration of the energy flow of the same chakra in the companion.

Most people only live sexuality through the second chakra. In man, too, the energy of the radical chakra plays a dominant role as a physical instinctive force. However, if sexuality is limited to the lower chakra, it becomes a rather one-sided experience, from which both companions are basically weakened and dissatisfied, and have a tendency to quickly separate and continue on their own. It's as if, on a string instrument, only two strings are crossed, but the full range of sounds was never taken out. From an energetic point of view, in limited sexual practice, in this way a lot of energy is actually consumed, since energies are extracted from other chakras and transformed into sexual energy, and then irradiated through the second chakra. The energies are unable to take their natural path upwards and simultaneously enter the seven chakras to fill them with additional vital energy.

The most natural way to dissolve the blockages that prevent a perfect sexual union in all planes is an exchange of energies of the heart chakra. When both partners radiate the love of their hearts freely and without fear, their own energy system, just like the other person's, is harmonized in the eyes of their own energy system. Blockages caused by distress dissolve, and it is possible to exchange the planes of the seven chakras.

Here's the deeper reason why the sexual union is experienced as very satisfying when, in addition to physical attraction, there is a feeling of deep love between the couple's partners. The higher frequencies are activated and sexuality rises beyond being purely bodily together, to become a spiritual union.

This is the art of tantra, taught and practiced for millennia. Here we come to a wide-ranging violent orgasmic experience that is generally considered possible. Such an experience actually leads us to areas of another dimension of experience and feeling. Suddenly we are aware that sexual energies are not enclosed in our genitals. They exist in each of our cells, just as the game of female and male forces exists in all forms of manifestation of creation. The perfect union with a beloved partner leads us to the experience of inner uniqueness with the life that throbs in the universe. And in the instant of orgasm, when duality is suppressed for a moment, we live in unity with the absolute and amorphous being, which constitutes the permanent basis and the goal of polarities.

The First Chakra And Its Correspondences

Keywords: Physical energy and will to live. Survival instinct. Fight, strength, stability, integration. Setting goals on Earth. To be and to have. Be. Material consciousness, the limitation for manifestation, discipline.

Development and nutrition. Rest and food. Simple physical comfort, pleasure, and health.

- **Location:** In the perineum, between the anus and the genitals.
- **Sanskrit name:** Muladhara.
- **Sound:** lam
- **Phoneme:** o
- **Verb:** I have.
- **Colors:** Blood red activates it, green calms it.
- **Foods:** Proteins in general (meat, lentils, soy).
- **Essential oils:** Patchouli, cedar, cloves.
- **Gems:** All red (garnet, red jasper, obsidian, smoky quartz).
- **Corresponding element:** Earth
- **Sensory function:** Smell
- **Symbol:** Four-petal loto
- **Basic principle:** Bodily will for being (as a polar opposite to the spiritual will to be in the seventh chakra).
- **Body correspondences:** All solid, such as the spine, bones, teeth and nails; and, rectum, large intestine, prostate, blood and cell structure.

- **Corresponding glands:** Adrenal glands

The adrenal glands produce adrenaline and norepinephrine, which have the mission of adapting blood circulation to specific needs by regulating blood distribution. In this way the body is prepared for action and can react immediately to the demands posed. In addition, the adrenal glands have a predominant influence on the body's thermal balance. Astrological correspondences:

- **Aries/Mars:** Reboot, original vital energy, force to impose, aggression.

- **Taurus:** Linkage with the earth, possession, sensory enjoyment.

- **Scorpio/Pluto:** Unconscious link, sexual strength, transformation and renewal.

- **Capricorn/Saturn:** Structure, resistance.

In Ayurveda, the radical chakra is also assigned to the Sun, as the original giver of life.

Mission And Operation Of The First Chakra

The radical chakra binds us to the physical world. It directs cosmic energies on the earthly corporeal plane, while simultaneously the earth's energy flows through it into the non-material energy system.

Here we come into contact with the spirit of "Mother Earth," we experience her elemental strength, her love and her patience.

The fundamental needs of life and survival, both individual and global, on this planet fall within the scope of action of the first chakra.

The "if" to life on earth, to physical existence, and the willingness to act in harmony with the energy of the Earth and learn from it are gifts of a first open chakra.

Thus the radical chakra is assigned to the earth element, its color is the red of energy and activity, of the most intimate nucleus of our planet. It gives us earthly security and the "safe ground" under our feet, on which we can build our lives, and simultaneously provides us with the energy necessary for creative activity in the world. It also gives us the strength to impose ourselves and perseverance.

The construction of existence, material assurance and the "preservation of one's own species" through the foundation of a family also fall within the scope of action of the first chakra, as well as sexuality as a bodily function and as a means for Procreation.

The radical chakra forms the most important foundation of life and the source of vital energy for the upper chakras. Here we are united with the inexhaustible energy reserve of Kundalini energy. It also starts the three main channels, Sushumna, Ida and Pingala. Like our heart in the physical body, the basal chakra is the central point of our non-material energy circulation system. In addition, it is where the collective subconscious settles, to which memorized knowledge we have access to here. It should be compensated with the seventh chakra, to maintain the inner balance of man.

Harmonic Operation

When your radical chakra is open and functioning harmoniously, you experience a deep and personal union with the Earth and its creatures, an unclouded life force, a being based on yourself and life, satisfaction, stability and inner strength. You feel immersed in the natural cycle of life, in the alternation of rest and activity, of death and of the new birth. Your actions are carried out by the desire to participate creatively in the configuration of life on your mother planet, in line with the generating power of the earth, with life in nature. It's easy for you to accomplish your goals in the world. Your life is driven by an imperturbable original trust. You live on the earth as a safe place where you receive everything you need: dedication, food, safety and protection. Thus you open yourself with confidence to life on this earth and accept gratefully all that she has in her right standing for you.

When there is a unilateral accentuation or dysfunction of the radical chakra, your thinking and action revolve predominantly around material possession and safety, as well as around sensory stimuli and pleasures, such as: good food, alcoholic beverages, sex, etc. Everything you long for, you would want to acquire without thinking about the consequences. At the same time, you may find it difficult to give and receive frankly. You have a tendency to protect yourself and delimit yourself. Not infrequently the non-detachable and the desire to retain manifests itself on the body plane in the form of constipation and overweight.

Your action is predominantly aimed at satisfying only your own needs. And you ignore, or unconsciously overlook, the needs of others and your own body for a healthier and more moderate diet, sufficient rest, and a balanced, harmonious way of life.

In the extreme case, you cling to certain ideas and ambitions from which you cannot part. When your bindings are challenged by circumstances or others, you react by easily extolling and getting angry. And in extreme situations, also in an angry and aggressive way. The violent imposition of one's own desires and ideas also falls within the scope of a deranged radical chakra.

Anger and violence are ultimately defense mechanisms that point to an original lack of trust. Behind it is always the anguish of losing something or even not receiving something, which transmits security and well-being.

The Earth is, for you, a place that must be dominated and exploited, to ensure the survival of man. Thus, the prey that is exercised today with the forces of the
Earth, and the destruction of its natural balance, are symptoms of a radical chakra alteration in most modern men.

Hypofunction

With a locked or closed radical chakra, your body build is quite weak and you have little physical and mood resistance. A lot of things in life worry you, and you know the feelings of insecurity all too well. You may also have the feeling of not stepping on dry land, you feel "elevated" or "not present." It's not easy for you to deal with life's challenges, and you often lack the capacity to impose yourself as well as stability. So often life on this earth seems to you as a burden and not a joy. You almost always yearn for a life that is easier, more enjoyable and less demanding.

In case you have unilaterally developed your upper chakras, a hypofunction of the radical chakra can convey the feeling of not belonging very well to this Earth. Since you can only hardly capture the earth's elemental vital energy through your radical chakra, a macros (anorexia) occurs (sometimes in combination with the sacral chakra and solar plexus chakra blockages) in some cases—an escape reaction. However, you will continue to face the problems of "earthly life" until you have learned to accept them as milestones of a comprehensive evolution.

Possibilities Of Purification And Activation Of The First Chakra

Natural experience

The contemplation of a rising blood-red sun and shimmering dawn or twilight acidifies and harmonizes the radical chakra and unleashes constrained structures that fall within its field of action.

To communicate with the reassuring, stabilizing and uplifting energy of our planet through the first chakra, sit in the position of the loto, or the tailor; on the bare earth and consciously breathe in its smell.

If you can combine both nature experiences with each other, there will be an optimal integral effect on the radical chakra.

Sound Therapy

Musical form: Music with monotonous and strongly accented rhythms is ideal for activating the radical chakra. The archaic music of many primitive people best expresses this form of music. Likewise, their dances also aspire to establish the union with nature, its forces and its creatures.

To harmonize the radical chakra, you can use the sounds of nature.

In case you don't have the "original sound" at your disposal, these sounds are currently recorded on a multitude of magnetospheric tapes and discs.

Vocal: The radical chakra is assigned the vowel "u". It is sung with the deep C tone of the musical scale. The "u" sound triggers a downward-facing movement in the direction of your roots. It leads you to the depths of the subconscious and activates the original earth energies of the first chakra.

Chromotherapy

The first chakra is activated by a clear and bright red. The red color warms, enlivens, and provides vitality, dynamism and value. When red is mixed with a little blue, it helps you penetrate vital instincts with intellectual strength.

Gemmotherapy

Agate: The agate provides seriousness, endurance and balance. It helps to dissolve negative emotions and protects the inner being. It awakens the evaluation of the body itself and acts constructively on the organs of reproduction. Agate discs with crystalline inclusion introduce a growing life (whether a physical or spiritual child), as well as safety and protection. They provide confidence and facilitate deliveries.

Hematites: Hematites give strength, have an uplifting effect on the body, and mobilize hidden forces. Therefore, they help in states of weakness and provide support for healing after an illness. In addition, they promote a healthy formation of blood and cells.

Blood Jasper: The blood jasper, green and red, binds you with the elemental strength and patient love of the "Mother Earth." It teaches you non-utilitarian character and modesty, strengthens the blood, brings vitality, stability, endurance and patience. It purifies and transforms the physical body, and conveys the feeling of security in the natural cycle of life, from which energy and rest can be created.

Granite: The granite brings active energy, will intensity, self-confidence and success. It opens the view for the occult until you reach clairvoyance. It stimulates sexuality and contributes to modify it in a transformative and constructive force. At the body level, it contributes to diseases of the sex organs and stimulates blood circulation.

Red Coral: Red coral provides fluid vital energy and strength. It has a stimulating and life-giving effect and promotes hematopoiesis. It gives stability, and at the same time favors flexibility, so that you can have selfsecurity while simultaneously following the course of life.

Ruby: Ruby transmits a life-giving, warm and creative energy that leads to clarification and transformation. It establishes a harmonious link between bodily and spiritual love, between sexuality and spirituality, through which new experiential forms are opened.

Aromatherapy

Cedar: The rough aroma of cedar oil unites you with the earthly forces and essences of nature. It helps to collect energy, transmits tranquility and the feeling of security within "Mother Earth".

Spice Nail: The smell of spice cloves helps dissolve the stagnant energies in the radical chakra.

It favors the willingness to release structures that constrain, arising from the need for delimitation and security, and to be open for new and fresh energies. In this way, it brings transformation and renewal if you let the message of its vibrations enter you.

Forms Of Yoga That Act Primarily On The First Chakra

Hatha Yoga: Development of consciousness through the purification and stimulation of the body base through certain exercises and physical postures linked to breathing exercises.

Kundalini Yoga: Awakening of the so-called energy of the snake, which runs from the coxal bone parallel to the spine and which, in its ascent, activates and vivifies all other chakras. For this there are different physical and spiritual exercises.

The Second Chakra And Its Correspondences

Keywords: Emotions. The change and how I adapt to it. The movement. Pleasure. The desire. Sexuality, orgasm. The protection. Empathy and sociability. Creativity. This place of the body needs to feel acceptance and love for itself that allows it to be its refuge affectionately and positively.

- **Location:** Below the navel.
- **Sanskrit name:** Swadhisthana.
- **Sound:** Vam.
- **Phoneme:** U
- **Verb:** Sorry.
- **Colors:** Orange if you are looking to activate it, blue if you want to calm it down.
- **Foods:** Liquids.
- **Essential oils:** Ylang-ylang, sandalwood.
- **Gems:** All orange, coral, carnelian, opal.
- **Corresponding element:** Water
- **Sensory function:** Taste
- **Symbol:** Six-petal loto
- **Basic principle:** Creative propagation of being
- **Body maps:** Pelvic cavity, reproductive organs, kidneys, bladder; all moods; such as: blood, lymph, digestive juices, sperm
- **Corresponding glands:** Sexual organs: ovaries, prostate, testicles. The role of sexual organs is the formation of male and female sexual characteristics and the regulation of the female cycle.

Astrological Correspondences:

- **Cancer/Moon:** Wealth of feelings, fertility, sensitivity.

- **Pound/Venus:** Dedication to you, sensory, relationships, artistic sensitivity.

- **Scorpio/Pluto:** Sensory ambition, the transformation of personality by overcoming the self in sexual union.

Note: Some writings indicate the spleen chakra as the second chakra. However, such a chakra is an important secondary center that matches its operation with the third chakra. This deviation from the original system has its beginning in the denial of sexuality in some esoteric schools. Subsequently there was sometimes a mixture of the systems, so that today the realm of sexuality is often assigned to the spleen chakra and sometimes to the radical center.

Mission And Operation Of The Second Chakra

The second chakra is the center of original unfiltered emotions, sexual energies and creative forces. It is assigned to the water element, from which all biological life has arisen and which in astrology corresponds to the scope of feelings.

Water fertilizes and continually brings about new life in creation. Through the Sacro chakra, we participate in the fertilizing and computing energies that go through all nature. We experience ourselves as part of a perennial creative process that manifests itself in us and, through us, in the form of creative feelings and actions.

The sacred chakra is often regarded as the authentic sensing position of Shakti, the "feminine" aspect of God in the form of creative force. Its field of action includes in the male the organs of procreation, which carry within themselves the impulse for the creation of new life. In women we find here those areas where she receives the creative impulse and brings forth new life, and the place where the new incipient being is protected, fed, and where everything the child needs to prosper is provided.

But the water element also purifies, dissolves and drags how much it is gripped and opposes its flow alive. This is manifested, within the body scope, by the detoxifying and excretory activity of the kidneys and bladder. On an animian plane we live it through liberation and letting feelings flow, so we are willing to experience life always in an original and new way.

Our interpersonal relationships, in particular, those relating to the opposite sex, are decisively marked by the functioning of the second chakra. The multiple varieties of erotic play also belong to their field of action as well as the abandonment of the limited ego and the experience of greater unity through sexual union.

Harmonic Operation

Flowing naturally with life and feelings shows the harmonic functioning of an open sacral chakra. You will be open and natural to others, and especially for the opposite sex. The sexual union with a loved one is for you a possibility to enter with your vibrations in the dance of the male and female energies of creation, in order to experience a superior unity with all nature and grow towards an inner integration.

You feel that the flow of life also flows into creation through your body, your soul, and your spirit. Thus, you participate in the deep joy of creation, and life always fills you with wonder and enthusiasm. Your feelings are original—your creative actions. Both bear fruit in your own life, as well as the lives of others.

A sacral chakra dysfunction often originates from puberty. Growing sexual forces cause insecurity, as parents and educators are rarely able to provide proper management of these energies. Often, in the earliest childhood, they have also lacked delicacy and body closeness. This can now lead to a denial and rejection of sexuality, so uninhibited expression loses its creative potential and energies manifest inappropriately. This often occurs in the form of sexual fantasies or repressed institute, which make their way in from time to time. Another possible impact is that you use sexuality as a drug. Your creative potential will not be detected here either, and it will deviate. In both cases there are tensions and insecurity against the other sex. Your sensory perception is relatively rude and you have a tendency to put the satisfaction of your sexual needs first.

Perhaps you simply live in a continuous longing for a fulfilling sexual relationship, without realizing that the cause of this desire not being realized lies in yourself.

With the loss of naivety and innocence in dealing with sexual energies, you also lose the candor to express or manifest these energies in creation, for the play of yin and yang forces and, therefore, for childish wonder for the miracle of life.

Hypofunction

The function of the sacral chakra arises in most cases from childhood itself. Your parents probably already suppressed their own sensuality and sexuality, and you lacked sensory stimulation, contacts, caresses and tenderness.

The consequence was that you completely retracted your antennas in this area.

Then, in puberty, you completely blocked the sexual energies that struggled to get out. Through your repression "crowned by success" you come to a lack of self-esteem, numbness of emotions and the coldness of sexual feelings. Life seems sad and unworthy of being lived.

Possibilities Of Purification And Activation Of The Second Chakra

Natural experience

Moonlight and contemplation or contact with transparent water in nature activate the second chakra.

The Moon, in particular, the full moon, stimulates your feelings and makes you receptive to the messages of your soul, which want to be transmitted to you in images of fantasy and dreams.

Calm contemplation of a natural and transparent watercourse, a bath in those waters or small sips of a freshwater fountain help you purify the soul, lighten it and free it from emotional blockages and stagnation, so that life can flow in you more freely.

If you can join the contemplation of the moon and contact with the water together, you will have an optimal effect on the second chakra.

Sound Therapy

Musical form: Any type of appropriate music is suitable to activate the second chakra, which awakens the carefree joy of living. Also, fluid rhythms and popular and coupled dances enter this therapy. On the other hand, any music that brings out your emotions suffices.

To calm and harmonize the sacral chakra, you can listen to the song of the birds, the murmur of the water flowing in nature, or the singing sound of a small indoor fountain.

Vocal: The radical chakra is activated by a closed "o," just like the first "o" of the word "sofort." It is sung in the rekeying of the scale. The vowel "o" triggers a circular motion. In its closed form, which approaches the "u" sound, it awakens the depth of feelings and leads you to the circular whole, in which yin and yang, the female and male energy, reach unity by the fluid harmony of forces.

In our language, the exclamation "Oh!" expresses an admiration laden with feeling. Similarly, the ability to surprise us by the miracles of creation is enlivened by the sound "o."

Chromotherapy

A light orange color activates the second chakra. Orange conveys a life-giving and renewing energy and releases numb emotional patterns. It promotes a sense of self-esteem and awakens the joy of sensory pleasure. In Ayurveda it is said that orange is the interior color of the water.

Gemmotherapy

Coralline: The coralline unites you with the beauty and creative force of this earth. It helps you live and promotes concentration. It brings back amazement at the miracles of creation, causes life to flow again, and activates the capacity for creative expression.

Moonstone: The moonstone opens you up for your richness of inner feelings. It unites you with your sensitive, receptive and dreamy essential side, and helps you accept and integrate it into your personality. It absorbs the fear of feelings and has a harmonizing effect on emotional balance.

On the body plane, it supports the purification of blocked lymphatic pathways, and in women it is responsible for maintaining an adequate hormonal balance.

Aromatherapy

Ylang-ylang: This refined oil extracted from the flowers of the ylang-ylang tree is one of the best-known aphrodisiacs. It has a relaxing effect and at the same time opens you up to more subtle sensory sensations. Its sweet aroma conveys a sense of security, from which you will re-trust the flow of your feelings. Stagnant or excited emotions are dragged and dissolved.

Sandalwood oil has often been used in the East to increase sexual energies and elevate the union with a loving couple to the plane of a spiritual experience. In addition, it stimulates fantasy and awakens joy for creative action. The vibrations of sandalwood produce the integration of spiritual energies into all planes of our thinking, feeling and acting.

Form Of Yoga That Acts Primarily On The Second Chakra

Tantric Yoga: In tantra all nature is considered as a game of the female and male forces, shakti and Shiva, who in a perpetual creative dance, generate the world of appearances or phenomena.

By opening all the senses, by means of complete "yes" to life, and by the use and elevation of sexual experience, tantra aspires to a union with this "cosmic sexuality."

The Third Chakra And Its Correspondences

Keywords: The ego. I am. The own territory. Power and will. Energy. The transformation.

The personal mind. This place needs to understand the situations that it lives in a clear, direct way and with a certain rational lucidity that flows in harmony with the intuitive mind.

- **Location:** In the pit of the stomach.
- **Sanskrit name:** Manipura.
- **Sound:** Ram.
- **Phoneme:** A
- **Verb:** I can.
- **Colors:** Yellow to activate it and purple to calm it.
- **Foods:** Cereals.
- **Magic with candles:** Between the "three wishes" in front of the birthday cake and conscious meditation.
- **Essential oils:** Lavender, rosemary, bergamot, sage, carnation, cinnamon, daisy, sunflower.
- **Gems:** All yellow, topaz, citrine, amber.
- **Corresponding element:** Fire.
- **Sensory function:** View.
- **Symbol:** Ten-petty loto.
- **Basic principle:** Configuration of the being. Body correspondences: Lower back, abdominal cavity, digestive system,

stomach, liver, spleen, gallbladder; vegetative nervous system.

- **Corresponding Gland:** Pancreas (liver).

The pancreas plays a decisive role in the processing and digestion of food. It produces the hormone insulin, which is important for the balance of blood sugar and for the metabolism of carbohydrates. Enzymes secreted by the pancreas are important for the metabolism of fats and proteins.

Astrological correspondences:

- **Leo/Sun:** Heat, strength, fullness, aspiration for recognition, power and social position.

- **Sagittarius/Jupiter:** Affirming vital experiences, growth and enlargement, synthesis, wisdom, integration.

- **Virgo/Mercury:** Subdivision, analysis, adaptation, selfless or altruistic service.

- **Mars:** Energy, activity, disposition for action, the imposition of one's personality.

Mission And Operation Of The Third Chakra

The third chakra finds different denominations. There are also different indications of where it sits. It is the main chakra and several secondary chakras that, however, intertwine so closely in their functioning that all of them can be considered together as a main chakra.

Thus, the third chakra has a complex scope of functions. It is assigned to the fire element; fire means light, heat, energy and activity; and on the spiritual plane, also purification.

The solar plexus chakra represents our Sun, our energy center. Here we absorb the energy of the Sun, which among other functions has to feed our etheric body, also nourishing the physical body with vitality and sustaining it. In the third chakra we enter into an active relationship with the things of the world and with other people. It's the area from which our emotional energy flows out. Our interpersonal relationships, sympathies and antipathies, and the ability to establish lasting emotional bonds are broadly governed from this center.

For the ordinary man, the third chakra is the personality seat. It is the place where he finds his social identification and tries to confirm himself by personal strength, the will for performance and the aspiration of power, or by adapting to social norms.

An important function of the third chakra is to purify the instincts and desires of the lower chakras, to consciously direct and use their creative energy, as well as to manifest in the material world the spiritual fullness of the upper chakras, and achieve a degree of maximum consummation in life at all levels.

It is found in direct union with the astral body, also called the body of desire or ambition, and which is the bearer of our emotions. The vital impulses, desires and feelings of the lower chakras are deciphered here, "digested," transforming into higher energy before being used in conjunction with the energies of the higher chakras for the conscious configuration of our lives.

We can find a corresponding principle in the physical plane in the liver area. In conjunction with the digestive system, the liver has the function of analyzing the food ingested, separating the useless from the profitable, and transforming the user into usable substances, transporting them to the right places in the body.

The conscious affirmation and integration of feelings and desires and our life experiences lead to the détente and openness of the third chakra, with which light continually grows in us and our life, and our world become increasingly enlightened.

Our general mood depends very intensely on how much light we let into us. We feel enlightened, cheerful and satisfied inside when the third chakra is open; on the contrary, our mood is unbalanced and bleak when blocked or deranged. This feeling is continually projected into the outside world, so that all life can seem enlightened or dark. The amount of light within us determines the clarity of our vision and the quality of what we contemplate.

The increasing integration and inner totality cause the yellow light of intellectual understanding to gradually transform into the third chakra into the golden light of wisdom and fullness.

With the solar plexus chakra, we also perceive the vibrations of other people directly, and then we react accordingly to the quality of such vibrations. When faced with negative vibrations, here we often experience imminent danger. We recognize this because the third chakra is contracted unintentionally, as a temporary protection mechanism. However, it becomes superfluous when the light within us is so large that it radiates intensely outward and surrounds our body as with a protective envelope.

Harmonic Operation

When the third chakra is open and works harmoniously, a feeling of peace, inner harmony with yourself, with life and your position before it, is transmitted. You can accept yourself with all your being and you are able to respect the feelings and peculiarities of other people.

You have the natural ability to accept feelings, desires and vital experiences, to recognize their function for your evolution, to see them "in the right light" and to integrate them into your personality in a way that leads you to totality.

Your action spontaneously comes into line with natural laws that are effective throughout the universe and in man's own. As it encourages evolution, it helps to open wealth and fullness for you and your fellow people, both indoors and outdoors. You're full of light and strength. The clarity in you also surrounds your body: this protects you from negative vibrations and radiates throughout your environment.

In combination with an open front and coronal chakra, you detect that everything visible is composed of different vibrations of light. Your desires are fulfilled spontaneously, since you are so closely bound with the luminous force of all things you attract like a magnet as desired.

Thus you realize in your life the knowledge that fulness is your right acquired at birth and your divine inheritance.

When the third chakra has a strong one-sided accent and dysfunction, you would like to influence everything according to your sense, control both your inner world and your outside world, as well as exercise power and conquer. But you find yourself driven by inner uneasiness and dissatisfaction. You've probably experienced little recognition in your childhood and youth. You have not possessed any true sense of selfesteem, and now you seek in the outer life that confirmation and satisfaction that have always been lacking inwardly. To do this, you develop a huge impulse of activity, with which you try to cover the corrosive feeling of insufficiency. You lack inner serenity, and you find it hard to free yourself and unwind.

Since you believe you are predominantly destined to gain recognition and external wealth, you will probably succeed.

The position that everything is feasible leads to the control and repression of "vicious" and unwanted feelings. Consequently, your emotions will stagnate. However, from time to time they will break that wall moved by rejection and control and will flood you without you being able to steer them properly. In addition, you exasperate easily, and in your excitability there is a lot of that anger that you have swallowed over time without processing it.

Finally, you must note that the mere aspiration for external wealth and recognition cannot give you any lasting satisfaction.

Hypofunction

When there is poor functioning of the third chakra you often feel defeated and unencouraged.

You see obstacles everywhere that oppose the fulfillment of your wishes.

The free development of your personality was probably strongly hampered as a child. For fear of losing recognition from your parents or educators, you have almost completely retracted the manifestation of your feelings and swallowed many things you weren't able to digest. Thus, "emotional slags" have been formed that mitigate the fiery energy of the solar plexus chakra and take away the force and spontaneity of your desires and actions.

Even today you try to gain recognition through adaptation, which leads to rejection and poor integration of vital desires and emotions. In difficult situations, you're invaded by a languid sensation in your stomach or you get so nervous that your actions are fickle and uncoordinated.

What you'd like most is to shut yourself down to new challenges. The unused experiences cause you distress, and you don't really believe in what's meant by a life struggle.

Possibilities of purification and activation of the third chakra

Natural Experience

The golden light of the sun corresponds to the light, heat and force of the solar plexus chakra. If you consciously open yourself up to their influence, these qualities will be activated in you.

The observation of a field of rapeseed or cereal ripe and resplendent by the sun also transmits to you the experience of the fullness manifested as resonance, caused by the heat and the luminous force of the sun.

In the center of the sunflower, in the unit of the moving circle, you find the moving spiral pattern, and on the petals, the golden light radiating outward. By imbuing yourself in it, the pattern of this natural mandala you experience in the inner experience of unity, there is a movement and activity full of meaning, orderly and at the same time dancers, who radiate outward with energy, joy, softness and absolute beauty.

Sound Therapy

Musical form: The third chakra is activated by fiery rhythms. Orchestral music, with its harmonic conjunction of a lot of sounds, can be used to harmonize the solar plexus chakra. In the case of hyperactivity, any relaxing music that leads you to your center is suitable to reassure you.

Vocal: The solar plexus chakra is assigned an open "o," as the second "o" of the word "sofort". Here too, the "o" causes a circular motion that is directed outward through the "o" opening. It favors the exterior configuration of the being from an interior whole. The open "o" approaches the "a" of the heart chakra. It provides breadth, fullness and joy in manifestation.

Chromotherapy

A light and sunny yellow activates and intensifies the functioning of the third chakra. Yellow accelerates nerve activity and thinking, and encourages contact and exchange with others. It counteracts a feeling of inner fatigue, joviality and serene ease. When you're in a passive or dreamy state, a light yellow will help you get actively into life. In addition, it promotes physical digestion and 'psychic digestion.'

The chromatic hue of golden yellow has a clarifying and sedative effect on psychic problems and diseases. It enhances intellectual activities and promotes that form of wisdom that is born only of experience.

Gemmotherapy

Tiger's Eye: The tiger's eye favors both exterior and inner visual ability. It sharpens understanding and helps you recognize your mistakes and act accordingly.

Amber: Amber provides warmth and confidence. Its solar strength leads you on your way to greater joy and clearer light. It conveys intuition to you and tells you how you can perform in life. In this way, amber gives you a lucky hand in the various companies you undertake.

On the body plane, it purifies the body, has a balancing effect on the digestive and hormonal system and purifies and enhances the liver.

Topaz: Golden yellow topaz fills you with flowing energy and warm sunlight. It brings greater awareness, wakefulness, clarity, joy and vivacity. It also eliminates the feelings of ballast and murky thoughts: an aid to anxieties and depression.

It strengthens and stimulates the whole body and promotes spiritual and body digestion.

Citrine: Citrine transmits well-being, warmth, vivacity, safety and confidence. It helps you process life experiences and integrates them into your personality, as well as apply intuitive perceptions in everyday life. It provides fullness, both indoors and outdoors, and supports you in the realization of your goals.

In the physical field, it favors the excretion or elimination of toxins and helps in digestive disorders and diabetes. It also activates blood and boosts nerve activity.

Aromatherapy

Lavender: The essence of lavender has a sedative and relaxing effect on a third hyperactive chakra. Its soft and warm vibrations help in the dissolution and processing of stagnant emotions.

Romero: The essence of rosemary, aromatic and rough, is particularly suitable in case of hypofunction of the solar plexus chakra. It has a life-giving and stimulating effect, helps overcome laziness and encourages the willingness to do so.

Bergamot: The vibrations of the oil that is extracted from the fruits of the bergamot tree contain a lot of light. Its fresh and lemony aroma enhances our vital energies. It gives us self-confidence.

A Form Of Yoga That Acts Primarily On The Third Chakra.

Karmic yoga: In karmic yoga we aspire to altruism in action, without thinking about the fruits and personal results of actions. In this way the karmic yogi opens himself to the divine will and concordats his actions with the natural forces of evolution, which reflect God's will for creation.

The Fourth Chakra And Its Correspondences

Keywords: Unconditional love, compassion, affinity, relationships, healing, breathing, devotion, the bridge. It is the center of love where we interact affectively with partners, children, family, colleagues, or friends. You need to give and receive love in all types of relationships where love is possible.

- **Location:** Heart.
- **Sanskrit Name:** Anahata.
- **Sound:** Lam.
- **Phoneme:** E
- **Verb:** I love it.
- **Colors:** Green and pink to activate it, intense green to calm it.
- **Foods:** Vegetables.
- **Essential oils:** Roses, jasmine, marjoram.
- **Gems:** All green or pink, green quartz, rose, rhodochrosite, moonstone.
- **Corresponding Element:** Air.
- **Sensory Function:** Touch.

- **Symbol:** 12-petal loto. (a)
- **Basic Principle:** Delivery of being.
- **Body Correspondences:** Heart, upper back with the rib cage and chest cavity, the lower area of the lungs, blood and circulatory system, skin.
- **Corresponding Gland:** Timo. The thymus regulates growth and controls the lymphatic system. In addition, it has the mission of stimulating and strengthening the immune system.

Astrological correspondences:

- **Leo/Sun:** Sentimental warmth, cordiality, generosity.
- **Pound/Venus:** Contact, love, aspiration to harmony, complementation in the "you."
- **Saturn:** Overcoming the individual ego, essential for selfless love.

CHAPTER 9

MISSION AND OPERATION OF THE FOURTH CHAKRA

The fourth chakra forms the central point of the chakra system. It links the three physical-emotional lower centers with the three psychic-spiritual upper centers. Its symbol is the hexagon, which represents very intuitively how the energies of the three upper and three lower chakras penetrate each other. The fourth chakra is assigned the element air and sense of touch. This signals the mobility of the heart, the movement towards something, the contact, the letting go, the being in contact with things. We find here the ability to emphasize and "feel with," to balance moods and to go into resonance with vibrations. Through this center, we also perceive the beauty of nature and the harmony of music, graphic art and poetry. Here, images, words and sounds are transformed into feelings.

The mission of the cordial chakra is the union for love. Every cripple of intimate contact, uniqueness, harmony and love is manifested through the cordial chakra, even when we come out in its form of sadness, pain, or anguish at the separation or loss of love.

In its purified and completely open form, the cordial chakra is the center of true and unconditional love, a love that only exists on its own, that cannot be had or lost. In combination with the higher chakras, this love becomes Bhakti, in divine love, and leads to knowledge of divine presence throughout creation, to uniqueness with the most intimate nucleus, with the heart of all things of the universe. The path of the heart towards this goal passes through "yes," full of love and understanding, towards ourselves as a premise for the "yes" to others and to life.

If through the third chakra and knowledge we have accepted that all life experiences, desires and emotions have a deeper meaning, and through it and the associated learning mission, we want to return to a broader order, we will find in the room chakra a loving acceptance emanating from the knowledge of the heart that all feelings and all manifestations of life have originally arisen from the longing of love, of union with life and, therefore, are ultimately a manifestation of love.

With every union, we generate separation and negativity. The positive and loving "yes" generates, on the other hand, a vibration in which negative forms and feelings, which dissolve, cannot be maintained and manifest. You may have already experienced the fact that an intense feeling of sadness, anger, or despair has been neutralized when you have dedicated your loving attention, without prejudice and integrity to that feeling. Try it some time.

When we suffer from difficulties or illness, we can see that, through loving dedication to the diseased organ or the part of the sick body, we can greatly accelerate healing.

In this way, through the cordial chakra, we have a great potential for transformation and healing: both for ourselves and for others. Love for ourselves, the acceptance of our whole essence from the depths of our hearts, can transform and heal us fundamentally. And it is a premise for a satisfying love for others, for "feeling with," for understanding and the deep joy of living.

The cordial chakra is a center whose force radiates with a particular intensity to the outside. An open, cordial chakra will have a spontaneous healing and transformative effect on other people (on the other hand, in a consciously applied healing activity the frontal chakra is also involved).

The cordial chakra radiates in the colors green and pink, and sometimes also in gold. Green is the color of healing, as well as harmony and sympathy. When an aura seer perceives, in a person's cordial chakra, a light and luminous green, it is for him an indication of a very marked healing ability. A golden aura, or with pink iridescent, indicates a person who lives in pure love and fully devoted to the divine.

Often, the chakra of the heart is called the door to the soul, since not only do our deepest and most vivid feelings of love settle in it, but through this energy center, we can also come into contact with the universal part of our soul, with the divine sparks in us. It also plays a decisive role in the refinement of perception, which is paired with the opening of the front chakra, the so-called third eye, since it is the delivery that makes us sensitive to the subtler realms of creation. This means that, in parallel with the development of the cordial chakra, the higher faculties of the frontal chakra are developed.

For this reason, many spiritual disciplines, both East and West, have specifically focused on the opening of the cordial chakra.

Harmonic Operation

When your cordial chakra is completely open and interacts harmoniously with the plus chakras, you become a channel of divine love. The energies of your heart can transform your world and unite the people around you, reconcile them and heal them. You radiate a natural warmth, cordiality and joviality that opens the hearts of your fellow citizens, awakens confidence and gives joy. Sharing feelings and a willingness to help are not over-the-top for you.

Your feelings are free from internal turmoil and conflict, doubts and uncertainties. You love for love itself from the joy of giving, without expecting anything in return. And you feel safe and at home in all creation. All in all, in what you do, "you put your whole heart."

The love of your heart also purifies your perception, so that you also perceive the cosmic play of separation and the new union in all manifestations of any plane of creation, a cosmic game that is ported and penetrated by divine love and harmony. You yourself have experienced that from the separation of the universal and divine aspect of life, and the suffering resulting from it is the longing for reunification with the divine. And that only through this prior separation can the conscious and complete experience of the love of God and the infinite joy in him come about.

You observe the events of the world from this wisdom of the heart, and you observe your life in a new light.

The love of your heart spontaneously supports all the aspirations that make love for God and his creation grow. You know that the whole life of creation lives in your heart. You no longer contemplate life from the outside as something separate from you, but as if it were a part of your own life.

The feeling of vivacity in you is so great that only now do you really know what "life" means in its original form: a permanent expression of divine love and glory.

Dysfunction of the heart chakra can be expressed in several ways: for example, you would like to give, always be there for others without having to be at the source of love. In secret (perhaps without being aware of it or without confessing to yourself) you still expect to receive recognition and confirmation in exchange for all your "love," and you are disappointed when your efforts are not sufficiently rewarded.

Either you feel powerful and strong and give others your strength, or you are not able to accept love yourself, to open yourself to receive. The tender and gentle will bewilder you. Maybe you'll tell yourself you don't need the love of others. This posture is often paired with a "ufano" chest, an indication of the internal armor and rejection of pain and attacks.

Hypofunction

The poor functioning of the cordial chakra makes you easily vulnerable and dependent on the love and sympathy of others. When you are rejected, you feel deeply affected; just when, for once, you had the courage to open up? Then you retract back into your shell, you're sad and depressed. It is true that you would want to give love, but for fear of a new rejection, you do not find the right way to do it, which affirms you again and again of your incapacity.

Possibly, you also try to compensate for your lack of love in a particular friendship, bringing you joy in a rather impersonal way to everyone alike, without letting yourself, however, introduce yourself deeper into people. But as soon as it really appeals to your heart, you react evasively for fear of a possible wound.

When your cordial chakra is completely closed, it manifests itself in dryness and disinterest, which can reach the "coldness of heart." In order to even feel something, you need a strong external stimulation. You're decompensated and suffering from depression.

Possibilities Of Purification And Activation Of The Fourth Chakra

Natural experience

Any silent walk through the green and untouched nature harmonizes our whole being through the cordial chakra. Any flower conveys to us the message of love and innocent joy and lets the same qualities flourish in our hearts. The red flowers are particularly suitable for gently activating and healing the energies of the cordial chakra.

A pink-tinged sky with delicate cloud formations lifts and widens the heart. Let yourself be wrapped and carried by the beauty and softness of colors and shapes of this image of the sky.

Sound Therapy

Musical form: Any classical music, "New Age" music or sacred music, both eastern and western tradition, which makes your heart dance along with life and creation, and awakens the heart force of love in your chakra, has a life-giving and harmonizing effect on it. Also, sacred or meditative dances, in their movements, manifest the harmony and joy of creation.

Vocal: The cordial chakra is assigned the vowel "a." Used in the scale f key. The "a" symbolizes the sudden discovery of the heart, as manifested in our exclamation "ah!" It is the most open sound of all, representing the greatest possible fullness in the manifestation of the human voice. In the "a" lies the unprejudiced acceptance of all events, acceptance from which love is born. It is also the most frequent vowel of babies, who's intellect cannot distinguish between "good" and "evil," when they "comment" on their experiences.

Chromotherapy

Green: The color of the meadows and forests of our planet provides harmony and empathy, gives us a conciliatory spirit, makes us feel sympathy and transmits to us a feeling of peace. It also has a regenerative effect on the body, spirit and soul, and brings new energies.

Pink: The soft, delicate vibrations of pink dissolve heart spasms. They arouse feelings of love and tenderness and provide a childish feeling of happiness. In addition, they stimulate creative activity.

Gemmotherapy

Pink quartz: The delicate and pinkish light of pink quartz favors softness, tenderness and love. It envelops your soul in a loving vibration in which they can heal the wounds of the heart caused by hardness, brutality or inattention, and can open your soul more and more to love and give it more love.

Pink quartz teaches you to love and accept yourself, open your heart to the manifestation of love and sweetness that is in you, in other people and in creation. It also makes you sensitive to the beauty of music, poetry, painting and other arts, and stimulates your fantasy and your ability to express creative expression.

Tourmaline: Pink-red tourmaline takes you out of indolent sentimental structures; opens and widens your heart. It also opens your conscience to the joyful and jovial aspect of love. It joins you with the feminine manifestation of divine love, which is expressed in the beauty of creation, in carefree joviality, in spiritual dance and in the game. In this way it integrates the different manifestations of worldly and divine love.

Pink tourmaline with a green flange is also particularly suitable for the cordial chakra, which is often cut into discs (watermelon tourmaline). Here, the qualities of pink-red tourmaline are embedded in the healing and harmonizing vibration of green.

Kunzite: In the kunzite are joined the delicate rose of superior love and the violet of the coronal chakra, which supports unification with the divine.

The kunzite opens your cordial chakra to divine love. It helps you grow your heart's love for altruism and perception. To do this, it provides guidance and always takes you back this way.

Emerald: Emerald is the love of the universe, since it intensifies and deepens love in all planes. It gives peace and harmony and puts you in harmony with the forces of nature. It also challenges you to make yourself equal to its radiant light and shows you the areas where it doesn't happen yet.

The emerald attracts healing energies from the cosmos in the direction of Earth. Regenerate, rejuvenate, refresh and reassure.

Jade: The soft green light of jade provides peace, harmony, the wisdom of heart, justice and modesty. The jade relaxes and calms the heart, makes you discover and live the beauty of everything created, thus fostering your esteem and love for creation. The jade helps in the face of restlessness and bewilderment, and encourages the reconciliation of peaceful sleep and pleasant dreams.

Aromatherapy

Rose Essence: There is no other aroma that has such a strong harmonizing effect above all our being as the precious essence of roses. Its delicate and loving vibrations mitigate and heal the wounds of our hearts. They awaken perception by the manifestation of love, beauty and harmony throughout creation. They reinstitute in the heart a deep joy and willingness for dedication. The essence of roses also causes stimulation and refinement of sensory joys, at the same time promoting their transformation for suprapersonal love.

Form Of Yoga That Acts Primarily On The Fourth Chakra

Yoga Bhakti: Bhakti yoga is the way that leads to the love of God and gives it to the individual for fulfillment in God. The bhakta deepens and intensifies his feelings and turns him to God. Everything he means, he sees it in all things and rises in love for Him.

The Fifth Chakra And Its Correspondences

Keywords: Sound, communication, creativity, creation, symbol ideas, telepathy, the media.

Harmonize with the divine will within, commit to telling the truth. You need to express your truth.

- **Location:** Throat.
- **Sanskrit Name:** Vishudha.
- **Sound:** Ham.
- **Phoneme:** i
- **Verb:** I speak.
- **Corresponding Element:** Ether.
- **Sensory Function:** Ear.

139

- **Symbol:** 16-petal loto.
- **Basic Principle:** Resonance with being.
- **Body maps:** Neck area, cervical area, chin area, ears, speech apparatus (voice), respiratory ducts, bronchi, the upper area of the lungs, esophagus, arms.
- **Colors:** Sky blue and turquoise to activate it, fuchsia to calm it.
- **Gems:** Turquoise, Aquamarine, Celestine, Blue Lace Agate.
- **Foods:** Fresh and dried fruits.
- **Essential oils:** Sage, eucalyptus, benzoin, frankincense.

Corresponding Gland: Thyroid.

The thyroid plays an important role in the growth of the skeleton and internal organs. It is responsible for the balance between physical and psychic growth and regulates metabolism, that is, the way and speed in which we transform our food into energy and in which we consume such energy. It also regulates iodine metabolism and calcium balance in the blood and tissues.

Astrological Correspondences:

- **Gemini/Mercury:** Communication, exchange of knowledge and experiences.

- **Mars:** Active self-manifestation.

- **Taurus/Venus:** Sense of space and form.

- **Aquarius/Uranus:** Divine inspiration, the transmission of wisdom and superior knowledge, independence.

Mission And Operation Of The Fifth Chakra

In the neck chakra, we find the center of human expression capacity, communication and inspiration. It is attached to a smaller secondary chakra, which is seated at the back of the neck and opens backward. Also these two energy centers are often considered as a single chakra. In its functioning, however, the cervical chakra is so closely linked with the neck chakra that we have integrated it into the interpretation of the latter.

The fifth chakra also forms an important union of the lower chakras with the centers of the head. It serves as a bridge between our thinking and our feeling, between our impulses and the reactions we have to them, and simultaneously transmits the contents of all chakras to the outside world. Through the neck chakra we manifest all that lives in us, our laughter and our weeping, our feelings of love and joy or anguish and anger, our intentions and desires, and also our ideas, intuitions and perception of the inner worlds.

The element that is assigned to the neck chakra is the ether. In the doctrine of yoga, it is considered the fundamental element from which the elements of the lower chakras are formed by compaction: earth, water, fire, air. But the ether is also the bearer of the sound, of the spoken word, and of the word of the creator; it is, in short, the transmitter of information on all planes.

Thus, the communication of our inner life to the outside is predominantly through spoken word, but also through our mimicry, and through other creative manifestations, such as music, graphic art and interpretive dance, etc. The creativity we found in the sacral chakra is joined in the neck chakra with the energies of the remaining chakras, and the forming power of the ether gives it a certain figure that we relay to the outside world.

However, we can only express what we find in ourselves. Thus, through the fifth chakra, we first receive the faculty of self-reflection. The premise necessary to be able to reflect is a certain inner distance. As we develop the neck chakra, we are more and more aware of our mental body, and we can separate its functioning from the functioning of the emotional body, the etheric body and the physical body. This means that our thoughts are no longer the hostages of our physical feelings and sensations, so objective knowledge is possible.

The ether is also defined as space (Akasha), in which the most compact elements deploy their effectiveness. The deepest knowledge is conferred upon us when we are open and unobstructed as infinite space, as the wide sky (whose light blue color is the color of the neck chakra), when we remain silent and listen attentively to the interior space and outside. The sensory function of the ear is associated with the fifth chakra. Here we open our ears, listen attentively to the hidden or unhidden voices of creation. We also perceive our own inner voice, come into contact with the spirit inherent in us, and receive its inspiration. And we develop unwavering confidence in the superior personal guide. We are also aware of our authentic role in life, of our dharma. We know that our own inner worlds are both the non-material planes of life and the outside world, and we are able to collect and relay information from the non-material areas and the higher dimensions of reality. This divine inspiration becomes a carrier of our selfmanifestation.

Thus, in the fifth chakra we find our individual expression of perfection in all planes.

Harmonic Operation

With a completely open neck chakra, you express clearly and without fear your inner feelings, thoughts and knowledge. You are also able to reveal your weaknesses and show your strengths. Your inner sincerity in front of yourself and in front of others is also expressed in your sincere attitude.

You have the ability to express yourself in a totally creative way with your whole being. But you can also remain silent when it is the right thing to do, and you have the gift of listening to others with your heart and with inner understanding. Your language is full of fantasy and, at the same time, it is very clear to transmit your intention in the most effective way to provoke a fulfillment of your desires. This voice is full. In the face of difficulties and resistance, you remain true to yourself, and you can also say "no" when you think so. You don't let yourself be convinced or dragged by other people's opinions, and instead you retain your independence, freedom and selfdetermination. Your absence of prejudice and your inner breadth make you open to the reality of nonmaterial dimensions. From here you receive, through the inner voice, information that leads you on your way through life, and you give yourself full confidence to this guide.

You recognize that all phenomena of creation have their own message. They tell you about their own life, their role in the great cosmic game and their aspiration to totality and light. You can communicate with beings from other existential realms, and the knowledge you receive from it, you sensibly relay to your fellow citizens without fearing their judgment. All the creative means of expression you use have the ability to transmit wisdom and truth.

From your inner independence and the free manifestation of your whole being, deep joy and a feeling of fullness and integrity are born in you.

When the energies of your neck chakra are blocked, the understanding between the "head" and the "body" is altered. This can manifest itself in two ways. Either you find it difficult to reflect on your feelings, and you often express your accumulated emotions through thoughtless actions; or you have encapsulated yourself in your intellectuality or your rationalism, you deny the right to life, and the wisdom of your sentimental world only allows you to pass the filter of your self-judgment to very crowded emotions, not allowing them to crash against the judgments of your fellow men. Unconscious feelings of guilt and anxieties prevent you from seeing yourself and showing yourself as you are and freely expressing your innermost thoughts, feelings, and needs. Instead, you try to disguise them with all sorts of words and gestures, behind which you hide your true self.

Your language is either unprocessed and rude, or even objective and cold. You'll probably stutter too. Your voice is relatively loud, and your words have no greater depth of content.

You don't allow yourself to give a weak appearance, you try to look strong at any price. In this way, you put yourself under pressure with demands imposed by yourself. It can also happen that the functions that life imposes on you at some point are too great a burden on your shoulders. Then, you arm yourself in your "scapular waist": you shrug your neck unconsciously to protect yourself from increased efforts, or arm yourself for a new "attack."

An inharmonic functioning of the fifth chakra is also found in people who abuse their word and their ability to express to manipulate their congeners, or who try through uninterrupted eloquence and loquacity to attract attention to themselves.

In general, people whose energies are stagnant in the neck chakra do not have access to the non-material dimensions of being, since they lack candor, inner amplitude and independence, which are the premises for the perception of these areas.

However, there is also the possibility here that you may have deep inner knowledge, but that, out of fear of the judgment of others or out of anguish at isolation, you do not dare to live and manifest them. Since they struggle to manifest themselves, spontaneous poetry, images or the like can arise from there.

Spiritual energies can also become stuck in the head. So its transforming force hardly finds access to your emotions, and the energies of the lower chakras do not give those of the superiors the necessary strength and stability to impose themselves, to realize in your life the inner spirituality.

Hypofunction

Also, in the case of hypofunction, you will have difficulty showing, manifesting and representing yourself. However, here you retract completely, you are preferably shy, quiet and withdrawn, or you talk only about things that are unimportant in your outside life.

However, when you have to externalize something you think or feel in the most intimate, you are easily tied up in your throat and your voice sounds coerced. More often than not in the case of inharmonic functioning, we find here the symptom of stuttering. You are unsure of other people and you fear the judgment they may make about you. So you're intensely oriented towards their opinions and often don't really know what you want yourself. You have no access to the messages of your mind and no confidence in your intuitive powers.

When in the course of life, the fifth chakra has not developed, a certain rigidity appears. The framework drawn by yourself, within which you pass your existence and in which you express your potential, is very small, because you only consider as reality the outside world.

Possibilities Of Purification And Activation Of The Fifth Chakra

Natural Experience

The clear blue of a clear sky evokes a resonance in your neck chakra. To fully embrace it in you, it is best that you lie relaxed outdoors and open your inner self to the infinite spaciousness of the celestial vault. You will notice how your spirit opens and becomes transparent and how any narrowness or stiffness in your neck chakra and irradiation scope gradually dissolves. You will be inwardly willing to receive the "heavenly messages."

The reflection of the blue sky in a crystal clear course of water also has the effect of expanding and releasing your feelings. The slight murmur of the waves carries the messages of your emotions and sensations hidden up to your conscious. Let yourself be completely penetrated by the vibrating energy of the sky and water, and spirit and feelings will unite in a complementary force.

Sound Therapy

Musical form: Music and singing rich in superior tones, as well as sacred and meditative dances accompanied by singing, will act with a hugely life-giving effect on the neck chakra. To harmonize and relax the fifth chakra, the most effective music is the "New Age" with acoustic effects. It provides release and spaciousness and opens the inner ear.

Vocal: The vowel "e" activates the neck chakra. It sings into the sun key of the scale. If your voice slowly goes from an "a" to an "i," at any given moment the "e" sound will emerge. Just as the neck represents a bonding channel between the head and the rest of the body, the "e" of the neck chakra unites the heart and understanding, "a" and "i," and channels its forces outward. As you sing the "e", you will notice that this sound demands maximum pressure from the voice and strengthens the energy of the ex-pressure in your fifth chakra.

Chromotherapy

A light, transparent blue is assigned to the neck chakra. This color fosters tranquility and

149

spaciousness and opens you up for spiritual inspiration.

Gemmotherapy

Aquamarine: The luminous blue color of aquamarine is like the sea in which a clear sky is reflected. Aquamarine helps the soul become a mirror for the infinite breadth of the spirit. It promotes communication with the innermost self and brings light and transparency to the most hidden Ancones of the soul. Its vibrations bring to the soul purity, freedom and breadth, so that it can be opened to visionary clairvoyance and an intuitive understanding, and also helps to express this knowledge freely and creatively. Under the influence of aquamarine, the soul can become a channel for selfless love and healing force.

Turquoise: Turquoise, the color in which the blue of the sky and the green of the earth come together, combines the high ideals of the spirit with the original strength of our planet. It helps to express intellectual ideas and knowledge and integrate them into life on Earth. In addition, it attracts positive energies and protects the body and soul from negative influences.

Chalcedony: White and blue chalcedony has a positive effect on the thyroid gland. It has a sedative and balancing influence on mood, and reduces irritability and hypersensitivity. Thanks to its sedative influence, it opens access to inner inspiration and promotes selfmanifestation through language and writing.

Aromatherapy

Sage: The fresh and rough aroma of sage sends healing vibrations to the "language dwelling area." It dissolves the convulsive contractions of the neck chakra, so that our words are expressed harmoniously and vigorously, and can transmit in the most effective way possible, the intention of our soul.

Eucalyptus: The refreshing aroma of eucalyptus brings transparency and breadth to the scope of the fifth chakra. Its vibrations open us for inner inspiration and give us self-manifestation, originality and creativity. Form of yoga that acts primarily on the fifth chakra.

Mantric Yoga: Mantras are meditative syllables that reflect in their specific form of vibration certain aspects of the divine. In Mantric yoga, mantras are repeated mentally uninterruptedly, recited high or sung. In doing so, the vibration of the mantra gradually transforms the practitioner's thought and feeling and resonates with the cosmic and divine power manifested in the mantra.

One exception is transcendental meditation. In this form of meditation, a technique is taught, with whose help the mantra is experienced in planes of consciousness less and less material and subtle, until the meditator overcomes even the most subtle aspect of the mantra, and transcends and reaches the experience of being Pure. This process is consumed several times during each meditation.

The Sixth Chakra And Its Correspondences

Keywords: Sight, intuition, clairvoyance, image, knowing, perceiving, insight, mastering, visualization, time, completing the karmic teaching of this life. Divine love and spiritual ecstasy. You need to live the personal experience of spirituality and unconditional love.

- **Location:** Slightly above the eyes, in the center of the forehead.
- **Sanskrit Name:** Ajna.
- **Sound**: Om.
- **Phoneme:** M or N
- **Verb:** I see.
- **Colors:** Ultramarine blue, indigo to activate it, to calm it, pale blue.

- **Foods:** None.

- **Essential oils:** Mint, jasmine, mugwort, anise, saffron, lavender.

- **Sensory Function:** All senses, also in the form of extrasensory perception.

- **Symbols:** 96-petal loto (twice 48 petals).

- **Basic principle:** Knowledge of being.

- **Body correspondences:** Face; eyes, ears, nose, sinuses, cerebellum, central nervous system.

- **Corresponding Gland:** Pituitary gland (hypothesis).

- **Gems:** All blue or violet, lapis lazuli, amethyst, fluorite.

The pituitary gland is also sometimes referred to as the master gland, since, through its internal secretive activity, it controls the functioning of all other glands. Like a conductor, it establishes harmonic conjunction of the remaining glands.

Astrological Correspondences:

- **Mercury:** Intellectual knowledge, rational thinking.

- **Sagittarius/Jupiter:** Holistic thinking, knowledge of internal relations.

- **Aquarius/Uranus:** Thought of divine inspiration, superior intuition, sudden knowledge.

- **Pisces/Neptune:** Ability to imagine, intuition, access (through delivery) to inner truths.

Mission And Operation Of The Sixth Chakra

Through the sixth chakra the conscious perception of being is consumed. It sets the superior psychic force, the intellectual capacity for differentiation, the capacity of remembrance and will; and on a physical level is the supreme command center of the central nervous system.

Its true color is light indigo, but yellow and violet nuances can also be detected. These colors indicate their different ways of functioning on different planes of consciousness. Rational or intellectual thinking can bring about yellow radiation here; transparent dark blue points to intuition and comprehensive knowledge processes. Extrasensory perception is shown in a violet hue.

Any realization in our lives presupposes thoughts and ideas that can be fed by unconscious emotional patterns, but also by the knowledge of reality. Through the third eye, we are united with the process of manifestation through force of thought. Everything that manifests itself in creation exists in pure and unmanifested form, similar to how in a latent state seed all the information from which the plant will arise is already contained. Quantum physics calls this area the unified field or the realm of the least excitation of matter.

The process of creation begins when the latent being itself becomes aware of its own existence. Then a first subject-object relationship arises, and with it the first duality. The amorphous being adopted a first manifest vibration pattern.

Based on this photo vibration, new differentiated vibration patterns are continually emerging through further awareness processes.

In us, men, are contained all the planes of creation, from pure being to compact matter, and are represented by the different planes of vibration of the chakras. Thus, the process of manifestation is consummated in us and through us.

Since the third eye serves as a seat for all the processes of awareness, here we obtain the power of manifestation until the materialization and dematerialization of matter. We can create new realities on the psychic plane and dissolve old realities.

However, in general, this process does not occur automatically and without conscious action. Most of the thoughts that determine our lives are controlled by our unreleased emotional patterns, and programmed by both our own and others' judgments and prejudices. In this way, often our spirit is not the one who dominates, but the servant of our thoughts laden with emotions, which can partially dominate us.

But these thoughts are also realized in our lives, for what we perceive and live outside is always and ultimately a manifestation of our subjective reality.

With the development of our consciousness and the growing opening of the third eye we can always consciously direct this process. Our power of imagination then generates the energy to fulfill an idea or a desire. Along with an open cordial chakra, we can now also emit healing energies and perform healings remotely.

At the same time, we receive access to all the planes of creation that lie behind physical reality. The knowledge of them comes to us in the form of intuition, through clairvoyant vision or through auditory or tactile clairvoyance. What we may have previously blundered vaguely now becomes a clear perception.

Harmonic Operation

In our time there are very few people whose third eye is completely open, since their development always has a development of advanced consciousness. But here the phenomenon that the sixth chakra works harmoniously even if it is not fully developed does occur in a clearly more marked way than in the chakras described above. This is shown in an awake understanding and in intellectual skills. Scientific research conducted from a holistic point of view can also be a sign of a partially open, harmoniously functioning third eye, as well as knowledge of deep philosophical truths.

You will probably also have a well-developed faculty of visualization and intuitively capture many relationships. Your spirit is concentrated and simultaneously open to mystical truths. You become increasingly aware that the outer manifestations of things are only a simile, a symbol in which a spiritual principle is manifested on the material plane. Your thought will be carried by idealism and fantasy. You may also notice from time to time that your thoughts and ideas are fulfilled spontaneously.

The more your third eye develops, the more your thoughts will rest on direct and inner knowledge of reality. More and more people are beginning to develop partial faculties of the sixth chakra, such as clairvoyance or tactile clairvoyance on certain existential planes; others are temporarily intuitions of other dimensions of reality: for example, in meditation or in sleep.

Describing the full panoply of faculties and perceptual abilities provided by a third open eye is not possible for us. It would fill a lot of bolts and we would have to rely heavily on data provided by other people. However, here's a general overview of what awaits you with a fully developed sixth chakra.

First of all, you will perceive the world in a new way. The limits of your rational understanding will have been far exceeded. Your thinking is holographic, and you will spontaneously integrate into the knowledge process all the information that comes to you from the different fields of creation.

The material world will have become transparent to you. It is a mirror for the dance of energies that runs in the most subtle planes of creation, just as your consciousness is a mirror in which the divine being is known. Your extrasensory perception is so transparent that you will be able to directly perceive the forces that act behind the surface of the outer appearances, and you will be in a position to consciously control these energies and bring about their own forms of manifestation of these forces. But in doing so, you will be subject to certain regular laws, the framework of which you will not be able to exceed, so that natural order is preserved.

Your intuition and inner vision open the way to all the subtlest planes of reality. You know that between the plane of material creation and pure being there are infinite worlds inhabited by the most diverse essences. Before your inner eye will develop a plural drama of creation, which will seem to have no end in its ever new forms and planes of reality. A deep fear will fill you as you contemplate the greatness of this divine drama.

The most common impact of inharmonic functioning is in this case, the 'head heaviness.' You are a person who lives almost exclusively through intellect and reason. By trying to regulate everything through understanding, you only give validity to the truths that your rational thought transmits to you. Your intellectual abilities are possibly very marked and you possess the gift of shrewd analysis, but you lack the holistic vision and the ability to integrate into a great cosmic relationship.

This is how you easily come to an intellectual preponderance. You only give validity to what is grantable with understanding and verifiable, and likely with scientific methods. You reject spiritual knowledge by being scientific and unrealistic.

Also, the attempt to influence people or things with the force of thought to demonstrate one's power or to satisfy personal needs falls fully into the realm of an inharmonic functioning of the third eye. In general, the solar plexus chakra is usually altered simultaneously, and the cordial chakra and coronal will be underdeveloped. When, despite some blockages, the third eye is relatively fairly open, these attempts may also take effect, but are not in line with the natural flow of life. A sense of isolation is installed, and in the long run the satisfaction to which it is sucked is not achieved.

Another impact of misdirected energies on the sixth chakra appears when the radical chakra (and with it the "grounding") is altered, and when there are other chakras whose harmonic functioning is blocked. Then it can happen that even if you have access to the most subtle levels of perception, you do not recognize in their true significance the images and information received. These are mixed with your own ideas and fantasies, which come from your unprocessed emotional patterns. These subjectively marked images can be so dominant that you see them as the only existence, project them to the outside world and lose the reference of reality.

Hypofunction

When the flow of energies in the sixth chakra is quite clogged, for you the only reality is the visible outside world. Your life will be determined by material desires, bodily needs, and unreflective emotions. Intellectual disputes will be found stressful and useless. You reject spiritual truths, for you they are based on foolish imaginations or dreams that do not represent a practical reference. Your thinking is fundamentally oriented towards prevailing opinions.

In situations that require a lot from you, you easily lose your mind. Possibly, you're also very forgetful. Vision disturbances, which often accompany a hypofunction of the sixth chakra, are a wake-up call to look more inward and to also know those areas behind the visible surface.

In extreme cases, your thoughts can be unclear and confusing and totally determined by your unreleased emotional patterns.

Possibilities Of Purification And Activation Of The Sixth Chakra

Natural experience

The third eye is stimulated by the contemplation of a deeply blue night sky full of stars. This natural experience opens the spirit to the immensity and infinite depth of creation manifested with its immeasurably varied forms of manifestation, and allows to glimpse the subtle forces, structures and regular laws that execute the celestial bodies in their cosmic dance by the immensity of space, and which are also effective after the apparent manifestations of our life on Earth.

Sound Therapy

Musical form: All the sounds that soothe your spirit and open it, and that evoke images and sensations of cosmic amplitude, are suitable to activate and harmonize the front chakra. Where you will most easily find the right pieces is in the music "New Age." But also some classical music from East and West, particularly Bach, can have the same effect.

Vocal: The radical chakra is activated by the vowel "i". It is sung in the key of "la" of the scale. The "i" triggers an upward-directed movement. It represents the strength of inspiration, which always leads you to new movements.

Chromotherapy

Transparent indigo affects the sixth chakra by opening and clarifying it. It gives the spirit inner tranquility, transparency and depth. In addition, it enhances and heals the senses and opens them up for more subtle planes of perception.

Gemmotherapy

Lapis lazuli: In the deep blue color of Lapis lazuli is inserted, like the stars on a night sky, golden inclusions of pyrite. It transmits to the soul an experience of security in the cosmos and opens it for infinite life in the universe. It guides the spirit inward, enhances its strength and helps you to know hierarchically superior relationships. By fostering intuition and inner vision, it allows us to recognize the hidden meaning and forces that act behind things; it also conveys a deep joy about the miracles of life and the universe.

Indigo Sapphire: A clear and transparent sapphire opens the spirit for cosmic knowledge and eternal truths. Its vibrations cause a purification, transformation and renewal of the soul and spirit. It is a bridge between the finite and the infinite, and it causes consciousness to flow along with the river of divine love and knowledge. It also gives transparency to the soul that seeks in a spiritual way.

Sodalite: The dark blue Sodalite clarifies the understanding and empowers it for deep thoughts. Its serene radiation brings serenity and strengthens nerves. Sodalite also helps to dissolve old thought patterns. It conveys confidence and strength to defend one's point of view and to transmit ideas and knowledge in everyday life.

Aromatherapy

Mint: The refreshing aroma of mint dissolves blockages in the scope of the third eye and helps to dissolve old and restrictive mental structures. It gives our spirit clarity and vivacity and promotes the strength of concentration.

Jasmine: By the subtle and outflowed scent of jasmine, our spirit opens to images and visions that carry within themselves the messages of deeper truths. Its vibrations refine perception and unite the energies of the third eye with those of the cordial chakra.

Forms Of Yoga That Act Primarily On The Sixth Chakra

Yoga jnana: Yoga jnana is the way of knowledge to the capacity of intellectual discernment between the real and the unreal, the eternal and the perishable. Yogi jnana knows that there is only one immutable, everlasting and eternal reality: God. In the individual's meditation, he is oriented only with the help of his power of discernment towards the absolute without attributes, to the unmanifested aspect of God, until his spirit merges with it.

Yanth Yoga: The yanths are figurative representations composed of geometric figures that symbolize the divine being and its powers and aspects. They serve as an auxiliary means for visualizations. The meditator delves into the represented aspects of divinity and patents them into its inner contemplation.

The Seventh Chakra And Its Correspondences

Keywords: Understanding, divine consciousness, cosmic consciousness, knowledge, transcendence, joy, liberation from the bonds to transcend karma.

Connection with the divine mind and understanding of the functioning of the universe. You need to experience the serenity and divine joy.

- **Location:** At the highest part of the head.

- **Sanskrit Name:** Sahasrara.

- **Sound:** None.

- **Phoneme:** n nasal.

- **Verb:** I know.

- **Symbol:** Lotus flower of 1,000 petals.

- **Basic Principle:** To be pure.

- **Body Correspondence:** Brain.

- **Corresponding Gland:** Pineal gland (epiphysis).

- **Colors:** Violet, gold, and white to activate, to calm, silver and pink, better iridescent.

- **Foods:** Fasting.

- **Essential Oils:** Frankincense, lotus, ylangylang.

- **Gems:** The most crystalline and pure, crystal quartz, amethyst, diamond, selenite.

The influences of epiphysis have not been fully clarified scientifically. It most likely influences the whole organism. When this gland fails, premature sexual maturity occurs.

Astrological Correspondences:

- **Capricorn/Saturn:** Intuition, concentration in the essentials, penetration of matter with divine light.
- **Pisces/Neptune:** Dissolution of boundaries, delivery, unification.

CONCLUSION

The auric field is the usual name given to each person's complete energy system. It consists of seven major chakras and seven energy bodies that are in charge of assimilating the different types of energy that they nurture and that are processed in each of the levels.

This individual auric field is not a closed or isolated redoubt. It works in resonance with the environment, with other living beings, and with the Divinity. This is done in such a way that it constantly interacts by giving and taking energy and multidimensional information from the different fields that make it up. Furthermore, it also interacts with surroundings and their respective inhabitants.

Despite the differentiations, the chakras work as a team and connect with the rest of the centers. The state of harmony, known as health, is always rooted in the harmonic balance of the openings and expressions that occur in the seven main centers. Having one chakra very open and another functioning half-closed produces a distortion that inevitably leads to disharmony and brings problems in some areas of life.

By paying due attention to your energy state, you can begin to improve the control of the chakras, using different tools that are easily accessible to improve our general state and begin to enjoy harmony.

Achieving harmony in our life is no-nonsense. The balance between everything we are, everything we have and everything we want to achieve is essential to have optimal well-being. And how could it be otherwise? To find order and peace in our life, we first have to find it in ourselves. The chakras are the energy centers of our body, a kind of door through which energy flows. A decompensation of our chakras can bring fatal consequences since it produces an imbalance between our energy which causes us to go into crisis.

REIKI HEALING FOR BEGINNERS

Become Your Own Self-Therapist Using the Best Alternative Therapeutic Strategies to Increase your Energy, Happiness and Mindfulness While Relieving Stress and Anxiety

Sarah Allen

INTRODUCTION

Reiki is one of the highest vibration energy ranges amongst all Universal Energy. Like all others, it tends to harmonize with the other ranges, and it being high vibration is very powerful. It is curative and restorative of physical and psychic situations that somehow do not flow. There are energies that surround us and that we call negative because they are more difficult to master. It seems that they dominate us, not leaving us free to be able to discern what we really want, and how we can achieve it.

Reiki energy is in constant motion around us by wrapping us in full and uniting us with all the living beings of our planet along with the entire Universe. But to be able to take advantage of it, you have to be aware of it, receptive and receive it with humility, openness and total acceptance. With it, we can walk towards integration into the Universe, in the Whole, from our human condition.

Reiki is a millennial medical art, rediscovered by Dr. MIKAO USUI, a monk and dean of a small Kyoto University. Its tradition dates from the Sanskrit sutras more than 2500 years old.
REIKI is a Japanese word which means "universal energy of life." "Rei" means "universal energy of life," and refers to the spirit or soul to the cosmic energy essence that interpenetrates all things and

surrounds all places. "Ki" means "a part of rei," which flows through everything that lives, the individual vital energy that surrounds our body, keeping it alive and is present in every living being. When the "ki" energy comes out of a body, that body ceases to have life.

This word, "ki," corresponds with the "Light" for Christians, the "Chi" for the Chinese, the "Prana" for the Hindus, and also to what has been called bioplasma, bioenergy, or cosmic energy.

Reiki is a generic Japanese word and is used to describe any type of healing work based on the energy of the life force.

Among the benefits it brings, we can find the following:

-   Relaxation of body and mind; recognizing the spirit.
-   Increased vital body energy and creativity.
-   Unlocks tensions and unleashes emotion.
-   Regenerates organs and tissue formation.

Balances energies and develops new capabilities - Acts on the causes of the disease - Healing of the whole being.

CHAPTER 1

EVERYTHING YOU NEED TO KNOW ABOUT REIKI

It is very important, when deciding on reiki therapy, that we go to a specialist in this field and, if necessary, do not leave the medical treatment we are already following.

Reiki is a traditional Japanese therapy that means " hands-on treatment." This method was first practiced by Mikao Usui in the early 1900s and subsequently developed by his disciple, Churijo Hayashi.

Reiki treatments have a very noticeable and positive effect on the mind, body, and emotions of the patient. Reiki energy moves through the receiver, balancing its chakras, and raising its vibrational frequency.

This energy has its own intelligence and travels to the parts where the patient needs it most.

Reiki Benefits

First, Reiki is a compound Sanskrit word that means universal energy (rei) and vital energy (ki). This practice helps the energy to flow through hands, massages or postures applied by the specialized therapist. Thus, the practitioner acts as a channel of universal energy, with the aim of harmonizing the physical, emotional, mental, and spiritual levels of the person.

Thus, reiki can act at the following levels in the body:

- **Physical:** Improving injuries and metabolism.
- **Emotional:** Relaxing the person and giving emotional balance in cases of depression.
- **Mental:** Helping with insomnia and stress.
- **Spiritual:** Granting balance, harmony, and inner peace.

This is a therapy that can be used on anyone, from a child to an elderly person, and even with pregnant women. However, it should be taken into account that this therapy is applied in a complementary way, never as a substitute, for conventional medical or psychological diagnoses.

Keep in mind that reiki is related to the theory of the chakras or energy centers of the body. Simply with hands, the therapist can easily know in which energy center the problem is. From there, they can proceed to work by aligning and harmonizing the energy centers, eliminating blockages that impede the flow of vital energy.

What Is Reiki For?

Chakra is a Sanskrit word that means wheel. The human body has 7 main and secondary chakras.

With the passage of time, it is normal for our bodies to deteriorate. Thus, negative emotions, traumas we have suffered, or bad habits, can end up hindering the circulation of vital energy through these vortexes of vital energy or chakras. This is where Reiki intercedes, promoting again the correct flow of vital energy and helping to improve the state of health.

On the one hand, when our vital energy is strong, it is easy to find ourselves physically, mentally, and spiritually healthy. On the other hand, when our vital energy is clogged, we can easily become unbalanced or sick.

One of the ways in which we can replenish ourselves with vital energy is by using Reiki. Therefore, Reiki is a holistic technique since it harmonizes and unlocks all the planes of the human being: physical, mental, emotional, and spiritual. It does not attack the body in any way or create addiction or side effects. This is because only vital energy is used, which is present in all living beings; no chemicals or foreign elements are used on the body.

In summary, reiki can be used to:

- Release repressed emotions.

- Provide physical vitality.
- Revitalize the organism.
- Increase the effects of medical treatment when used in a complementary way, never replacing it.
- Reduce or eliminate anxiety.
- Help eliminate daily stress.
- Help eliminate migraines, depression, menstrual cramps, constipation.
- Help cleanse the body and mind of all kinds of toxins.
- Help with pregnancy and postpartum.
- Help animals and plants.

It is not necessary to be sick to use reiki. Therefore, it is a practice suitable to provide relaxation in times of stress. With this method, we can help our body to be healthier, calm bad thoughts, and increase feelings of joy.

Reiki In Healing Crises

A healing crisis is, in a nutshell, a process that is activated in our being. Consequently, through this, our physical body releases toxins that negatively affect our organs, and our mental-emotional body releases emotions and generates negative thoughts.

Symptoms We May Experience

Some of the emotional symptoms we can find in healing therapy are:

- **Sadness**
- **Fear**
- **Hate**
- **Anxiety**

It is also possible that, among the physical symptoms that may occur, we experience:

- **Excessive sweating**
- **Increase in urine**
- **Vomiting**
- **Cold or flu**
- **Headache**
- **Fever**
- **Sorrows of the past**

Each person responds to the treatment in a different way. Therefore, usually for a healing crisis to appear, a multi-session treatment must be performed.

A Reiki Session

The practitioner's hands become hot with the flow of vital energy, especially when placed on a part where there is a blockage. Thus, the practitioner can know where there is a problem.

To begin, during a reiki treatment, the patient lies on his back comfortably. Then, the therapist uses reiki energy to eliminate energy blockages and balance the patient's life force.

Reiki treats the physical, mental, emotional, and spiritual parts of each person, helping to cure the disease at the root. It can also help the patient set aside the limitation of negative thoughts. Do not forget that continued negative thoughts can become blockages. Therefore, this tendency to negativity can impede our progress in life.

Most people experience a feeling of deep relaxation while receiving reiki therapy. Then, once the session is over, they feel calmer, connected to their ground pole, refreshed, and energized.

Finally, a couple of other things you should know about this therapy:

- First, a reiki session can last approximately one hour. During this session, the patient will lie on a stretcher, barefoot, and dressed.

- Second, during the session, the practitioner can use other techniques, such as massage or acupressure, soft music, and aromas such as incense or essences.

Do you dare to try it?

CHAPTER 2

THE UNIVERSE IS ENERGY

The sages and seers of all times and cultures have always known it, and science is taking a little longer to really understand this: everything in the universe is energy—vibration.

Sri Aurobindo, one of the greatest seers of the last century in India, describes the universe as something that is ultimately consciousness. Consciousness is at the same time energy and a force. The higher the divine one's consciousness, the higher the divine of one's own energy body, its own vibration, and the greater its own power to the point of omnipotence. For Aurobindo, a very important part of spiritual development was the mastery of all vibrations on all levels. He perceived the physical plane as the one that resists the divine transformation the most, i.e., possesses the greatest inertia.

Health, illness, positive and negative life experiences, including accidents and strokes of happiness, are nothing more than a reflection of our own energy field. If this energy field is in a vibration of order and harmony, then the outer life must necessarily proceed accordingly. Conversely, disharmony and disorder in one's own energy field also attract corresponding energies from the cosmos and lead to unpleasant experiences.

Contrary to the general notion that we are influenced by the external circumstances of life, Sri Aurobindo clearly shows that our lives are determined the other way around, from the inside out. Mastery in one's own energy field then also means the mastery of external events, health and illness, and possibly even the aging process and death. These findings of a great Indian seer are wonderfully explained in the book "Sri Aurobindo or the Adventure of Consciousness" by Satprem, O.W. Barth Verlag.

There are infinite examples of mastery that show us the potential in our human spirit: when the mother, the companion of Sri Aurobindo, once went up to close the windows with him, since the monsoon rain had set in, she had to admit that the peace in his room was so powerful that the storm could not penetrate, even when the window was open.

Sai Baba, a famous Indian saint, is known for the manifestation of objects that he creates by the power of his spirit.

Indian sadhus master the art without losing a drop of blood, not only to guide a small spear through the cheeks, but even to cut off the tongue with a knife and put it back on a few seconds later without blood flow, and without blood, there remains no scar.

The Karmapa, one of the greatest Tibetan masters, is able to give precise information about where he will be found in his next incarnation, in a letter he writes. For example, how his father and his mother will be called in the next incarnation and where they live.

The crowning glory of all these abilities can be found in the highest yoga of Tibetan Buddhism. The consummate masters of the Dzogchen are known to manifest a so-called rainbow body: when they feel that it is time to leave the body, they retreat to a room for 7 days for undisturbed meditation. After 7 days, only the hair and nails remain in the room, and everything else is transformed into the essence of the elements, into rainbow light. There are various reports of this phenomenon, Namkhai Norbu writes about it in his book "The Crystal Path," Diederich's Yellow Series, p. 178.

H.H. the Dalai Lama has confirmed such cases of rainbow bodies several times, among others in "Dzogchen, The Heart Essence of the Great Perfection," H.H. Dalai Lama, 2000, Snow Lion Publ.

Well, the patient reader will slowly ask himself, what does this have to do with Reiki? And it is true that Reiki is certainly not about extraordinary paranormal phenomena as I have just described them. What I want to show are the limitations and inadequacy of our previous worldview and the unimaginable potential that is actually in our human mind. And thus also, the spiritual potential, which will be developed much more in future generations, in order to help people in their healing process. Reiki is just one way among many that are rapidly spreading in our time, and support the healing processes with the help of energy and light. Our ideas, our rationally oriented world view to date, are often too limited to explain everything we experience. Therefore, for all the down-to-earth discernment, it makes sense to at least assume the possibility that we have so far understood very little of life, and that we must constantly seek a higher perspective in order to understand. We must keep letting go of our limited ideas along these journeys.

A world view that understands evolution, life in the universe, as an interaction of vibrations, as a manifestation of consciousness—this is necessary in order to grasp and understand Reiki in its full potential.

Even though my ability to really comprehend all this is quite low, I would like to try to build on what Albert Einstein also taught with $e=mc^2$; matter equals compressed energy on a very low vibrational plane, the potential and the re-use of Reiki.

The Science of Biophotons according to Prof. Fritz A. Popp

... Is a further step to grasp consciousness in a scientific approach on its way to becoming matter (and thus also health or disease). Popp's realization in simple terms means: the molecules as such are stupid; they do not know what to do; only the biophotons that move between the molecules and the light = vibration = information = consciousness radiate and turn it into a functioning organism. Popp has shown that food emits different levels of light (life energy/life force) depending on whether it is conventional or biologically produced.

But one by one. Leading in the field of so-called biophoton research is Professor Fritz A.Popp, who has empirically demonstrated with the most sensitive methods of measurement that cells emit light, in other words, there is light in all cells of living beings. We as human beings are in some ways light beings. Popp called it biophotons, and photons are light quanta, the smallest physical elements of light, and bio of bios-life as they control the cells. The quality of this light corresponds to the laser light and is, therefore, able to transmit information. So Popp came to the realization that the molecules themselves are, so to speak, stupid, and only the biophotons, which move between the molecules at the speed of light, tell them what to do. The light field, therefore, controls the molecular field. Thus there is a kind of radio communication in this light body, which ultimately controls all processes in the human body. This light is not only to be found within the body but also outside—we radiate light. It would then be easy to link to the theory of morphogenetic fields according to R. Sheldrake fork, which means that we also exchange light, energy, and information with each other as living beings, without us constantly being aware of this.

The experienced and sensitive Reiki channels will probably only be able to smile because, for us, this is a fact of experience that we absorb and release energies and that the quality of these energies influences our whole being. Both in our own (light) body and in the energetic exchange with the entire environment, we become more and more conscious through the Reiki practice, and one can also say more brightly sensitive or clairvoyant.

With our hands, we can perceive not only the amounts of energy like the instruments in biophoton research but also the quality, the inner harmony of an energy field. The instruments are not able to do this, they can detect particularly strong energy, for example, in the case of cancer, but the unpleasant perception that this is a sick energy field can tell us that the measuring instruments are always limited to the amount of light emitted. However, such measurements could

185

certainly detect the life energy that a food product has, and Popp has noticed large differences in the light quality of food, depending on whether it came from the supermarket or from organic farming.

Research is now being carried out worldwide in the field of biophotons, and science hopes to find a key to many unresolved questions.

In connection with Reiki, biophoton research is interesting in that it has now been scientifically proven that we are light beings and that light food, i.e., the universal life energy of the Reiki, can positively influence, and even nourish us.

The light of the biophotons controls the entire organism of the human body, so one can even say scientifically that we are beings of light. There is a constant exchange of biophotons, light, information, and life energy between the individual and the cosmos.

Does this mean that Reiki could be explained and proven in the scientific field? But I have, at the beginning, already explained in detail that the seers, the saints and wise in perhaps all cultures and times had long recognized our existence as beings of light…

CHAPTER 3

THE HUMAN ENERGY BODY FROM A BUDDHIST POINT OF VIEW

Mikao Usui lived in Japan from 1865 to 1926 and is considered to be the founder of Reiki or, rather, the Usui Teate. He spent most of his life studying Buddhism and taught his students, depending on his ability, a simple lay version of Reiki, or a higher Buddhist or Shinto reiki practice.

A channeled book by Lama Yeshe (Richard Blackwell), which has been published only in English, explains the medicine Dharma Reiki on the basis of Buddhist texts and explanations from (alleged) records of Usui and his disciple, Watanabe.

(Lama Yeshe had promised an independent review of the (alleged) originals of Mikao Usui until the summer of 2002. However, he remained guilty until the end of the year, which led to him becoming implausible in removing various websites from the MDR, and its students unfortunately doubt him and the authenticity of the teachings of the MDR. Regardless of this, the explanations given on the energy body are quite coherent and interesting, Richard Blackwell has spent many years studying Buddhism and spiritual healing.)

187

All rights to Usui's texts, as depicted in Lama Yeshe's book, are protected by copyright, so, unfortunately, I cannot provide a verbatim, complete translation to the German reader. But in the following, I would like to make an effort to give a clear representation of Usui's text about the essence of the universe as a vibration, in my own words:

The Buddhist declares our true timeless being, which has always been and is perfect, as the presence of the pure, clear light. If we have really realized this, we are enlightened, freed from the painful cycle of death and rebirth. The Christian idea of a soul punished or praised by God does not exist here, but the knowledge of karma, of the self-responsibility of each individual does. This is on the basis of our own self-created obscurities and obstacles, which are based on ominous action, the pure clear (light) being that we actually become ignorant and tainted.

The Buddha taught the existence of three Kayas, three bodies, and three levels of consciousness, the ultimate subtle plane being the Dharmakaya. From the Dharmakaya arises the Samboghakaya, our human energy body. On this energetic plane, infinitely more or less unconscious interaction takes place between the individual and the universe. The physical plane corresponds to the Nirmanakaya, our appearance.

The impurities in our consciousness continuum cause deformation in our energy field. This energy field, in turn, determines the state of our physical body. This view is not only taught by Buddhists but is also widely accepted in the Western world of Lightworkers. The teaching of biophotons is even able to demonstrate this scientifically.

Again, in other words, all that represents our physical body arises from our energy body, which in turn is created by our own, more or less, painful and imperfect consciousness. Usui cites another very interesting legality: the interaction on the energetic level takes place not only between the individual and the cosmos but also between all the embodied and unembodied beings with whom we have a karmic connection. The interpersonal struggle for energy is also well explained in the well-known New Age book "Celestine's Prophecies." Usui extends this to the connections we have to beings that are not currently incarnated in a body.

There are many examples of this in our daily lives that show this legality, that we constantly (more or less consciously) exchange energies with others. The more we are permeable and telepathically receptive, the clearer our perception in this field becomes. Ultimately, it is karmic causes that make other beings to withdraw energy from us or to direct ominous energies at us. According to the text of Usui, this is one of the causes of illness.

Our subtle vibrational body develops negative, unredeemed areas, which in turn manifest themselves in the physical body or on the emotional level. This is what we call illness. Western conventional medicine is capable of having a healing effect on the physical plane. Reiki, on the other hand, has a healing effect on the energy body, which can then also affect the physical body and the psyche.

The Reiki treatment cannot correct the cause in the body of consciousness, i.e., dissolve the citric stains. However, a correction in the subtle energy body also affects our consciousness, allowing our thinking and feeling to orient itself new and more healingly. This is not only pleasant, but some suffering is necessary to purify body and mind, an idea that we find not only in Buddhism but also in Shintoism and Christianity.

Usui had already said it at that time, which is now revealed in the biophoton theory: every being, whether human, animal or plant, has its own vibration, (I had already quoted Sri Aurobindo on the page "What is Reiki?": Vibration = Energy = Power = Consciousness). Illness means a false, negative vibration in the energy body, which can possibly be dissolved by the pure, clear, positive vibration of Reiki. The healing process, therefore, involves a change in the vibration, the information in the energy body, which is also caused by bach flowers and homeopathy, for example. Provided that karma can be dissolved, and the individual does not block the effect of purification in the energy body (and the necessary new orientation in consciousness), healing is possible. Healing in this context, we must understand as being pure in light (the plane of Dharmakaya) and not just as an absence of inconvenience to the body or the psyche.

Usui had treated a number of war-wounded with Reiki, and the recovery of those who received Reiki in addition to surgical treatment had gone much faster than those who had not received Reiki. Consequently, complete healing is achieved not only through the treatment of the physical plane, but also in the energy body, order must be restored.

Even more healing in the holistic sense is possible if the individual is placed in the position, through initiation in Reiki, to constantly attract healing energies from the cosmos. This means purification and promotion on all levels. That is why Usui not only treated many people who came to him in search of healing with Reiki, but also initiated them in the first degree. The positive effect of such initiation in Reiki is also not limited to the purely physical or emotional level, but a seed is laid for spiritual development and for a balance of all three levels mentioned at the beginning of this chapter—human existence.

I understand this in the sense that the Tibetan Masters and Sri Aurobindo also taught it accordingly in their spiritual practice: we are particularly efficient, skillful and successful when we learn to master things on the pure vibrational level. The thinking, feeling and the physical body follow this. In the course of years of Reiki practice, we become even clearer and more conscious in our perception. In the so-called invisible, the whole world of vibrations must be discovered.

This text by Usui about the world as a world of vibrations explains very well the statement in his Reiki Hikkei with questions and answers from the collection of Ms. Koyama, that we are working with Reiki on a completely different level than conventional medicine and other known forms of therapy. While they treat healing at the level of appearance, Reiki works at the level of Samboghakaya, which is brought, if possible, in harmony with the level of Dharmakaya. If the energy body is in harmony with the universe, the physical and psychic body follows it. All attempts to understand and regulate Reiki from the worldly level do not do Reiki justice and must fail, because Reiki only begins beyond this level. However, we cannot learn to understand this level until we have acquired a clear perception in our own development of consciousness in the realm of Samboghakaya, the pure energy, and its connection with the Dharmakaya, with the completed truth.

Then Reiki becomes not only a technique of relaxation and activation of the self-healing powers but also a spiritual path that leads to the completion of happiness and well-being, to the bliss of Samboghakaya, as Usui also discovered in Reiki, defined in its rules of life.

CHAPTER 4

PRACTICE REIKI DAILY - FOR A LIFETIME

"The (Buddhist) teachings explain to us what must be realized by us, but then we must go on our own journey in order to achieve a personal realization. This journey may lead us through suffering, obstacles, doubts of all kinds, but this will be our best teacher. Through them, we will learn the humility to recognize our limitations, and through them, we will discover the inner power and fearlessness that we need to go beyond our old habits and patterns and surrender to the greater vision of true freedom offered to us by the spiritual teachings." (Rigpa/Sogyal Rinpoche)

Why do we take part in a Reiki seminar, alternative therapies, shamanic journeys, initiations, and Darshans—all the booming esoteric events? What is the real reason for this? We are all looking for happiness, love, sense-finding, the mastery of fate; let's call it the search for the quality of life. Much is touted to be the immediate solution, the only, the best solution of the inner emptiness. And if it doesn't work out right away, then something else is being tried, and again something else, and in the end, where are we? A few nice, some painful, memories, but nothing has really changed.

The consumerism and rapidity of this time are also often found in the Western world in the field of spiritual search, so I write these lines to show which factors are responsible for the success of our search for the quality of life.

In all ways of self-experience, it is the same phases and the same trials and obstacles that we encounter. Whether it is holistic psychotherapy, yoga, Mother Meera or Sai Baba or the practice of Tibetan Buddhism, Zen or Reiki, what do we do after the initial phase of enthusiasm, what happens next?

So easily we allow ourselves to be caught up in all the distractions of everyday life, all the supposed necessities that have to be dealt with first, but when we die, what is left for us? Can we really say that we have used our human potential with all its lightness and divinity? Have we created causes for future happiness and developed our own being towards the light?

So if we assume that human existence acquires meaning and thus quality of life only when we try to recognize our true (inner) being and try to change accordingly, many external things that we have previously considered so important, and that seem to take full care of our daily lives, will become rather inconsequential.

"More, more, more" is the motto of our outer consumer world, which we are often influenced by. In the inner world, it is more about a reduction, where more satisfaction, simplicity, modesty, and clarity would be desirable goals. Or serenity, patience, the ability to be loving, compassion, truthfulness, etc.

If we take a close look at our lives, it runs from the inside out. Everything that we experience and recognize on the outside, that is ourselves, is a mirror. So if I really want to change my quality of life, I have to change something within myself, and that means swimming against the current of habits, becoming less empty, and more relaxed.

Again and again, we look for new suggestions that do not help us, but rather a patient and persistent daily practice will. And I think Reiki makes it so easy for us. Thanks to the initiation once received, this clear light is always at our disposal for a lifetime, we just need to lay our hands on and let Reiki flow.

Reiki is indeed universal as a practice on the way to light because it nourishes and heals (in the sense of being a heil- =whole) the Christians, Mohammedans, Buddhists, shamans, and even the atheists. Reiki also gives us strength, blessing, and support at all stages of development. The beginner who tries to relax for the first time, as well as the advanced, who has been meditating for 20 years, does 2 hours of Tai Chi every day or whatever.

Always. Both experience through Reiki a promotion in the development of their human potential.

And if I only pause once a day for 15 minutes, look inward and relax with Reiki, I will experience blessed support in the search for quality of life due to its positive impact on my life. Reiki makes it so easy for us, we just have to lie down, then lay our hands on ourselves—without otherwise having to practice an intense discipline and abstinence—and so we come back to rest, into our midst, in balance, in relaxation and regeneration.

In order to continue in the phases when, after the initial enthusiasm, our practice is less of a selfsufficient one, I try to use these lines to make clear what it is all about.

Reiki is a path of self-knowledge, self-experience and self-mastery. "In good times as well as in bad times ...", it says so beautifully, and this also applies, of course, to the daily practice on our spiritual path. It is not more, but rather less (ego, selfishness, selfcenteredness) that needs to be developed. This cannot be done without resistance, and one could even say that, by means of resistance, I can see whether I am really taking a step further or not. Integration of one's own shadow is sought in psychology, and this means looking at the pages that are unpleasant and uncomfortable. One mask after another wants to be seen through, and I have to clean up patterns again and again until a new persona is formed, more viable, lighter, and more loving than the old one of the past. All that has been suppressed in the past, perhaps even traumatized from being conscious, many illusions about the inside and the outside, want to be experienced again, recognized, and this knowledge integrated.

Reiki is such a great help, and it gives us unconditionally new strength and blessing, support from above. In its perfection, the Reiki force is able to guide us in the wisest way. But my own mind must also be vigilant and open to this leadership, ready to work on myself, to be mindful that every day becomes a day of quality of life. In many, many everyday situations, the blessing of Reiki can unfold. Life runs from the inside out: if I have found peace within, I experience this also in everyday life. In the end, every moment is a divine moment, and every breath is bliss. But first of all, a great deal is already achieved when I experience that Reiki helps me in one or other everyday situation to be more relaxed and loving, more grateful, and with confidence in the good in all beings, and thus to interact with others in a positive and more salutary way. Each impulse has the property of attracting similar energies, and small steps ultimately have a great effect.

Every Buddhist practice attaches great importance to gaining the right motivation and to remind ourselves why, from what insight, we want to make Reiki every day. The Reiki Rules of Life are a good guide to this, and it is important to also deal with where we want to develop. Occasionally we experience such particularly clear and luminous moments, in which there are no doubts, conflicts, or problems at all. These moments must be recorded as orientation. After that, we often sink back into old (painful and self-referential) patterns. But if we work persistently on our own unfolding, the state we once experienced in a particularly luminous moment will one day become our everyday being.

If today I really tried to be peaceful, without worries, grateful, loving, and sincere, it was a day that gave me the quality of life. If, on the other hand, I have lost myself only in external things, I am missing something afterward, and if I continue to do so for a long time, I must finally realize that my life has become only stress and suffering and that I have the chance to master my life.

I would also like to mention one more obstacle here: our expectations. If we have had a pleasantly relaxing and soothing experience with Reiki for a while, we are happy to expect this as a matter of course. Then suddenly the relaxation is absent, some even think that their Reiki no longer works.

That is certainly not the case with a correct Reiki initiation, but our expectation blocks the reception of Reiki. So again: let go, let it happen, let yourself be guided, just be a channel.

Reiki is experienced differently every time and my ego cannot take over this therapy in order to bring about certain effects immediately. In the development of a living connection to and communication with Reiki, we find the same laws to which the connection to the wise, the Divine, and the Higher Self, are subject. In order to understand this relationship and to make it blessed, the study of the I Ging and, of course, the encounter with the Holy Mother Meera, H.H. Dalai Lama, and others were a great help to me. The cartouche cards are also a good tool.

We have so many possibilities here in our Western world, and hardly anyone has to put all their life energy into pure survival, as so many beings on this planet are doing. For all the bustle and speed of Western life, Reiki can help us in a very simple way to take a step back, experience and realize the true quality of life. But we must also (really) want it, strive for it persistently and patiently, and orient our lives accordingly. It is beautiful to be able to fall asleep in the evening with a feeling of gratitude in my heart for all the blessings I have received and passed on. This is a good starting point for the (inner) wealth the next day.

I wish you light and blessing in all your ways.

CHAPTER 5

THE PATH TO HAPPINESS AND WELL-BEING

The Reiki Rules of Life are the only documents we know in the handwriting of Mikao Usui, which state that Reiki is the path to happiness and well-being. What does this mean? What does it really mean?

Suzuki-san, one of the students of Usui still alive today, told us that the focus of the Reiki practice in Japan at the time was to train in accordance with the rules of life in its own spirit, day and night. Also, in the Usui Reiki Hikkei, there is a hint, a statement from Usui, about this. He said, "First the mind is healed, then the body follows."

In the following, I will try to explain this in more detail.

Usui taught a path to enlightenment, to perfection in the Spirit. Reiki, which is popularly known in the West, is more dedicated to relaxation and well-being and healing by laying on of hands. Originally, the focus was on the schooling of one's own mind with the aim of finally leaving all suffering behind, and finding lasting happiness and well-being that is independent of the ups and downs of life. Happiness then means that the inner being, the own mind, is always stronger than the outer destiny. Well-being is also a state of being that takes place inside, in one's own heart.

The 2nd and 3rd-degree symbols are the key to perfection. The mental symbol is the root mantra of Amida Buddha (Amithaba), and "Namo Amida Butsu" is the Nembutsu, the mantra by which the blessing of Amida Buddha is invoked. (Amida is the Buddha of boundless light and, according to Mariko Obaasan, who is a personal disciple of Usui, is said to have been the main practice of Usui. In particular, the Buddhism of the Pure Land (Jodo and Jodo Shin) practices in Amida.)

A direct translation of the HSZSN, which is mistakenly called the remote symbol, reads: "the very essence of being is pure mindfulness." This, too, is an indication of the enlightened state of the human spirit, empty and absolutely present. The coming and going of thoughts and feelings is in this state like writing on water, it also immediately dissolves back into the state of pure mindfulness. The energy follows my attention and intention, and imagination alone is enough for the 2nd Reiki degree to be able to send a remote treatment. The HSZSN is not necessary as the key to establishing a remote connection at all. Usui's disciples learned to experience the Ki of unity in this symbol, which, in the state of pure mindfulness, is a level beyond duality on which there is no separation at all, and thus, everything is connected. Therefore, meditation in the HSZSN can be very helpful in experiencing a transcendent level beyond dualistic, value-giving thinking.

The master symbol of Reiki is a reference to the great all-pervading light, to the lightness of our mind, here too an enlightened state is meant, which must be realized. The master symbol is associated with Dainichi Nyorai, with the Buddha Samantabhadra. This is the so-called Urbuddha, which carries in itself all the enlightened qualities of the five Dhyani Buddhas without having specifically trained them.

When we think of the Reiki symbols in this form, they are a key to entering an enlightened state, in order to train our own minds in such a way that we constantly experience happiness and well-being within us and that all the suffering belongs to the past.

In the application, this means that with the Reiki force, we target our own (!) to develop an awareness that all suffering has been overcome forever. And this is, of course, a very different objective and motivation than is usually taught in western Reiki.

It is beautiful if Reiki even helps to relax a little better, to find a little leisure and inner peace. Lying down and enjoying Reiki is so beautiful. But the potential that we receive with the Reiki Initiation goes far beyond that, and perhaps we should take more care of this and also appreciate it.

In this way, Reiki helps us to connect with the inner teacher and to realize love, harmony and healing on all levels in inner and outer life in inpatient and purposeful practice. Then Reiki, as simple as its application is, is a perfect guide to happiness and wellbeing, as Mikao Usui put it.

Be good to you!

Usui defined Reiki as the path to happiness and wellbeing. And that's what we all aspire to when we regularly give ourselves Reiki. We want to feel comfortable with ourselves and with what life gives us. And we want to experience happiness, and walk happily through life.

It sounds so simple, yet it's so hard. A universally valid recipe cannot be given for happiness, because everyone is at a different point in their development, one trying to relax for the very first time, and the other meditating for three hours every day for a long time. And yet, in my many years of treatment practice, I was able to identify and accompany certain processes and learning tasks over and over again. Depending on where we are in our own development, being good to ourselves means something completely different.

And so, I would like to share a few observations with you from my work and also from my own learning process.

At the beginning of the path of self-experience, it is fundamentally important for the vast majority to feel themselves again. Life will only be experienced in thought. One's own strategies of justification, doubts, condemnations and even self-destructive ways of thinking determine the whole life. The cause of the problems is seen only in others and not in itself. The experiences of childhood have led many people to a happy and satisfied existence that has come a long way. To be good to yourself then means to reconnect with oneself, to feel the feelings again, to uncover repressed and compensated feelings, to give yourself a space in the relaxation of Reiki, in which all feelings, even the less socially capable, are one. All that has not been healed and deliberately released in the past, much that has been suppressed and held back, must first be made conscious, felt, relived. Layer by layer, until breathing is free again and all muscle parts are relaxed again. Guilt complexes, feelings of inferiority, various fears, these are some obstacles to overcome in order to be able to feel authentic again. I had to lead many people out of impotence into anger and then on into the sovereign mastery of conflict situations. Some (desperation) screams had got stuck in the throat and had to get out. The inner child, the little boy, the little girl, had been lost and had to be found again. Sometimes the pain had been so great that this part had completely moved away from the conscious personality. What needs healing is no longer present in the body or psyche, and must be specifically captured and integrated with a technique of retrieving lost parts of the soul.

The next step is to embrace good and evil with all that is there, lovingly. Only when I have lovingly accepted the shadow does it no longer lead its idiosyncratic existence as a troublemaker, but can be transformed. And then we have to practice positive, life-affirming, constructive patterns. It's easy, then with relapses into old stories, the mental symbol can be good support for us. Be good to you, but it's not that easy. What's really good for me?

"Be good to you" means at this stage of development, to accept yourself as you are, stop making yourself small, as your father or mother did with you. This is quite difficult because we have often adopted such ways of thinking with breast milk. A replacement ceremony for mother and father can make things easier and show new perspectives. So many parentchild relationships have been manipulative, overwhelming and unloving, and abuse is also a common topic. Reiki can support the therapy wonderfully because, at the same time, we receive very positive, loving and peaceful input from working on our shadow.

Trust is a very important point, even in the Reiki rules of life, it says: don't worry! Again and again, mistrust and old fears or doubt, which is a form of hatred, eat up every new positive impulse. Patience, loving patience with oneself is a characteristic that we must develop. In general, we must learn to be a good loving mother to ourselves, a benevolent, but sometimes also the strict father. Integration is the right keyword, not exclusion and self-punishment, but everything that is in me to accept with the help of Reiki and bring it to the right place.

Only when we have resolved the themes with father and mother, anima and animus come to their place and become consciously tangible. If we can love ourselves again, then, and only then, can we approach spiritual development, orient ourselves upwards, receive higher guidance and inspiration, yes, then we occasionally begin to fly. But a path begins with other maxims, with the themes of self-discipline and selfpurification. Then it is no longer a question of giving space to all feelings, but of reorienting feelings and thoughts with care and overcoming all self-centeredness. It is the path of self-mastery, the path of WuWei, of non-action. Compassion and selfless devotion to others are then what we have to strive for, and the good heart must be developed, whether it is a Christian, Buddhist or shamanic.

Thus, if one's own being has achieved a certain degree of stability and clarity and integration, if the psyche can constantly give us positive impulses for the mastery of everyday life, then the path of purification and higher development begins. Certainly also in the initial phase, the turn to the divine light can be helpful, so there is no clear dividing line to be drawn. Often, however, we want to be higher, further, more holy than we actually are. This is not helpful, because our shadow catches up with us again. "Be good to you" means being sincere and seeing your own level of development clearly without embellishment. What I get mirrored in the outer life shows me where I stand in my development. Some simply do not want to see or hear this, they remain unreachable, and therefore they make no progress at all in their healing process.

Reiki, when we have learned again to relax, to let ourselves fall, leads us into higher states of consciousness and lets us experience infinite peace, and inner happiness in a form that we have never known before. Most especially, luminous moments reveal to us our true being. And if we remain patient and disciplined in our daily practice, then this particular light experience, which we have had at an inauguration, for example, will be our everyday life after five or ten years. In this phase of development, it is no longer a matter of simply giving space to all the feelings, whatever they may be. On the contrary, it is beyond being in the world, and no longer of the world. The causes of the problems are only searched within one's own and no longer projected onto the outside world. Then it is a matter of seeing through the nullity, transience, and sorrow of all the impulses we have in mind, not to put them on the back of it. We are detached from the collective, which is a very, very lonely phase, and then we go down the path of inner truth. What we want to develop is, at first, still hidden behind the veil, only occasionally visible. Our divine, eternal being is not yet tangible. We must reverently ask for support and guidance so that we can find the right way forward.

This phase also brings many obstacles and resistances, and sometimes it goes back to the trauma of another incarnation in one treatment. The self-will, the desire to determine one's own life, is a major obstacle and requires many years of purification. Psychic abilities that manifest must not lead to an ego trip or too confused states. Again and again, I have to remember: "be good to you" means to develop a good, pure heart for others, nothing else. Then I gradually develop a spirit that is stronger than the ups and downs of external destiny, a spirit that can endure equally unpleasant situations, if not into positive learning experiences and spiritual growth.

And then... one day ... The veil lifts, and we enter into a life in the light and are now permanently connected with the Divine. The spiritual world becomes our home, our food, our whole aspiration. Completion is achieved when every impulse, every thought, every feeling in us is then good, salutary and blessed for all beings, myself included.

CHAPTER 6

THE INAUGURATION IN REIKI

The most important moment in Reiki is the so-called initiation or attunement, which means the opening and activation of the student to the Reiki channel. Only then can Reiki flow out of his hands; only then is it a protected channel that transmits only Reiki and no personal energy. This has great advantages over other forms of energetic healing: without any daily retreats, diets and other disciplines, the Reiki channel is immediately functional; the transmission of Reiki is always healing and blessing, you can do nothing wrong, you cannot overdose or enter inappropriate vibrations. Provided the Reiki initiation was correct, the practitioner is protected from the sick energies of the patients and is strengthened even when giving Reiki.

Thus, at initiation in Reiki, we receive a great blessing, a divine gift with immense healing potential. Initiations exist in many cultures. Generally, these are transfers of consciousness, energy and spiritual blessing from the Master to the disciple. For example, I have also received initiations from H.H. Dalai Lama in high Buddhist deities and their practice.

In the following, I would like to explain some things about the inauguration in Reiki because this topic is not always understood and presented correctly. Some Reiki Masters claim: "Only when you have received 4 tunings to the 1st Reiki degree have you received a proper Reiki Initiation." This is complete nonsense and an unsightly way of supposedly securing more market shares. Usui had given the Reiju—that is, his kind of initiation in Reiki—to the student once, but repeated it weekly. In the western Reiki, there are many different initiation rituals. In the Reiki Alliance after Takata/Furumoto, the first degree is tuned four times, and the ritual to Ishikuro and the Tibetan Reiki is tuned once. At Tera Mai there are three attunements, at Karuna, it is one attunement; each ritual is slightly different, but they all work well and give the student a permanent and protected Reiki channel. So it should be: if you are tuned four times in the 1st Grade, you get a Takata/Furumoto-style initiation, no more, as other Reiki shapes and lines transmit more healing power and a higher vibration.

Many different initiation rituals are known in Reiki, for the activation of the Reiki Channel. And they all work wonderfully, they connect the student with Reiki for a lifetime and have many beneficial and healing qualities for the development of one's own potential and for the transfer of the Reiki power to others.

Some rituals are quite simple; others quite extensive and complicated. The Reiki force is anchored by the master in different positions such as crown chakra, palms, heart chakra, feet and others, by intention, by symbol or via the breath in the student. At the end of the ritual, the student has his own direct connection to Reiki, which is energetically independent of the initiating master. Even the Master is only a channel at the inauguration, a helper, and he holds the space for the spiritual world, so to speak. After the initiation, the student is directly connected to the source of the Reiki and can pass on the Reiki power through his hands, through the breath, the eyes and through mental ideas.

A very important difference between the original Japanese Reiju by Mikao Usui and the western Reiki initiations is the following: the Reiju transmits the entire spiritual potential of the teacher with all the psychic abilities so that the student can access the channel, even with targeted exercises. After the western Reiki initiation, the canal is immediately ready and can be applied. The channel is and remains at the level that the master could transmit; it does not become any more or better over the years; only the perception of the student improves with regular practice. Both the Reiju and the various Western Reiki initiation rituals connect the student with Reiki, but each in its own way.

After the inauguration, it is decisive whether the student also practices Reiki—whether he finds a way to integrate his Reiki applications into everyday life. Only with regular use is progress noticeable, a development towards improved well-being. Reiki is not a sect, and it is up to the student to decide how often he practices, when and where he is completely free. Even if a unique initiation in the (Western) 1st, 2nd or 3rd Reiki degree is sufficient to absorb and pass on the healing power of this degree for a lifetime, it is also quite possible to receive multiple initiations to the same degree and to benefit from repetitions of the initiations. The personal development towards the light is promoted with each initiation. As a master, you can also initiate yourself again and again.

Exchange with other lines of tradition can also be a good extension, and the healing power is actually different in the various forms of initiation. I offer a Reiju once a half-year when I don't see the light. And everyone is welcome to repeat an initiation to a rereceived Reiki degree on a donation basis.

And something else: is it possible to remove a Reiki initiation? This is a hot topic. Some teachers say a Reiki initiation is forever and can never be deleted again. Others have specialized in removing Reiki initiations, claiming that Reiki is fundamentally bad. And there are even seals with which Reiki masters try to prevent their students from receiving further initiations elsewhere, a dark chapter in Reiki.

Well, with a proper Reiki initiation, there is no reason to remove it, because it always has a positive, healing, and beneficial effect. But unfortunately, in recent years, there have also been other initiations that are not in order. Where the protection against the assumption of the symptoms of the patient does not work, in which one feels crushed afterward, constantly sloppy and tired, gratuitously aggressive, manipulated, or feels alienated, because other beings who are not full of light have crept in. Sometimes even a brief touch through a dark channel is enough for all the light to disappear, all the joy of the spiritual, and it is a difficult test that people then experience. This can be done with false Reiki treatments, but also with healers who work differently than with Reiki. And this is not limited to healers, even from an English media training and spiritualist association, I know this.

But I don't want you to be afraid here. The vast majority of Reiki initiations are good, and heal and strengthen our well-being!!! Occasionally, however, there are false initiations, which can be seen by their effect. And these can also be removed. As a Seichem Master, I have the ability to do this, and I have been able to successfully remove several ominous initiations, not only from the Reiki but also, for example, the "Light of the Akasha Crown." This is not always a harmless matter, but it is vital for the psyche and sometimes the entire existence of the wronglyinitiated.

It should be clear from the foregoing that the initiating Reiki Master bears a great responsibility. If the initiation has been carried out correctly, it is always healing and is a beautiful light work that has already given tens of thousands of people around the globe an infinite amount. But if the initiation has been distorted, the mental health of the student is endangered. The pupil is also called to carefully choose his teacher and his initiation.

A correct Reiki initiation is a great blessing of heaven, and for very, very many people, the first Reiki Initiation is the first step into a new chapter of life with more light, love and meaning in inner as well as in outer life. The initiation is a central element in Reiki and is given in different rituals depending on the line of tradition. The Master bears the responsibility for the quality, but the student is also encouraged to look for a good teacher and better overcome his inertia.

Western Reiki initiations have a different quality than the Japanese original Reiju, as Mikao Usui regularly transmitted to his students almost 100 years ago. The Reiju is rather a transmission to the development of the entire spiritual potential, not only for channeling the Reiki power. Thus, repeated initiations in the same Reiki degree, also from other lines and from other teachers, are quite useful, and even more, a repeated reception of Reiju. Reiki is a path of self-experience and spiritual development, on which an initiation every time means a special blessing and help from above.

A Reiki Initiation is a gift from heaven. May it always have a salutary effect on all beings…

CHAPTER 7

FEELING COMFORTABLE MEANS BEING AT HOME

Feeling really comfortable in our skin, isn't that exactly what we're always looking for? What do we want? To rest in our own way, to be at home, to be at peace with what is and with what is not. To be stronger within than the ups and downs of external fate.

There is outer life with the fields of work and leisure, family, and relationship. And there is the inner life of our feelings, thoughts, consciousness, and psyche. Whether we end up experiencing heaven on earth or hell depends only to a small extent on how our outer life is going, but much more on our inner condition, on the way we know how to deal with the ups and downs of outer life.

That is why I love Buddhism so much, it shows us how we can train our own minds to experience true (inner) happiness and to free ourselves from the shackles of outer life on our own. And in this respect, the message of Mikao Usui's Reiki and the handling of the Reiki rules of life is also to be understood when Usui says: "Reiki is the medicine for all diseases."

We all know this: If we are newly in love, work is good for us, we fly through the day. If, on the other hand, we are in a bad mood, very simple things of everyday life easily bring stress and frustration. This clearly shows us how much we depend on our happiness in our lives and how we deal with the things of everyday life internally. If I am grateful for all the blessings, I live in abundance. If I do not waste my energy on fears, hopes, and worries, the vitality is fully available to me to cope with the tasks. If I am sincere with myself, truthful and not complacent, I can make progress on the spiritual path and from year to year, make more friends with myself, and feel more and more comfortable in my skin. Reiki is a blessing of heaven, a light and an unconditional love that we can receive every day once we receive a Reiki Initiation.

Relaxing in Reiki and enjoying it to the fullest, leads to us being less annoying, less worried, and capable of feeling the love in our hearts. But what if, after some practice, there is no real improvement in the quality of life? Then we must be more skillful and use the blessing of Reiki to train our minds consciously and purposefully.

It is not the external circumstances that are responsible for the fact that I do not have time, or that anger at my neighbor is in my heart, or that the circumstances of life make regular Reiki practice impossible. It is always my own mind, for which I am solely responsible, that is decisive of whether it is a good day or a bad day. If I take the time and use Reiki for my spiritual development, my life will change for the better. I can become more and more calm, peaceful and loving from day to day, and from year to year. And therefore in the course of life, I can learn to be at home in me, to feel really comfortable with myself and in my skin.

First of all, I have to find a distance to create a space in my life for the encounter with myself, my own mind, my innermost thoughts, feelings, and motivations. The decisive factor is the recognition of how important my inner condition is for my happiness in life, so how blessed it is to deal with myself. Then a firm decision must be made to make a daily effort to make one's own mind lighter with the help of Reiki. In this way, I can connect the worldly everyday life directly with the spiritual. The events of everyday life become a mirror of the progress of my spiritual practice.

The more I have realized the meaning of my own mind, my inner condition for experiencing happiness and fulfillment, the more effectively I can work with myself and align myself lovingly towards the Light.

Reiki is the medicine used to cure all diseases, Usui said. But only if we are willing to change our conditioning, our inner attitude. Usui learned that many patients relapsed after some time because they did not want to change. And that's why he gave them the Reiki rules of life.

Depending on how far we get with ourselves or not, we need to seek professional help to get rid of the programming we are at the mercy of. It is not always possible to do this on your own. Others, on the other hand, can use oracles such as the I Ging or Cartouche to learn more about themselves. And if I have defeated the worst troublemakers in me, seen through mother and father issues, then I can continue on my own and be a teacher and good friend to myself.

With the blessed help of the Reiki force, I can then learn to develop a truly good heart and to tame my own mind. More and more, I will feel comfortable in my skin and be at home in myself. Ultimately, this will have a positive impact on my external life, on work and on relationships. Because in reality, life runs from the inside out. Paradise on earth can only be found in one's own heart, or, as H.H. Dalai Lama said: "The mystical land of the Buddhas Shambala is not to be found on a map, but only in one's own spirit."

With this in mind, I wish you a bright development and good guidance on your way home. The blessing power of the good heart or: The importance of an altruistic attitude for one's own happiness.

In July 2007, I was lucky enough to participate in the teachings and the Manjushri inauguration of H. H. Dalai Lama in Hamburg. At the end of this event, H. H. asked all participants from teaching professions to include in their function the importance of wisdom and compassion, the importance of an altruistic attitude for their own happiness, and also that of the whole world on their own teaching material.

What does this have to do with Reiki and the path of Reiki, as well as with faith? To what extent are healing and well-being through Reiki possible in both practitioners and patients, without having this wisdom and compassion in their hearts? I would like to look at these questions a little below.

Mikao Usui taught in the introduction to the Reiki Rules of Life: Reiki is the way to happiness and well-being. This is a common paraphrase in the introductions of traditional Buddhist teaching texts for the path of liberation from all suffering, for the Buddhist path. Should this also have been meant by Usui? I think so. It is now well known that Usui Sensei has been a Buddhist throughout his life and never a Christian, as Mrs. Hawayo Takata had falsely claimed.

But by this, I do not want to make Reiki an exclusively Buddhist practice, but in the sense of Buddhist spiritual training, I want to show a few laws that apply independently of the religion to the individual and to all who have spiritual healing, happiness, and strive for true well-being.

Usui Sensei gave blessed and healing energy transmissions to both students and patients, but always in conjunction with the Reiki rules of life. Spiritual healing without changing consciousness, one's own mind, is impossible! Healing is much more than just relaxation and often involves not only energy work in the human energy field but also a conversation to clarify the cause of suffering in the patient's thinking and feeling.

Spiritual healing is always associated with a change in the nature of the patient. After all these years, I can say from experience: patients who are full of gratitude, kindness of heart and integrity often experience astonishing miracles in the healing treatments, while those who expect much without wanting to recognize and change are unwilling to see the self-responsibility for their lives, that they have created their own (unconsciously) problem, experience only a little relief and relaxation, but rarely a miracle. Thus, even these healing miracles have a system, are subject to legality, and are thus directly connected with the maturity of a soul. Of course, there is light and darkness in each of us, just as there are light and dark phases in life.

The decisive factor in whether blessings and healing are received from above is an openness to the Higher—to the Light.

The Buddhist defines healing much more comprehensively as a way to freedom from all suffering, to lasting happiness and well-being, to become completely independent of the ups and downs of external life. This is then the perfect mastery of fate, which can only take place in one's own mind. The overcoming of all suffering and enlightenment aspired by the Buddhist means a development into myilucity rather than what is often sought in the world of the New Age as so-called self-realization.

Life means learning and growing; our human existence is a learning process and not just consumption. We must explain this carefully to the patient during the treatment if we want to achieve lasting improvement and not just temporary relaxation. Spiritual healing is thus, in addition to pure energy work, always teaching, a show of the need for higher development.

Higher development, healing, and true realization always mean increasing love, compassion, forgiveness and tolerance. The real cause of the disease, as well as for all suffering, is negative mental poisons, and the Buddhists call them suffering emotions: these must be recognized and overcome. Thus, no lasting cure can happen if the patient does not see his own responsibility and is willing to change. Sometimes this change of consciousness happens by itself in relaxation during energetic treatment, and sometimes a conversation is also necessary to show these connections.

Being able to receive spiritual healing also means accepting the existence of something higher, which is rarely the case in our (godless) world. "Please and you will be given," the Bible says, but this request is not so easy. To this end, arrogance must be transformed into humility, the heart must be purified, and self-righteousness and expectations are also counterproductive. The healer is, therefore to a large extent, dependent on the cooperation of the patient and thus always only the companion. The patient (as well as the student) does not have to believe in Reiki in the first place for it to work, but he must be open to something higher that cannot be subject to his selfish will and control. A certain degree of receptivity is necessary. The greater the devotion, the better.

The central point of this form of healing is the good heart: only with an open heart can it be possible to receive help from above, blessing, compassion and wisdom, as H. H. Dalai Lama taught. To understand this is universal and completely independent of religious affiliations, "Temple needs it in people's hearts," he says. The ancient Tibetan master Shantideva, in whose tradition the Dalai Lama stands, taught: "All suffering arises from the fact that I find happiness for myself; all my happiness comes from wishing this for others." When we look at the laws of karma, it is easy to understand this, and this is a purely logical process, not a matter of faith. Real peace, lasting healing and a fulfilled existence we find in altruism, in a wisdom that has overcome self-centeredness and developed true compassion.

And this applies to the one who is spiritually aspiring on the path as well as to the patient who comes to the healer because of physical or psychological problems. Healing takes place according to the plan of the soul and the maturity of the heart. The real cause of all diseases is to be found in consciousness, in negative, painful emotions and thoughts, in attitudes of life that do not fit into the whole. The Buddha has named them exactly as the enemies of happiness: they are desire, hatred and ignorance. Which brings us back to the Reiki rules of life...

In this sense, I wish you a bright development, good food for the heart, and all the healing you desire.

CHAPTER 8

THE TEACHING CONTENT OF REIKI

In traditional Reiki, there is the first, the second, and the third degree, in addition to the teaching master's degree. Unfortunately, I often found that pupils did not meet basic requirements because they had been incompletely trained in their Reiki seminar.

That is why I would like to try to give a list of the teaching material that a certain Reiki degree should contain. This is based on the most famous western transmission lines and, of course, on my own pieces of training in Western Reiki traditions. Whether you need a whole Reiki weekend or just 1 day for the 1st, 2nd or 3rd Reiki degree depends, in my opinion, on the size of the group and the personal preferences. The pure teaching material with the achievement of the learning goal of the respective Reiki degree is in a few hours and does not always require a whole weekend. Of course, it is always nice when there is enough time to experience and internalize the blessing of Reiki. A Reiki seminar in the length of 1-3 hours is always too short, and during this time, the learning goal that the student is able to carry out the applications independently afterward cannot be achieved.

The Reiki seminars only provide the student with theoretical knowledge and practical applications according to the degree. The actual learning only begins after the seminar through one's own practice. We grow into matter piece by piece; it is a learning and growing process on all levels. And it is a process that takes time, years of practice. It is good if the teacher is available after the seminar for further questions and supervision on the path of the student.

The following is a list of the teaching contents of the 3 degrees of Reiki, which I think makes sense:

The 1st Reiki Degree

- A correct and also intense initiation in the healing power into the 1st Reiki degree.

- A correct theoretical understanding of the mode of action of Reiki is fundamentally important: How does Reiki work?

- The Reiki rules of life are an essential part of the tradition of Mikao Usui.

- A little on the history of Reiki.

- A form of whole-body treatment and chakra treatment, as well as chakra balancing, are included. Intuitive treatment is not possible for every student to practice the same, so I find it helpful for the beginner to learn these basic forms of treatment. Later on, when the clairvoyance develops, you can drop this form again and treat it purely intuitively.

The 2nd Reiki Degree

- A correct and also intense initiation into the 2nd Reiki degree, which is also intense in healing power.

- An explanation of the healing process in the sense of holistic growth, in order to understand the application of the symbols.

- Explanations of the 3 symbols of the 2nd Grade: CKR, SHK, and HSZSN. Application of the symbols in treatments. A symbol is drawn once and the corresponding mantra is recited three times, not the other way round.

- Mental treatment, Usui called it the "healing of habits." Working with the mental symbol is an essential part of the possibilities of the 2nd degree and should really not be missing, as is, unfortunately, the case more often.

- Remote treatment techniques and room cleaning as well as other possibilities of applying the symbols, e.g. to a specific topic.

The 3rd Reiki Degree

- A correct and also intense initiation in the healing power into the 3rd Reiki degree, into the Master symbol.

- Explanation of the DKM in the sense of perfection of the Mind, a guide to spiritual development.

- Psycho-energetic healing.

- Meditation and possibly also energetic exercises.

Dao Reiki - 1st degree

The High Art of Hand Laying

It's been a long time, but I can still remember my very first Reiki seminar and the joy and gratitude in my heart that I associate with it: in 1987, I went from northern Germany to the Austrian Kleinwalsertal for a seminar of the 1st century. I did grades with Ulla Oberkersch, a student of Phyllis Lei Furumoto (Reiki Alliance), and one of the first Reiki masters in Germany. A whole weekend from Friday evening to Sunday noon in a group of a good dozen participants, all but me from the southern German region. The obligatory 400- D-Mark plus accommodation and food was a lot of money for me at that time, but I liked to give them as well as later 1200- D-Mark for the 2nd degree. I liked Ulla immediately and there was a lot of space and time to get to know the others. It was May 1st, there was still snow in the mountains and we could walk nicely. A beautiful group atmosphere had formed a tense expectation of meeting the saint, and everyone felt at home. Of course, I was told Mrs. Takata's fairy tale of the Christian Usui even then. And for hours, we practiced the same hand positions again, and again, all of them could be memorized afterward.

Today I have to smile when I remember the importance attached to these hand positions. Also, a few years ago, I was in Hamburg with the so-called GrandMaster Phyllis Lei Furumoto, who admonished us to do exactly these hand positions every day and nothing else for a lifetime. The actual teaching material of the then 1 Reiki grades could have been taught in a few hours; actually, I learned little for a whole weekend, considering this from today's point of view.

Only many years later, since 1999, new information about the original reiki of Mikao Usui Sensei from Japan came to the West and so much was put into a different light. It turned out: The hand positions come from Dr. Hayashi, Usui has never used them in this shape. And even Hayashi, after a few years of practice, has dropped these positions and worked intuitively.

So the question alike came up for me: How do I teach how to treat in my seminars on the 1st Reiki degree? — I continue to show my students the well-known hand positions, not in the absolutist form of the alliance, but merely as a helpful framework for the beginner, who can also drop this form of treatment as soon as his perception improves and he can handle it intuitively.

A year or two ago, I came across material from the Jin Shin Jyutsu and the Japanese healing currents, special treatments, and positions based on the ancient Asian knowledge of the meridians, which are subtle energy channels in the human body. These positions can be combined very well with Reiki in a simplified form, without intensive years of study.

CHAPTER 9

REIKI IS PEACE AND SILENCE

That still, peaceful life in our world often runs out, and many hardly get ahead. Reiki, of course, hits a very important point in our lives and can satisfy a very significant and often neglected need. It helps us to relieve stress, to find peace, to go inside, and to feel ourselves again instead of just being in thoughts. Reiki is also so simple: easy to learn and easy to practice.

Many people only use Reiki occasionally to do something good for themselves, or because they are less well off. But we can also use Reiki as a source of strength throughout everyday life to consciously develop further and higher, as Mikao Usui had intended with the alignment of the mind according to the rules of life. Reiki, as the way to happiness and well-being, then means to strive daily for the salutary and blessed contents of one's own mind.

All things ultimately exist only in our own minds, no other is to blame for our suffering. The only trigger, the most important factor, lies in ourselves, and how we react to it. How we deal with life, whether we can cling to or let go, whether we are longing for more, or are content and grateful with all that the day gives us: this is what determines our happiness in life. Reiki can show us a lot, help us, and be a source of strength if we consciously analyze our thinking and feeling, and nourish and maintain healing content.

The happiness of life, the fulfillment of our existence, is always our own responsibility: we can strive to become a little more peaceful and loving every day, to remain more relaxed, to keep a smile instead of being grim, hard, or stubborn. No mental state, relationship crisis, unemployment, illness—no situation is permanent. Everything changes, arises and passes again. If we really become aware of this and learn to let go, we can simplify our lives, as well as increase serenity and inner peace.

The moments of silence are so helpful: to pause, to breathe, to perceive the thought or the feeling and let go again, and to let the moments of silence become longer and longer. This silence must be practiced, and it does not come by itself, certainly not in the urban world in which we live today.

At the beginning of the Reiki practice, it makes sense and is very good to take a longer break every day to give yourself Reiki. Afterward, we are always a bit more relaxed and satisfied. Slowly we get out of the hustle and bustle, and get back to ourselves. Some feelings come up, which had been suppressed. So much that has accumulated in the unredeemed, must first be made conscious again.

And at this stage, inner resistance sits part of the way, and they are part of it. After a certain period of regular practice, those who stick to it have to carry a less heavy backpack with them and experience everyday life in a more relaxed and fulfilling way.

Once the calm has returned to the interior, collection and mindfulness have been found, and it is time to observe one's mind vigilantly in all everyday situations and consciously strive for a positive change in thinking and feeling. Then, every situation is a chance to implement Reiki. At the very first moment, I can choose not to get angry at all. If I recognize fears, hopes, worries and doubts as enemies of my inner peace, I can immediately make them disappear from my head before they have settled down or even become a habit. Every thought and every feeling, can be consciously perceived and immediately let go of without any identification with it. In this way, one preserves inner freedom, serenity and also sovereignty.

Out of this silence, consciousness is present in everyday life. If something was less salutary in thinking or feeling, you don't have to go down for it, constantly evaluate yourself or even compare yourself with others: you become aware of what was less coherent and simply choose to make it better next time. In this way, one remains in a positive and constructive state of mind. This is the only way to a stable self-esteem that can exist independently of internal and external factors of neurotic appearance.

And so the same world in which ten years earlier we were exposed to constant stress, fears, worries and doubts, now, constant conflicts look much more beautiful. There is the outer world, and there is the inner world. Both are relative and in constant transformation. Whether one perceives life as joy or as a burden depends greatly on the inner attitude. Reiki can serve us throughout our lives as a source of power, as a light and as a blessing, and thus be a great help to increase positive content in thinking and feeling and to reduce the power of ominous patterns in us. Supported by Reiki, every moment in everyday life can be consciously used to increase the light in us, and also in others.

The Mental Symbol In The 2nd Reiki Degree

The name "Mental Symbol" for the SHK already states that we are hereby healing on the mental level. But what exactly does this mean? Originally at Usui Sensei, it was called the "healing of habits." To understand this, I need to take a little while explaining Buddhist knowledge of the nature and functioning of the human spirit:

The pure nature of the human spirit is empty and open like the sky, in a meditative state. Thoughts and emotions pass by like the clouds in the sky, without the sky feeling disturbed. The worldly spirit, on the other hand, is trapped in the clouds, trapped in desires and dislikes, and ignorant of its true origin, the clear sky. So is all habitual thinking and feeling, the mental symbol in the 2nd Reiki degree. Thus all habitual thinking and feeling, all identification, any expectation, fear, or hope are only as real as we ourselves give them power over our minds. And so our thinking, our feeling is nothing but a habit, they do not possess an absolutely objective reality, even if we often act in this way in everyday life, and thus every way of thinking, every conditioning can also be changed. I can be annoyed or patient. I can react indifferently and dismissively or lovingly and compassionately to any human situation. I can be selfrighteous and proud, moody and arrogant, or exercise humility in dealing with my neighbor. Especially in everyday dealings with one's own family or partner, little attention is paid to the vulnerability of the other and there is a lack of mutual respect and appreciation. However, it's nothing but habits, conditioning, the pattern in which we involuntarily function in a compulsive manner, and we struggle to be different in intense situations, to think differently, or less emotionally.

And that's where the healing power of the mental symbol comes in. Its power penetrates deep into the subconscious and can initiate changes in the mind from there, which after a while, also take hold in more difficult life situations and are stable. Pure reflection may often lead us to want to change one way of thinking or emotion, but the power of habit keeps us falling back into the old patterns. The mind is quickly distracted on the outside, the mindfulness is lost inwardly, and already we are again entangled in old patterns and endless dilemmas from which we cannot really escape, with distractions, self-justifications, or rationalizations. With the mental symbol, we have a very effective and helpful tool to finally solve old conditionings and establish new healing ones.

But now for practical application: How is the healing power of the SHK used correctly?

Clear, simple, and very insistent is the method from the original Japanese Reiki, as Usui Sensei is said to have taught and practiced it herself. You sit upright and are clear and free from any distractions in the mind. Without this mindfulness and focused attention on this practice of healing habits, however, this technique hardly works, so the ability to keep one's mind focused is a prerequisite. The Hara is the center of our being, from there everything happens. And so one hand lies before the Hara, the other hand on the forehead. The mental symbol is entered in the hand on the forehead, and in this hand, I also enter the idea of the desired redeemed way of thinking and being. If the hand on the forehead is programmed and

239

charged in this way, I then place it on the other hand, on the Hara, and let the energy act from the Hara in my body and on all levels. Here, too, I am free of distraction; quiet and clear.

In western Reiki, other techniques of mental treatment are taught for self-treatment, for the treatment of others as well as for remote treatment. In most cases, the mental symbol and the power symbol are drawn at the top of the head into the crown chakra, the hands are placed, and the name of the recipient is said three times. Then, the affirmation is entered and concentrated on for a short time, after which the hands remain on the head and let the affirmation continue to act.

So far, this is a very simple technique. When entering the affirmation, however, one should observe certain rules, so that it actually arrives at the recipient effectively and salutary. The affirmation must always be formulated exclusively in a positive way and should be clear and concise. But what arrives in the subconscious is also always the whole image, the felt idea that is entered! As we recite the phrase affirmation, the image and feeling must also be purely positive and redeemed, because this works much more than the words we say.

When someone enters: "I am patient and loving in the care of the mother-in-law," but actually feels: "Oh God, the poor, now she also has to look after the mother-in-law," the latter arrives and makes them depressed rather than happy. We must, therefore, take great care that the emotional energy and the presented image are also redeemed during the input, and are purely positive. The emotional energy affects the receiver even more than the energy imaginable. When we know this and use it accordingly, the mental treatment is very powerful and can convert many old habits into new redeemed ones. So a sentence should not only be said but there should be an intensely felt (!) presentation in conjunction with the sentence. Then, such a mental treatment is very effective and beneficial.

In most cases, a whole series of mental treatments with the same affirmation is recommended on consecutive days, preferably in the morning, at noon and in the evening, so that even deep-seated habits can be changed. I always recommend a book about affirmations by Louise L. Hay: "Heal Your Body." In this small booklet, body areas and illnesses are psychosomatically assigned to the wrong unredeemed ways of thinking, and suggestions are given for corresponding positive affirmations. The assignment of the individual vertebrae to body zones and ways of thinking is also helpful and revealing for the professional practitioner.

After a mental treatment, it makes sense to keep silent about it, so as not to draw disturbing thoughts of others to this healing process. As is so often the case with spiritual exercises, all beginnings are slightly endangered by external influences of the doubt of third parties. The thoughts of others can have a disturbing effect on one's own development. This is the reason for secrecy, that one keeps silent about things such as a mental symbol, even certain Buddhist teachings and certainly initiation experiences, and does not talk about it with those who are far-left.

After years of practice, faith in the light is confirmed many times by experience, a powerful connection is established on the inner plane to the spiritual world, and then we are also so consolidated that thoughts of others can no longer make us waver. In this sense: May your heart connection to the light strengthen and intensify a little more every day, and may all the healing that you want, happen, according to the plan of the soul.

CHAPTER 10

PRACTICE DAILY FOR A BETTER WORLD

H. H. Dalai Lama is an embodiment of Avalokiteshvara, the Buddha of infinite, perfect compassion. The Dalai Lama is tireless in his quest to help all beings in the best possible way, out of pure, selfless compassion with all suffering beings. The radiance of such a consummate saint is probably not unaffected.

Towards the end of the event in Nottingham in May 2008, the Dalai Lama was asked the following question from the audience: "H. H. was so kind to us, how can we do something for Him?" And his answer was direct and clear: "Practice sincerity! Become more harmonious and create a better world."

This shows parallels to the Reiki rules of life and can also be applied to our daily Reiki practice. This is what all spiritual traditions are all about. This is the essence of the search for the Higher and for a sense of life: tame your own mind, develop a good heart, and thus make the world a little more loving.

Developing the quality of heart is what it really is all about. And that is perhaps the only thing that can actually make our world better and more beautiful, both inside and out. In the New Age, a person who can almost fly has incredible clairvoyance abilities etc., and a higher species with advanced magical and psychic traits were sometimes predicted for 2012. It is often overlooked that these properties are only a side effect, and if the self identifies with them, they are even an obstacle on the path of higher development, because the essence has always been the same since the beginning of the day: the quality of the heart develops through Self-mastery, devotion and purification. The result is completely unspectacular and reveals itself precisely by its simplicity.

What does this mean? It means to regard the others more important than learning humility, to reduce one's attachment and defense, and to be more compassionate and loving in dealing with all, no matter how they behave towards us. The Holy Mother, Meera, says, "Become a little more loving and peaceful every day."

But how can we implement this in everyday life? We have to motivate ourselves first: Why did I start Reiki? What am I looking for? What happiness do I want to experience in life? What really matters in my life? And then it quickly becomes clear that, on the one hand, we have ups and downs in external life that can only be controlled to a limited extent, but ultimately the internal constitution decides whether or not we are satisfied and happy with what is and what is not. In this way, we realize how helpful and significant daily Reiki practice is.

Of course, it is also perfectly okay if you only give yourself Reiki occasionally, when something is hurting, you feel miserable or just want to relax a little bit. But a development towards heart quality, and increased well-being and happiness in life requires more effort and as regular reiki as possible, especially on days we don't really like and prefer distraction.

The inauguration in Reiki is a great gift from heaven, it is made so easy for us: to lie down, lay hands, relax and feel good, to just let it happen, and let go. And afterwards, we are in a more loving and peaceful constitution. This is done on its own. But of course, we can also do more and always align ourselves with the rules of life in everyday life, using Reiki as a source of strength for our own process of higher development. All beginnings are difficult, but if I have consciously exercised patience in place of anger a few times, this too becomes a habit. When I realize what a beautiful divine blessing I have received through the Reiki Initiation, I remain in humility and gratitude, and so more and more blessings can happen. And in times when I struggle, I recognize the value of sincerity towards myself. Only in this way, I can continue along the path.

Reiki helps us to nourish so much inner peace and a warm, kind heart so that we can feel love and compassion in our hearts, and this also has a

245

beneficial effect in all our encounters. This, in turn, also comes back and strengthens us. After 10 years, our life looks very different, both inside and outside the light of the soul begins to shine. H. H. Dalai Lama would also enjoy this...

The Hand Positions In The Reiki

Since 1999 we have learned that Reiki still exists in Japan and that Mikao Usui has encouraged his students from the very beginning to be intuitive in the treatment and either let their hands be completely guided by Reiki or to use the hands to identify energetic disturbances in the human energy field and then treat them in a targeted manner. Hayashi, as a former doctor, first developed position sequences for certain diseases, but dropped them in later years and instead worked only purely intuitively. Ms. Takata met hand positions at her Reiki treatments in Tokyo, brought them to the West, and either herself or her granddaughter Furumoto then declared this sequence of treatments absolute.

We know more about Suzuki San, who has been with Usui for 12 years, as opposed to Hayashi, who has only witnessed the last 9 months of Usui: Usui has worked intuitively, much more purely mentally, so without direct contact. From the very beginning, he taught his students to work intuitively, to learn to distinguish energy fields in the body. And this ability was also particularly supported and promoted by the regular Reijus, the original form of initiation that Usui has repeatedly given to his disciples, and which is very different from the western form of initiation in Reiki.

A special form of treatment, but rather unsuitable for the beginner, was actually used by Usui Sensei, according to Suzuki San. I find this magical, and it is incredibly effective: without touching the body at all, all meridians, all zones, all organs, all systems, all levels of man are treated via only 5 imagined head positions. Combined with the blessing of the healing Buddha Binzuru, there are 5 mudras that are imagined at the head of the recipient and treat specifically all 12 meridians in the body. If my information about Reiki in Japan is correct, in Usui's time, this is the only original Reiki treatment form, apart from the purely intuitive treatment. It is much more difficult to apply than western whole body treatment, but it also goes much deeper and is more comprehensive. Their healing effect amazes me again and again. And so you also train the ability to see the meridians directly in the body and then place energies in disturbed areas of a meridian. However, this type of treatment requires mental abilities in order to be effective accordingly.

For a professional treatment, I discovered another treasure a few years ago: treatment points on the meridians, as they are applied in Japanese healing streams and in Jin Shin Jyutsu. This is the main subject of the seminary Dao Reiki 1. Here, as in an apprenticeship as a physiotherapist, the student must be able to learn a lot about the respective position and also in treatment, which of the 18 positions is the one that the client needs at the moment. Then it can be worked very effectively, and one or two of these hand positions achieve more than several whole-body treatments according to the classic traditional Western Reiki system.

CHAPTER 11

REIKI IN THE PRESENT DAY, REIKI FOR THE EXHAUSTED SELF

The achievements of modern civilization allow us to live more and more in a man-made artificial world, in a world away from nature, away from natural rhythms and far from silence and pause. Has man really improved his world with it? Environmental protection has found its place and is trying to limit the damage caused by the exploitation of the planet. But what protects people's minds and psyches? Modern medicine and psychology speak of new diseases such as ADHD (attention deficit syndrome), anxiety neurosis (pain of social isolation) and CFS (chronic fatigue syndrome), and now also of the exhausted self. The exhausted self—a symptom of our modern meritocracy—and how Reiki can be helpful and healing should be the subject of this book.

The human psyche has also long been under pressure to perform in the economy, which is constantly geared towards growth. The classic definition of economics is a system for meeting human needs. This has become completely self-sufficient and a system of creating more and more needs that never end. But should we not then be allowed to ask the question, to what extent this system actually increases human happiness or even destroys it? Bhutan is the only state on the planet that has anchored the pursuit of inner happiness at the forefront of its legislation and political leadership. But this is not to become a political text, only the background of the social system in which we spend our daily lives should be pointed out for a short time so that we can see to what extent we ourselves are manipulated by it or not. The external life of increasing productivity has also had an impact on the inner level of man, and stress is part of everyday life; nature is a luxury.

Outer inspiration is also reflected on the inner plane: an always strenuous attitude in life, one's own self must always get better, and the persona constantly optimized. This restless optimization of the self, whether conscious or unconscious, leads to the fact that hardly anyone can love and accept themselves as they are. But also, the handling of oneself is performance-oriented up to the grotesque spectacle of his own body to further and further optimize the gender marketplace in order to have better chances of winning. So many people are becoming more and more estranged from themselves. They are only in their heads and without connection to the heart and their belly. Once they pause the constant distraction and pressure to perform, they find only emptiness, futility, and have no connection to themselves, only to the optimization goals of their self. Inner satisfaction, which accepts everything lovingly and gratefully as it is, seems to exist only on another planet.

It is not surprising that the demand for therapy in both classical and alternative forms has increased very strongly at the moment. Especially the interest in all kinds of life support, in order to find a way of selftherapy, and to reconnect with the inner being and a sense of life within itself. Always being at work, won't work in the long run. But to pause and simply enjoy the moment in the here and now as it is, is very difficult.

The strenuous attitude has become a powerful habit; the miraculous and fulfilling experience that was lingering in the unity of giving has come a long way. Instead, most feel overwhelmed, not good enough for this world, they orient themselves to external things and have lost touch with their own inner beings. Heart and stomach have to function according to the ideas and expectations of rational thinking, and their messages are ignored (if there is a pain signal, just take a tablet and carry on). On the other hand, if one senses inwardly and gives space and attention to the inner conflicts and alternating impulses, a solution can be found even without the control of thought. As the saying goes: Only with the heart one sees well. This is also to be applied to the handling of oneself! But if everything is conducted only from the head and is always tensely subordinated to the striving for optimization, the inner conflicts manifest themselves as illness and pain, and our modern society also has its typical modern diseases such as ADHD, Anxiety neurosis, cancer and allergies. The new psychological concept of the exhausted self is a sign of the times, a signal for rethinking: this is simply no longer the case, the vitality is exhausted, nothing is possible anymore. How long must one have disregarded the messages of the body in order to get to this point?

Sometimes we feel that balancing and switching off are important, that we have to relax again and leave the pressure of performance and optimization behind. Regenerating and letting go at all levels is possible, to the point of the desire for nothing more, which alone can really give us peace. Reiki can be very helpful and healing for everyone. You can go to a practitioner and also get Reiki treatments, attend a Reiki seminar and from then on, give yourself reiki every day. Reiki is easy to learn and practice, and there are no exceptions at all; anyone can do this. Reiki helps us to go inside again, to feel ourselves again instead of just thinking. Reiki is regenerating, brings back calm and strengthens all levels and systems of man. And there is nothing wrong: For Reiki directs, guides, leads and lets everything happen, so one does not work with one's own will or energy but is a channel for a pure divine light that always works salutary on all levels.

Many people are looking for something that will help them to find themselves again, and Reiki is ideal because it can be learned in a few hours and enjoyed without any special effort during treatment or selftreatment. Reiki takes over the work, so to speak, we just have to let it happen. The universal life energy that we receive in a Reiki treatment strengthens us on the energetic level and supports any form of development of our own potential. Whether you are spiritually oriented or not, old or young, sick or healthy, Reiki can give something to everyone in his or her own individual way through life. With Reiki, we can easily take a break to regenerate and find ourselves again. Finally, we can switch off again. Even the exhausted self can lie down to Reiki and treat itself, thereby regaining strength and meaning. However, a good practitioner can also support this process of healing the soul particularly well by seeing exactly where the person is standing, making him aware of this, and then pointing out targeted solutions.

Sometimes there is not so much that needs to be changed in one's own life in order to be able to experience peace and contentment again. Only a little space is needed for Reiki, for pause, and to find one. The exhausted self needs food from within, a space without incitement, where self-love and value-free acceptance of all that one is will be experienced as a counterpoint to all the demands that outer life places on one. In this way, the exhausted self can find its way home, and relive being at home. Reiki is a very simple and perfect way to create this space in your everyday life and to come back home.

Sometimes, the beginning is not so easy, because, like addicts, people are directed outward and programmed for consumption and distraction. Often it takes a life crisis to wake up and ask yourself: Isn't there anything else that can make me happy and satisfied? A distraction-free silence and a direct encounter with oneself, can hardly be endured and inside feels empty and dead. Some have completely lost touch with themselves in their wholeness. But even at this point, Reiki makes it very easy for us to regain access to ourselves. Reiki is then an inexhaustible source of power, which builds us up every day and supports us on our way. It gives us peace and relaxation, light and blessings.

CHAPTER 12

WIRELESSLY HAPPY? REIKI SHOWS US HOW

Some Reiki students were rather skeptical at the beginning of their first Reiki seminar, but in the end, everyone had an inner experience that Reiki is doing well. In any case, I know only one instance from my almost 15 years with infinite reiki initiations, where the doubtful spirit was so overpowering that nothing had been experienced except for one's own neurosis.

However, the differences in how Reiki works and how it is experienced are great, and one can relax very well and drop very quickly the other struggles experienced with it at first. Even with the same person, Reiki is experienced differently and anew every time. So we need patience, and then it becomes easier and the condition in everyday life becomes more relaxed and lighter. If the Reiki student finds a way to integrate Reiki into his everyday life and regularly practice Reiki, only then will a positive change in the inner and outer life take place. The eyes begin to glow and get depth— the depth of the soul.

Those who practice Reiki seriously will make progress year after year, and it is a growth process in which all levels of the human being participate. And occasionally, there are particularly deep and dissolved states in which one never wants to reappear. This is not possible, but it is possible to become aware of the quality of this state and to aspire to it in the further life as the truth, as the light, as the essence of being, or as Usui defined it in the introduction to the Reiki rules of life. : As the path to happiness and well-being, which is a classic description of the Buddhist path, liberation from all sufferings and the realization of the spirit of enlightenment.

Many Reikians have experienced such a little satori before, but the meaning has not become clear to them at that moment. In deep relaxation, all worries fall, all fears disappear, there is nothing to be annoyed about, love in the heart is there for all and also gratitude. This IS the truth: no more ego and no more will or pushing away; everything is okay as it is. The distinction between I and You also dissolves, and we experience unity.

Many experienced such conditions in the Reiki, and yet they went down again as soon as the treatment was over, and discursive thinking had regained the upper hand. It's a pity because we could learn so much from it. It is possible to be unconditionally happy, to be at home within so that one is no longer looking for something outside. It is a state of desirelessness, an experience of undesired happiness.

In Buddhist doctrine, Dukha is spoken of, which means as much as not fulfilled—unsatisfied. All-consuming thinking, and all desires create tension. And so, in the end, we live our whole lives in a state of Dukha, of non-fulfillment. Everything you desire creates tension and restlessness. In the deep relaxation that Reiki sometimes gives us, we come into this state of desirelessness, the outer life is still the same, and yet it can no longer disturb our inner peace.

You experience such a feeling of deep peace in the Reiki, everything dissolves and falls away from you, why then do you start to put so much stress on yourself afterward? Reiki shows the way to happiness, to inner happiness in the heart. There is nothing more to be desired, hoped for, or feared. There is only the pure being, the being in the here and now, in unity.

Any deep relaxation in Reiki can show us that there is another way to happiness and well-being, to happiness without desire. Well, if one is made aware of this again and again and aligns one's own mind according to it, then year after year, even higher enlightened experiences of being can arise, in perfection that one cannot yet imagine. It is always up to ourselves, whether we aspire to this inner happiness in our hearts or the world of external desires. Reiki shows us the way inward.

Reiki - The Path To Happiness And Well-Being

Reiki treatment is soothing and very pleasantly relaxing, easy to use without being able to do anything wrong, and without having to train for years. And so it is very helpful even in today's hectic times to be able to reduce stress in this way and to come back a little to rest. Traditionally, the 1st Reiki seminar teaches different ways of laying on hands in order to be able to treat oneself and others with Reiki. In addition, the Reiki rules of life are always an essential part of the daily Reiki practice.

However, the potential of the Reiki is far from being reached, the introduction to the Reiki Rules of Life states: Reiki is the "path to happiness and well-being." It is probably no coincidence that this very formulation was chosen by the founder Mikao Usui. The "path to happiness and well-being" is a classic description of the Buddhist path, the way to liberation from all sufferings and the pursuit of enlightenment.

And so, for the practice of Reiki, we can also use some very basic rules of Buddhist lifestyle and thinking, without having to change religion and take refuge in Buddhism. The Buddha's teaching shows us the laws according to which true well-being and happiness of life are to be attained, according to which our being, which is primarily spirit, functions. The better we understand how our minds work and thus shape our destiny, the better we can consciously develop with Reiki.

The pursuit of happiness is universal; all living beings have this in common and desire this. For the intelligent Homo Sapiens, lasting and stable happiness is to be found less in the outside than in one's own mind, as the Reiki rules of life point out to us.

Reiki, as our universal source of power, can be used even better in everyday life by realizing how our minds work and then training our own minds to get used to positive attitudes that are helpful and healing.

Only when one becomes aware of the phenomena working in one's own psyche can one also transform them and take a lighter and more loving path. The inner troublemakers, the emotional and mental constraints, can be gradually purified by loving and constructive dealing with one's own being until they lose their power over you.

Our self-image is usually a neurotic element, which always has one's own self first in its attention, and either makes itself larger and more important out of this self-relationship, combined with an unrealistic and unteachable self-righteousness, or making itself smaller and less inferior, which can be increased to self-pity and the play of the poor self. Both neurotic components of our minds must first be recognized and then overcome in a clever way. But how???

Reiki teaches us to let go: If I do not follow these thought processes of self-centeredness further, but let them move on relaxed again, then calm and associated clarity will arise. Then, I can experience myself as big and small, without my self-esteem changing. Thereafter all the attention is no longer used to make myself bigger or smaller, but I can begin to constructively establish a connection with myself, at the end of which I no longer take myself so seriously but have realized that my own Well-being depends on how far I love others in my heart and am more interested in their happiness than my own.

How much stress is there every day around this selfimage? How much am I trapped in pride or in compensating or rationalizing thought patterns, and can lose my composure so quickly? How many times has the self-image changed, everything seemed great when it was a good day, or horrible when my hypocrisy had suffered? So much revolves only around one's own self-image, which ultimately turns out to be pure conceit, but which is often difficult to see through.

All these projections and fixations, the Buddha calls spiritual poisons, that come from the patterns of fear and hope, from the will to have or the defenses. I can be conscious of every single reaction in my being and try to see through it, so I modify my attention inward rather than outwardly: How much true happiness and well-being does this habitual reaction really give me?

It is very important in this self-experience that we treat ourselves lovingly, that we learn to be a good "Reiki" friend to ourselves: "Okay, that was not good, tomorrow we will do better." And then let go again. So I stay on a constructive level with myself. I find a wise and loving way of dealing with the self, and that feels much more beautiful than constantly getting bigger or smaller, or even going into guilt complexes or devastating thoughts out of self-rejection.

Inward attention makes us realize how quickly we want to reach for something that promises amenity or to fend off something that goes against the grain of self-centeredness. This is how we live in the constant change of fear and hope. The path of Reiki, on the other hand, can show us how beautiful it is to be loving, grateful and serene simply by letting things be as they are. This is great art if we have fully internalized this, we are enlightened and free from all sufferings.

The more one deals with the importance of the Reiki rules of life for the daily practice of Reiki, the more it becomes clear that this is a long way, that it is spiritual development, and that this, in turn, means recognizing the tyranny of the ego in the first place, and ultimately defeat. The Spirit is constantly concerned with fear and hope, with desire and defenses and is extremely tricky in this endeavor. This requires sincerity towards oneself— the fourth of the rules of life. "Don't worry today" means something else: to actually use your mind skillfully and not to constantly worry about superfluous and stressful thoughts.

Reiki helps us every day to come into serenity, to look carefully into the here and now, mindful of the inward and is an inexhaustible source of strength on this journey. Using Reiki gives us a blessing that simplifies and makes life more beautiful, lighter, and more loving.

May all the healing you want, happen according to the plan of the soul.

CHAPTER 13

THE REIKI-GRADE

Defining the term "Reiki" clearly and universally, and in doing so thinking more than receiving and transmitting light, is quite difficult in all the different forms that are taught and practiced under the name Reiki. And the "scholars are also at odds with each other" on a definition of the term Usui Reiki that is valid for all. Usui Reiki is also available in many variants, in Western and Japanese traditions.

One of the characteristics of all traditions of Reiki is that it is taught in three successive degrees— Reiki 1, Reiki 2, and Reiki 3. Also, in the writings of Mikao Usui, the founder of Reiki Ryoho, the Reiki healing method, there are three degrees, three levels in which he taught his disciples, namely, shodes, okudes and shinpads. In terms of content, however, these deviate from the degrees that have spread widely in the Western world known as Reiki 1, 2 and 3.

The first Reiki degree (in Western traditions) allows the introduction to reiki practice. In addition to a theoretical understanding of how it works, intention, and history teaches the student the practical application by placing his hands on both his own body and another person's. A one- to one-and-a-half hour full-body treatment with certain hand positions and a short chakra treatment are part of a Reiki-1 seminar. So are the ideals, the Reiki rules of life, the prayer that Mikao Usui and his students recited to common practice.

After the seminar, the actual practice begins for the student, because only if Reiki is applied in a reasonably regular form in everyday life, can its blessing and healing power have an effect on personal development and general well-being. The practice of hand laying after the inauguration to the Reiki canal means not only an increased opening of the hand chakras from which Reiki flows out but, as is the case with all the other chakras of the human energy body, the hands will also be used in the course of the time to become a trained perceptual organ for energetic vibrations.

If, after a certain period of Reiki practice, the whole being has opened up to the light of Reiki, there is an interest in further applications and a certain sensitivity to the flow of energy has been developed, the student is ready for the second Reiki degree. This may take half a year or a whole year, but it varies quite differently individually.

In the second Reiki degree, there are symbols that make specific energies available. Their applications are taught and three symbols are common, namely, a force symbol, a mental symbol, and a so-called remote symbol. With the help of these symbols, the

Reiki 2 student can give more targeted, comprehensive, effective, and much more powerful treatments, as well as energetic room cleaning, remote treatments, mental treatments far beyond the reach of his own hands and much more. The power symbol alone reinforces its Reiki many times compared to the first degree.

Other symbols for grounding, karmic healing, inner peace, the purification of psychic energy and angelic work, and a symbol for back treatment are added to the 3 traditional Reiki symbols. These are from Tera Mai and Karuna Reiki, respectively.

Even after the Reiki 2 seminar, one's own practice and experience are very important, because it is only in the course of time that we grow into this world of the so-called invisible and are able to develop a clear perception in the realm of energies and vibrations. This goes hand in hand with one's own spiritual and emotional development and is a process that takes time. It is an inner development towards the light, which wants to be nourished and supported. Reiki is a great, unconditional help and a source of power—a heavenly blessing.

Since I understand Reiki as a development process and not just as a technique, it is not my style to teach all three degrees in quick flow in a few weeks or even days. The time from the second to the third Reiki degree lasted up to 7 years for me personally, and only then was the time ripe for the next step, the inauguration to the Reiki Master. A minimum of one year of Reiki practice should, in my opinion, definitely pass between the second and third Reiki degrees.

The third Reiki degree is the full opening to the Reiki channel, and the initiation into the energy of the Master symbol is a big step in personal development. It is possible to make the third degree exclusively for your own Reiki practice and development and, thus, to have the full power of Reiki at your disposal. Others, on the other hand, train as re-masters in order to be able to give their own initiations in Reiki and seminars. In some traditions, this is referred to as a Reiki Master Teacher or as a fourth degree. In the third degree, further techniques for treatment are taught, including psycho-energetic surgery, as well as a particularly intensive breathing technique and meditation for the training of one's own energy body.

To be a Reiki master and to teach others in Reiki is a responsible task that we can only do justice to if we are willing to work on ourselves in accordance with the fourth Reiki rule of life, and this is certainly a wonderful development of one's own being towards the light. Daily meditation in the energy field of the Master symbol is one of many ways to promote development at all levels of one's being.

Building on the Master's degree, a whole series of other initiations are possible, sometimes referred to in the literature as the Reiki Grandmaster Degrees. This is another step on the path of Reiki, more to the higher Reiki Master degrees on the next page.

In the years 1999 to 2002, we learned that the founder of Reiki in Japan, Mikao Usui, also taught a system of mainly 3 Reiki degrees, but its content and objectives differ from the Western Reiki practice. The degrees and levels of Reiki, as originally taught by Usui Sensei himself in Japan, can be learned in the seminar URR & Usui Teate.

More Reiki Master Grades

With the big step to the Reiki Master Initiation, the road is far from over; on the contrary, now the learning really begins. All the more so when the Reiki Master decides to teach others in Reiki and thus assumes a responsible task.

Building on the master's degree, other so-called Grandmaster grades have been developed by various people. So these are not symbols, and initiations that can be traced back to the founder of the Reiki, Mikao Usui, but rather further developments of Western Reiki masters, which are reflected in the inner level of spiritual and emotional development and can be very helpful with treatment.

I myself prefer to call these initiations "only" further or higher Reiki master degrees. Officially, at most, the president of the Usui Reiki Ryoho Gakkai would have the right to bear the title of Grand-Master. Some egos in the Reiki scene feel bigger with the Grand Master title, I deliberately do not want to promote this, so I call these initiations, as beautiful and powerful as they are, more master degrees.

The wisdom symbol comes from a Hessian Reiki master named Helmut Ernst and rightly bears his name. With our gaze into infinity, we are able to recognize higher connections and experience a serenity that alienates us from the consciousness of everyday life. For me, the first meditative practice with the wisdom symbol was as if the legacy of a thousand years of Buddhist meditation suddenly became available to me. The message of the wisdom symbol is: "the knowledge of this world is at your disposal." Wisdom, intuitive knowledge, spiritual guidance, and deep insight are promoted with this initiation and subsequent practice with the symbol.

The 4th Reiki degree (Radiance), the heart symbol, has the message "Light and love shine from my heart" and is beautiful for our heart. The energy of the symbol opens and purifies in the area of the heart and neck chakra and allows us to be back in love. The development of intellectual abilities is one side; one's own kindness of heart, and also the unconditional joy that comes with such a heart is certainly no less important. An injured or sorrowful heart can be led back into harmony and joy with the symbol of the heart. Another aspect is the ability to let heart energy radiate freely to the delight of others as well as of one's own. According to my research, this symbol comes from the lineage of Barbara Weber-Ray, who made it from a source in Japan (Mieko Mitsui or Iris Ishikuro—who knows more exactly?) and integrated into their radiance system.

The 5th Reiki degree (Radiance), the neck chakra symbol, comes from the Barbara Ray line, i.e., from the A.I.R.A., later renamed Radiance. This Grand Master's Inauguration energizes, as the name suggests, the neck chakra. All areas and levels of expression, communication and truthfulness associated with this chakra are opened to the light. The message of this symbol is: "the divine powers are expressed." I find remarkable the connection between the opening of the neck chakra, the voice, and the quality of inner truthfulness. This can be experienced in the energy of this symbol and was also experienced by Ray's students (The Reiki Factor - Barbara Ray). As the phrase says so beautifully: "to be coherent."

The 5th Reiki degree, The Great Harmony, as well as the 6th degree, the Great Division, is attributed to two Reiki masters living in Germany; Raj Petter, and Jay Arjan Falk. There are many stories and rumors circulating about the origin of these degrees and unfortunately, there is no clear explanation of the origin of these degrees of Petter and Falk together. After repeated, extensive research also in the context of the emergence of these degrees from the years 1990 to 1992, the puzzle seems to me to be composed and the following about the origin of these two degrees crystallized:

The 5th and 6th degrees developed in two steps in their present form. A Buddhist monk named Serge Goldberg, a white-haired, nearly eighty-year-old American who had practiced Zen Buddhism for many decades, had the energies and mantras (or just selfinitiation technique?) in the 1940s in a Japanese Reiki School. Raj Petter, who had been with Osho in India, met Serge Goldberg in India and brought these energies and mantras, as well as technology, to Europe from India.

In Germany, the energies and mantras were then passed on in a Reiki scene in the Frankfurt area in the early 1990s. A. Falk also came into contact with it and, according to Norbert Kuhl, simply took a Japanese dictionary and took symbols in Japanese kanji from it. Falk's own depiction varied, and his claim that the symbols were created in collaboration with a Japanese woman was unlikely because the sign of the mouth (a figure similar to the square) in the kanji would never be written in this way by any Japanese man in this form. So I suspect it was just a dictionary. With a ceremony, the symbols were then charged together with the mantras of Falk and the inauguration in the 5th and 6th degrees, as many Reiki masters have received since then, mainly in the German-speaking area, was created. This should have been 1993 or 94.

Anyway, the name of the 5th Grade, The Great Harmony, actually says it all — a beautiful healing harmony in the heart. Love is the greatest of all forces. Saint Amma of India says that 90% of all sufferings and illnesses are due to a lack of love, which is easy to understand. To be back in love with all my heart is healing on all levels par excellence. The great harmony is an energy, a force that makes the quality of heart and unity tangible. In treatments, I have been able to experience beautiful healings in people's hearts with this energy.

The 6th Reiki-Grade, The Great Division, is also from the line Serge Goldberg/Petter & Falk and belongs together with the Great Harmony. Higher levels of awareness and clarity become tangible as soon as the essential is separated from the inessential.

The 7th and 8th Reiki degrees, are a further development of W. Keil and a Japanese student of mine; Dai Ji Yu, The Great Freedom, and Dai Hey Wa, The Great Peace. W. Wedge, initiated by Raj Petter in the Reiki Master, has received these two energies and with the help of Makiko, a Japanese Reiki student of mine, and a kanji dictionary, we have found matching symbols that are then found in a sacred ceremony of W. Keil and me (E bull) and that were connected to the energies. In the initiation ritual customary for all higher master degrees, since then, more precisely, since the year 2000, these initiations have been preserved in the 7th and 8th degrees. They have proved to be very blessed and particularly fine and high-swinging. They can be shared or passed on one after the other.

Dai Ji Yu, The Great Freedom, supports clarity in spirit, calm and free of attachment, and rejection to see things as they are. This is the freedom that lies in the sublime.

Dai Hey Wa, The Great Peace, gives security. Security in infinite, unconditional love. An "all-round feelgood," in its intensity far more powerful than what can be conveyed with the second or third Reiki degree. This is the power and divinity of the sublime, beyond all duality.

All initiations into the symbol of wisdom, as well as in the 4th, in both 5th, and in the 6th, 7th, and 8th degrees are an enrichment for any Reiki master both for his own inner development as well as for use in treatments. I am happy to pass on these degrees on a donation basis to interested Reiki masters, and appointments can be arranged individually.

Prerequisite is an initiation in the 3rd Reiki degree, in the Reiki Master symbol Dai Ko Myo.

Often, a rather high price is demanded for these inaugurations, up to '40,000—for the heart chakra symbol at Barbara Weber-Ray. Giving these initiations on a donation basis, yes, that is still true for me, after I have initiated Reiki masters from many lines in it since about 1997. This is because I would like to make these degrees accessible to all interested parties, regardless of their material situation. What was not intended with the donation base, however, is that these grades will then be resold at double to almost five times the price of what was donated to me. From September 2003, the rule was, therefore, applied that the transmission of these initiations must not be more expensive than the donation made—which I actually take for granted, or don't?

All other Reiki master grades are very powerful and blessed, and they serve the spiritual nourishment and development of the master, e.g., in meditation.

These particularly intense energies can also be used in treatments. It is an enrichment for every Reiki master with and without teaching skills. I am glad to be able to pass on this blessing.

And so I would like to conclude this text with a quote from Ayya Khema from her book with "Instructions of the Buddha to Happiness":

"What we do with love is well done. In reality, what we do with love is spiritually done. What we do without love can still look so spiritual, but has no spiritual content. Holiness is to be whole and nothing else. Bliss is bliss. We all have the skills to do so, but we have to work towards it and realize that it is possible... and leave this world a little more pure and beautiful than we found it."

CHAPTER 14

REIKI LIFE RULES

According to Buddhist tradition, the Reiki practice is started and ended with a prayer, a recitation. This prayer aligns one's own mind, clarifies the motivation for doing, and is thus an effective attunement and orientation in order to create a specific cause for a certain effect. Every Buddhist practice, such as a meditation on the medicine Buddha, begins with a prayer to clarify motivation. The text is always repeated at least three times, and the hands are folded in the prayer posture (Gassho) in front of the heart.

The full version of this text by Mikao Usui Sensei only became known in the West in the late 1990s. Ms. Hawayo Takata's previously learned version had been altered in the text. The Japanese version shown below was kindly provided by Ms. K. Koyama, former head of the Usui Reiki Ryoho Gakkai, in Tokyo.

Happiness, true well-being, healing at all levels is possible in the spirit of Reiki, in a spirit that has liberated itself to a universal being that clearly recognizes and lives in unity with the spiritual. In daily practice (especially today), certain guidelines such as peace, trust, gratitude, self-discipline and appreciation of others, hence the care of Buddhist (and also universally human) virtues in one's own thinking and feeling, are Prerequisite for attaining happiness. That is, to truly master his destiny, or, in the words of the New Age, to achieve self-realization. If the mind is in the right balance, the body must also follow and be healthy.

In my personal opinion, the Reiki rules of life contain typical Buddhist traits. So I would like to add a few suggestions from a Buddhist point of view.

At every moment (especially today — the clear alignment of attention to the here and now), we create our karma through thinking and acting on the inner and outer plane in the sense that it inevitably leaves traces in one's own consciousness. Sooner or later, we experience the effect of happiness or suffering. Therefore, at the beginning of an action, is a clarification of the orientation, the objective and the motivation. If we are aware that we are responsible for all the happiness and suffering we experience, a clear knowledge of what is to be promoted in one's own consciousness is most helpful. In this way, we can then promote happiness and reduce suffering. Qualities such as equanimity, trust, integrity and loving devotion to others are able to make our inner and outer lives healthier, more healing and lighter. Practice always takes place at this moment, in the here and now, and requires constant mindfulness, that is, work on ourselves. Thus, the blessing of the Reiki practice can not only bring about a little relaxation, stress reduction, and relief of pain and illnesses, but also show a path that leads us into the light, to true happiness.

The Gyosei, poems of the Meiji Emperor, which, like the rules of life in Usui's Reiki practice, were quoted together, can be found here.

Another translation and interpretation of the Reiki rules of life, all of which originated in the original text of the Meiji Emperor, comes from the transmission line of the Reiki Jin-Kei-Do. This is perhaps the version that most corresponds to Buddhist thinking.

The Buddha taught that all life is painful, is Dukha (Being Unsatisfied). The existence of negative ominous emotions and thoughts in one's own mind as the cause of suffering is a fact that is to be recognized and transformed from this knowledge with clever methods. Thus compassion is the antidote to hatred, while doubt and worry are overcome by mindfulness in the here and now. In the end, we can free ourselves from all attachments, recognize our true being directly and clearly, and thus free ourselves from many painful patterns. The practice of the art of life, to think and feel in a healing and happiness-bringing way, is what the Buddhist strives for at every moment, because in this way he can have a positive influence on his fate. Also noteworthy in this text is the reference to the direct connection between our thinking and feeling and our mental and physical health.

Dodrupchen teaches: "By practicing in this way, our spirit will become gentle. Our attitude will become tolerant. We will become very affable people. We will have a brave mindset. Our spiritual training will be free of obstacles. All adverse circumstances that occur will prove to be great and promise happiness. Our spirit will always be satisfied with the joy of inner peace. In order to practice the path of enlightenment in this age of decline, we must never be without the armor of this kind of training that transforms happiness and suffering into the path of enlightenment. If the suffering of worrying us does not plague us, then not only will other mental and emotional sufferings disappear - such as weapons that soldiers drop out of their hands - but in most cases, even the concrete negative forces, such as the physical diseases, disappear by themselves."

The saints of the past have said: "By not feeling anything and no one's dislike or dissatisfaction, our minds will remain untroubled. If our minds are not troubled, our energy will not be tarnished, and other elements of the body will not be bothered as well. Because of this inner calm and harmony, our minds will not be troubled, and the wheel of joy will continue to turn." They also said: "Just as it is easy for birds to inflict injuries on horses and donkeys with sore spots on their backs, negative forces will easily find an opportunity to harm those people whose beings are filled with fear of negative concern. But it will be hard to harm those whose beings are implemented by a strong positive attitude." (from Tulku Thondup, The Healing Power of the Spirit, Knaur Verlag, Men's Sana series. A book that explains health (well-being and happiness of life) from the point of view of a Tibetan Buddhist, and gives the reader many suggestions for a healing practice in everyday life. Not only suitable for Buddhists).

The History Of Reiki

The story of Reiki, as a unique form of energy work, of healing with light, is inseparable from the person of its discoverer, a Japanese named Mikao Usui. And so I would like to begin the chapter on history with the life and work of this man to whom the world owes so much.

Mikao Usui was born on 15 May 1898. He was born in Yamagata District, Japan, in a Chiba clan Buddhist family with an ancient samurai tradition. Usui had a son and a daughter with his wife Sadako, née Suzuki. Professionally, he had experienced many things, he had worked in the civil service, and also as a businessman, reporter, secretary of a politician (bodyguard?), missionary and probation officer. As private secretary to the politician Shimpei Goto, Mikao Usui must have had good connections with the upper classes.

The time when Usui grew up in Japan was marked by renewal. After centuries of isolation, Japan reopened to foreign countries and to progress, but also to various ancient traditions that were not the former state religion of Shintoism. Belonged. A synthesis of old and new, this has also been the life path and life's work of Mikao Usui.

But he was not interested in worldly success, and perhaps he had been less interested in it. Mysticism and spirituality were of great importance to him, and he studied Kiko, the Japanese Qi Gong, to a high degree, interested in Chinese medicine, learned martial arts, among them Yagyu Shinkage Ryu (Samurai Sword Fight) to the high degree of Menkyo Kaiden. He studied Tendai, Zen and Shingon Buddhism and also the ancient religion of Japan, Shinto. His interest was in medicine, psychology, fortune telling, and spiritual paths; he was an educated person with an awareness of inner qualities. He has also been to China and the West to learn, but it is quite possible that he has found much of his knowledge in the former imperial city of Kyoto with all its temples and libraries. Kyoto is a place with a very advanced cultural and spiritual heritage. Important companions of Mikao Usui include Morihei Ueshiba, the founder of Aikido martial arts, Onasiburo Deguchi, founder of the Oomoto religion, Toshihiro Eguchi, a good friend of Usui and also the founder of a religion, as well as Mokichi Okada, founder of the Oomoto religion. Johrei is the religion of spiritual light. Reiki is, therefore, a path of many that were created in this creative time in Japan.

CHAPTER 15
ON MOUNT KURAMA NEAR KYOTO

The life of Usui, for all his abilities and high education, was not particularly happy, and so he asked his spiritual teacher for advice, as is so common in Japanese culture. This led him to go on a retreat, i.e., to withdraw completely from the outer-worldly life and to practice "Shyu go," 21 days of fasting and meditation, a Buddhist practice that required a great deal of discipline and sincere effort. (The general form of meditation that Usui practiced is Zazen Shikan Taza, more on this in the URR and Usui Teate seminar.) A waterfall on Mount Kurama north of Kyoto was the perfect place to be undisturbed and practice. On the morning of the 21st day of this retreat, the light of Reiki unexpectedly came down to him and Reiki was born. Usui recognized and realized the Reiki healing method and had found himself, attaining a spiritual state of consciousness called "Anshin Ritsumei," which roughly means the following: one's own mind is perfectly at peace, it is clear what to do, nothing can disturb the inner peace and clarity anymore. I suspect this corresponds to Rigpa in Tibetan Buddhism.

This satori must have taken place between 1914 and 1922. The new healing method was first tested in the closest family circle, with such positive results, i.e., healing successes, that Usui decided to make this Ryoho, this healing method, freely accessible to all people. He deliberately did not want to hold them back as a sure source of income for his family and his descendants and kept them as a secret, thereby revealing his great spirit, his altruistic attitude to life. This is clear from the inscription (in German) at his grave in Tokyo.

In 1922, Usui had moved from Kyoto to Tokyo, and since Reiki had proved extremely helpful in various diseases and problems, he founded his first clinic, his first healing center. The interest in Reiki was immense, and people even had to queue in front of the house to get treatment from Usui or his co-workers. With his extraordinary abilities, Usui quickly became known throughout Japan, even though he explicitly did not want any publicity for Reiki. The treatments were open to all, which meant that they were not expensive if any fee was required.

In the few years that remained for his work with Reiki until his death, Usui taught and initiated well over 1000 people in this healing method, 17 of his students received the third grade, the 3rd or Shinpid degree.

The training in Reiki was initially divided into three degrees, and the first is called Shoden, the second Okuden and the third Shinpid. Shihan is the mystical teachings that are based on Shinpids. Only here, the disciple learned to give the initiations, Reiju. In addition, there are said to have been at least two higher master degrees, one without a name, the other meaning "bringing in the light." These empowerments can only be learned after many years of meditation practice and then passed on.

The second and even the third Reiki degree was awarded to the students only after a long-term collaboration with Usui Sensei, with their venerable teacher Usui. The student also had to demonstrate his sensitivity to being able to diagnose in the energy body (Byosen and Reiji Ho) in order to obtain further empowerment. The title "Sensei," venerable teacher, is bestowed on the teacher out of respect for his integrity and ability from the students.

Shoden, the first level of Reiki, was open to every student. People came to Usui to find healing; they received treatment from Usui and regular initiations (Reiju) in the first degree, in shodes. The higher degrees and empowerments, Okuden and Shinpids, and even more so, the even higher master degrees, were granted only after the student had demonstrated the necessary skills and character qualities. Years of cooperation and cooperation were a prerequisite, the Reiju, the attunement in Reiki, as well as a short form of Hatsurei Ho were regularly practiced. Even today, it may take up to ten years for a student in Usui Reiki Ryoho Gakkai to learn the second level, Okuden.

Mikao Usui placed great value on the spiritual side, the care of the inner spiritual qualities. His treatments were purely intuitive, sometimes he taught 5 head positions, as we have learned by now from the well over a 100-year-old student of Usui. He taught meditations and kotodamas, invocations to connect with special energies. If a student was not sensitive enough to do so, such as Hayashi, they were given the well-known 4 Reiki symbols as a tool.

Seventeen students have learned the Shinpid degree at Usui, 5 Buddhist nuns, 3 naval officers, and 9 other men, among them Eguchi, a close friend of Usui's. 5070 students learned the first part (Zenki) of the 2nd degree, 30 also learned the 2nd part (Kouki) of Okuden.

Usui Sensei's goal was and is to improve the state of people's body, mind, and soul, and promote health, well-being and happiness. Reiki was, therefore, not only intended to cure illnesses and relieve pain but also to promote, in a holistic, spiritual sense, health at all levels of the human being and a healing mental state that means true happiness in life, and finally the enlightenment of obtaining liberation.

Shinto and Kiko were the basis for the energetic Reiki practice, and the Tendai Buddhism provided the spiritual background. It may be that Shingon and Zen also had influence, but only secondary. On this basis, Mikao Usui developed a very simple way of purifying and strengthening the human energy body and various forms of meditation, spiritual training. Usui taught a path to enlightenment and spiritual development, the pure laying on of hands, which has become so central in the West, was only a side issue. Weekly, the Reiju, the initiation in Reiki, was given. Religious texts and prayers were quoted together, it was about training one's own mind in mindfulness and pure presence and thus developing all hidden qualities beyond the ordinary.

The so-called Reiki Rules of Life, or Reiki ideals, which corresponded to the five principles of the Meiji Emperor, served as clear orientation for the Reiki practice. They were regularly recited at the beginning of the common practice. So did Gyosei, imperial poems for spiritual inspiration. Usui chose those Gyosei that were interesting and helpful as Kotodamas to lead the students into certain states. The Hikkei, the manual that Usui handed out to his students around 1920, contained the rules of life, gyosei, and meditations, but not hand positions.

Usui Reiki Ryoho Gakkai in Tokyo

Later, after Usui Sensei died of a brain stroke in 1926, the Usui Reiki Ryoho Gakkai, a society for the spread of the Reiki cure to Usui, was born in Tokyo. It has now been proven that Usui was not named as the first president of the Gakkai until after his death.

Mikao Usui himself is named as the first president of this Usui Reiki Ryoho Gakkai, and his successors were Juzaburo Ushida, Kan'ichi Taketomi, Houichi Wanami and Kimiko Koyama. The current President is Mr. Masaki Kondo. If anything, only Mr. Kondo could call himself the Grand Master or Head Teacher of Reiki, but such a term is unknown in Japan.

The teachings of the Gakkai, presented by Arjava Petter, William Rand, and Hiroshi Doi as the original Reiki of Mikao Usui, do not represent the practice as Usui Sensei himself taught it, but are a further development within the Gakkai.

The former president of the Gakkai in Tokyo, Mrs. Koyama, who is now also very well known to us, has the version of Usui Reiki Hikkei, a handbook that Usui partly gave to his students. The Usui Reiki Hikkei answers questions about Reiki, and an English translation can be found on Rick Rivard's website, "Reiki Threshold." The Hikkei also lists certain hand positions for a wide variety of diseases. According to the latest research in Japan

(Usui Teate), the hand positions come from Hayashi's pen, hence the resemblance to the positions in his own Hikkei, and not at all from Usui himself. Students who learned directly from Usui—in contrast to the information of the Gakkai, which came from the 2nd hand and have been modified—have said that Usui taught only 5 special head positions, then the body was treated intuitively. More on the Usui Teate page.

The name Reiki consists of two kanjis, Japanese characters, Rei and Ki. There are several ways to interpret and translate these words:

Rei is the spiritual healing associated with spiritual growth.

Ki is the energy, the power to heal the mind and body. Here are the old and new definitions of the Kanjis:

A more literal translation, interpretation of the two Kanjis, is Rei: from heaven, the rain comes with lifegiving energy, which is composed of three parts, light, love, and wisdom. Ki: on the earth, a shaman stands with his arms stretched out to heaven.

Reiki is, therefore, reception of light, love and wisdom from above, from heaven, and passing on to the people of the earth. This applies both to the initiation in Reiki and the treatment with Reiki.

Other Sources - Kurama

Usui had certainly received inspiration from his studies of Zen Buddhism, as well as from Tendai and Shingon Buddhism. He knew other Japanese forms of light work and was probably also a member of the "Rei Jyutsu Ka," which was based at the foot of Mount Kurama. Usui Sensei was master (Menkyo Kaiden) in Japanese martial art called Yagyu Ryu. The account in some chapters of Usui's life story that he was secretary of a politician is probably a paraphrase of his work as a bodyguard.

Mount Kurama, an hour north of Kyoto, is a particularly sacred place in Japan, even called the spiritual heart of Japan. Many hundreds of temples are there, from all Japanese traditions, thus also their energies and helpers from the realm of light. Mountain Kurama is also a particularly sacred and blessed place for Japanese martial arts.

From 1922, Usui practiced Zen meditation for three years, several times he made a retreat, the frame of which is described in the Zazen Shikan Taza.

Perhaps the Satori that Usui experienced in March 1922 with the reception of Reiki on Mount Kurama was also inspired by the mystical history of the Kurama Sonten, which is connected to Mount Kurama and is still energetically effective there. The three deities of the Kurama Sonten embody different qualities and are represented by Sanskrit mantras. They are the divine attributes: light (Bishamon-Ten), love (Senju-Kannon), and power (Mao-Son). The mythology of the Kurama mountain has striking parallels to the degrees of Reiki! Sonten, depicted in kanji like the Reiki Master symbol, is the Universal Life Force, which permeates and nourishes the entire cosmos and manifests itself through the three properties of light, love and power.

The symbol of Senju-Kannon (a form of Avalokiteshvara, the thousand-armed Bodhisattva of consummate compassion) is the Hrih in Sanskrit and the source of the 2nd traditional Reiki symbol, the socalled mental symbol. It stands for the Amida Buddha (Amitabha), which is highly revered in Japan (Buddhism of the Pure Land). The Hrih embodies the blessing power of love in this trinity and is associated with the moon principle.

Bishamon-Ten is the power of light (light-strength is an essential property of the spirit of enlightenment) and is connected to the principle of the sun. Mao-Son is the third deity of the Kurama Sonata and means power. Mao-Son embodies the principle of the earth.

Also, the mantra of the master symbol is used daily in this temple on Mount Kurama for protection and invocation. The Dai Ko Myo, the Reiki Master symbol, represents the three principles of The Kurama Sonten: Love, Light and Power.

In 1923, Japan suffered a major, devastating earthquake, the Kanto earthquake, in which more than 100,000 people lost their lives. Mikao Usui was very committed to helping the victims to alleviate and heal their suffering with Reiki. To this end, he moved his clinic to the area of the earthquake in order to "extend the hands of love to the suffering people." This, too, shows that Usui Sensei was a man of the "Great Spirit" who, in a selfless manner, really practiced Bodhicitta, loving devotion. As an award for his services, Usui received a doctorate, honorably.

In 1926, Mikao Usui succumbed to a brain stroke. His grave is at the Saihoji Temple in Tokyo. Right next to the tomb is a stone with an inscription, soon also in the German translation of the inscription on the memorial stone, which reports on Usui's life and work. The discovery of this inscription, the discovery of Tokyo's Reiki-Gakkai, and two Japanese books on Reiki, made it possible at the end of the 20th century to obtain more coherent information about the history of Reiki and the life of its founder, Mikao Usui, in the West. The two Japanese Reiki books are the "Iyashi No Te" by Toshitaka Mochizuki and the "Iyashi No Gendai Reiki ho" by Hiroshi Doi. The book by Hiroshi Doi has been translated into English and is now available under the name "Modern Reiki Method for Healing." Further traditions of other Japanese Reiki teachers, who are not members of the Gakkai but can still be traced back to Mikao Usui or Chujiro Hayashi, have become known.

Thanksgivings/Proof of Source

Many have contributed to the news of the new information from Japan, most notably Frank Arjava Petter ("The Reiki Fire," "The Legacy of Dr.Usui" and "The Original Reiki Manual," all published by Windpferd- Verlag); and Hiroshi Doi, who trained with Usui Reiki Ryoho Gakkai now teaches this Reiki tradition in the West. I would also like to thank Andrew Bowling (Reiki History) from England for his history of Reiki and William Rand for Discovering the Roots of Reiki. At the end of 2000, the "Reiki Compendium" of Lübeck, Petter, and Rand were published by Windpferd-Verlag on this topic. Another tradition of Buddhist Reiki practice is Buddho-Ener Sense. It is based on a line of Usui's student Hayashi.

Meanwhile, thanks to Chris Marsh and the insights about the Usui Teate, an even clearer picture of what Usui practiced and what he did not. In particular, I would like to thank Taggart King for his work and support.

Mikao Usui Sensei practiced daily the recitation of the Reiki rules of life and a short form of Hatsurei-

Ho with his students and the initiation, which Reiju regularly repeats so that the ability to pass on Reiki has been increased more and more. It was clear to him that health and true happiness in life is inextricably linked to spiritual, inner values, and to spiritual development. He attached great importance to finding peace in one's own mind on the basis of ethically correct behavior and to act with a good heart and in inner silence as the great saints of all times for the good of men.

Reiki goes West, Hayashi & Takata

In this section, I would like to report a little about the transmission line from Reiki to the West. This line begins with Dr. Chujiro Hayashi and leads via Ms. Hawayo Takata to the U.S. and Europe.

Dr. Chujiro Hayashi, along with two other officers, Jusaburo Gyuda/Ushida and Ichi Taketomi, had been a student of Usui. Born in 1878, he had served as a commander in the Japanese Navy and as a doctor. In 1925, he learned (only) for 9 months Reiki from Mikao Usui and later ran a small Reiki clinic in Tokyo with 8 beds and 16 healers, who always gave two treatments. Hayashi had written his own manual, which was very similar in terms of treatment positions to Usui Reiki Hikkei. Both were probably made from Qi Gong materials, which were distributed in the Navy in 1927. The 3 officers were the founders of the Gakkai, but older students of Usui could not identify with what was practiced there. Eguchi was only with the Gakkai for 1 year, from which Hayashi probably learned the Reiju, the initiation, which he probably also modified.

The nationalist attitude of the "Officer Club" Reiki Ryoho Gakkai had even been too much for Hayashi, and so he went his own way and later was no longer a member of the Usui Reiki Ryoho Gakkai, but taught his own Reiki in the Hayashi Reiki Kenyu-kai from 1931. The spiritual dimension on which Usui Sensei had placed so much emphasis was not a central point for Hayashi, and he focused on the technique of laying on hands for the purpose of (physical) healing. Until his death in 1941, he had dedicated 17 students to the Master's degree. One of his students was Ms. Hawayo Takata, who graduated from the Masters in 1938.

Hawayo Takata arrived on 24 May 1898. She was born in Hawaii, the daughter of Japanese immigrants. Life on the sugar cane plantation was hard and had made her sick. When Ms. Takata was in Tokyo in her midthirties for family reasons and was examined in a hospital, she was diagnosed with a tumor, gallstones, and appendicitis. She was already lying on the operating table when an inner voice told her impressively that surgery was not necessary. She asked the doctor for another possibility and learned about Hayashi's Reiki clinic, which was directly opposite the hospital. Instead of surgery, she received daily Reiki treatments, and was completely healed within 4 months. So convinced of Reiki, she wanted to learn it herself and was able to get Hayashi to give her the first degree in the spring of 1936. For a year, Hawayo Takata worked at the Reiki Clinic in Tokyo and received the second degree at the end.

In 1937 she returned to Hawaii and began her Reiki work there. In the winter of 1938, Hayashi inaugurated her master's degree. The political situation during the Second World War, when the US and Japan had been opponents of the war, may have been the reason that Ms. Takata made Mikao Usui a Christian theologian. Pearl Harbour was all too well remembered by the Americans. In this situation, she would have had great difficulties if she had wanted to publicize something Japanese or Buddhist. So she began to tell a fairy tale and turned Usui into a Christian he definitely never was. The Reiki practice was also adapted for the West. The Hatsurei Ho, for example, she had learned from Hayashi but never passed it on to her students.

Usui would never have agreed that they, like other "line holders," would call themselves Reiki GrandMasters. He had deliberately created an open teaching system, called "Ronin," without leadership ambitions and open to anyone who had an interest.

Until her death in 1980, Hawayo Takata had inaugurated a total of 22 Reiki masters, including Barbara Ray, who founded the A.I.R.A., later Radiance, and her granddaughter Phyllis Lei Furumoto, who founded the Reiki Alliance. For a long time, these two organizations were leaders in the spread of Reiki in Europe, and it was only in the 1990s that it became possible to devote themselves as Free Reiki Masters to the mediation of Reiki. This abolished the high price level, one might also say, price cartels, and made Reiki accessible to an even greater number. The attempt by Phyllis Furumoto, the granddaughter of Ms. Takata, to patent the names "Reiki" and "Usui Reiki Shiki Ryoho" worldwide has fortunately failed because Reiki is now known and popular globally. The way in which she took on the role of Reiki GrandMaster is also doubtful.

Back to sources in Japan

At the beginning of the 21st century, a return to the origins of the Reiki takes place, and the western Reiki scene looks back at Japan to find out the true story about Reiki. In particular, it is thanks to William Rand, Arjava Petter, Rick Rivard and Hiroshi Doi that the socalled URR techniques have now become known in the West. Its source is the Gakkai, which—as we have seen—was created only after Usui's death and did not have the high spiritual level on which Usui had attached so much importance.

As at 2002, when I wrote these lines, 12 students of Usui still lived in Japan, the youngest of them was 107 years old. Chris Marsh has contact with them and passes on his research under the title "Usui Teate." I find this particularly exciting and I am very grateful that Taggart King has shared this teaching material with me in such a generous form, especially since Chris Marsh is very covered and has nothing to do with the Reiki boom. A move that makes him sympathetic to me and underlines his credibility.

Men Chhos Rei Kei, the medicine Dharma Reiki after Lama Yeshe alias R. Blackwell, another attempt to revive the original teaching of Usui, is based on documents found (allegedly?) in Japan. At the end of 2002, Lama Yeshe's details are questioned because he is not prepared to show the originals on which his teaching is based. It is now clear that Mr. Blackwell has proved to be implausible, as he has never kept all the promises to show the originals. Also, a high reincarnation, which he claims to be, is completely unknown in Bhutan and with H.H. Dalai Lama. Many of his students around the world have since distanced themselves from him, deleted the MDR websites and canceled the MDR seminars. The German Reiki Magazine, which had a translation of the book by Lama Yeshe alias R. Blackwell into German already in production, finally had to stop the project with financial losses.

Further Development in the West

In addition to the attempts to go "back to the roots" to rediscover the original Reiki practice, there are also a number of developments in the West. The higher Reiki Master grades, also called "Grandmaster Degrees" are very beautiful energies.

And other styles, such as the Tibetan Reiki (William Lee Rand), Karuna Reiki, and Tera Mai Reiki (Kathleen Milner), are also very interesting additions to the "traditional" western Reiki.

Many more Reiki styles could be mentioned, often interesting, and healing extensions. But some things in the esoteric scene should probably be called energy or light, not Reiki, because it has nothing to do with Reiki anymore. Partner merges and similar magic are not, in my opinion, a Reiki application. A very regrettable development through the publication of symbols and initiations in connection with a lack of respect and self-serving striving are distorted Forms of Reiki, which do not prove to be blessed. The term "Reiki" is not protected, and so, unfortunately, some things can run under the name Reiki, which do not deserve this name.

I hope that these excesses of the Reiki boom in the West are only very isolated cases, as Reiki is something so beautiful and blessed.

May the light prevail in order to make the world in which we all live a little more loving and peaceful. May we all strive for the great heritage of Usui to produce many salutary fruits in the spirit of its founder.

BUDDHISM
for Beginners

The Step-by-Step Guide to Overcome the Era of Anxiety and Stress Using Mindfulness Meditation and Zen Teachings

Sarah Allen

INTRODUCTION

The creation and control of the universe are unarguably from a higher source. This is a phenomenon that human beings have tried to understand over the years. Connecting with a supreme being and efforts to get connected to that source have made man experience forces beyond compare. There are various degrees of participation in the quest to discover the inner self that connects to a deity. This has been the hallmark of the factors that seem to unite all human beings in the world. Although not everybody believes in anything that has to do with the supernatural, someplace their beliefs in other philosophies. Science-based beliefs don't dwell on anything that cannot be proven scientifically. Of course, there has always been disagreement over the years on what should be believed or what ought not to be believed, what exists or what doesn't exist, or what can be seen or what cannot be seen. The spirituality of man and his embodiment in the physical has been interpreted by some people with beliefs in the supernatural to have a divine connection with a superior being. And this leads us to what we now know in the world as religion. We have various religions in the world, and there is a diversity that comes with people who place their beliefs in different things, both living and non-living. Despite that, there is one particular religion that is exceptional and based purely on practical terms, on what can be practiced, and the result is seen accordingly. This religion does not force you to believe, but it makes you see reality. It is convincing enough for you to admit the facts because they appear just as they are. Many people in the world are yet to discover themselves or know who they really are. The practice of Buddhism is quite different and exceptional in the sense that it is all-encompassing and consuming. It teaches the individual to identify himself with the possibility of physical and spiritual advancement. This will re-orientate him to have a different conception about life and see it from a more spiritual angle. This, with great authority, will show what is obtainable from the natural through spiritual concentration and communication with a higher source of power. Inevitably, it results in a practical approach to recognizing and communicating with the mind.

A Buddhist student will be transformed and given the necessary training and wisdom that comes with transformation. He becomes a new being capable of identifying and touching lives in magnificent and influential ways. The teachings, based on practical knowledge, evolve the way to self-actualization.

New knowledge transformation can also be traced and noticed in the individual's way of thinking and expression whenever the need arises. The Buddhist student becomes the epitome of knowledge of what an individual is capable of becoming, achieved within the space and time of practicing the knowledge imparted through Buddhism. The beginners who learn the art of Buddhism as a religion and practice it faithfully will become exceptionally outstanding among their peers. They will command authority with a different mindset and way of thinking that exceeds the ordinary citizen. In addition, Buddhists are masters whenever they make commentaries about life and how it should be lived.

While many religions successfully command followers, the Buddhist faith has successfully created more potential leaders because of its knowledge impartation. This actually goes with the practice that leads to the transformation of individuals. No matter their status, they are able to learn the actual meaning and truth about life, as well as how it should be lived. Self-examination, combined with a high level of spirituality, is very effective in Buddhism practice. This is one of the keys that guarantee great success when anyone applies the Buddhist system of belief and practice. When a student of Buddhism gets involved in the real practice of the Buddhist faith, this is the turning point in the life of such an individual. Many Buddhists are known all over the world to have the most effective and exceptional lifestyles. Almost all other religions can borrow a leaf from the way of life of the Buddhist. There is an enormous misconception about the term "Buddhism," especially from the Western part of the world. Buddhism has a deeply traditional and practical orientation. It is further believed to work perfectly in modern times. This is because it can be applied in the modern lifestyle to solve the problems of anxiety and stress through improved mindfulness mediation. Also, this is achieved by following the Zen pathway. Enjoy!

CHAPTER 1

Knowing Your Mind

How well do you know yourself? Before you can answer this question, you have to understand your mind. The mind leads to the success and failures of many people, but for a person who practices Buddhism, it helps the development of his mind. What causes the difference in many people around the world starts from the mind. It is based on mindsets that we can distinguish great people from people who are going to fail in their course. Every individual has a mindset level. Your mindset level of understanding or positivity can differ from another person's. This is why we will never stop having individuals with different mindsets. As long as we are different human beings, we are bound to have different mindsets. Now I will be taking you through the Buddhist system of mindset. Also, how it all begins and ends with the level of perception of the individual, which is responsible for the success and advancement of his destiny and which can impact greatly on him.

The mind is powerful in the sense that it determines who you are. The fact that you are resolute and wouldn't want to change your mind doesn't make you an exceptional individual. Rather, an exceptional individual is one who is able to adapt, adjust, and become more flexible to understandings and teachings. The mind is very powerful because it goes a long way to define a person's stance on issues. It also defines an individual's perception of life and how it can turn around to affect him personally, throughout his life. How well you discover your mindset and levels of seeing through the mind is something that is not easy to accomplish. Especially without some form of education and teaching that will help you to open up your mind. While a closed mind is a closed destiny, a lot has to do with an individual's acceptability and readiness to assume the position of a victor by being open. I say this because not many people are prepared to allow the impact of knowledge and teachings that can transform them.

Therefore, can you force knowledge on someone? It depends; if the age of knowledge is necessary, then yes, of course. But for an adult, it may not be easy— you cannot change him because he is already adamant. Most people have such problems. Opening up the mind to allow knowledge and training that will be very useful can be difficult for some people. However, this is not to say that we cannot have the knowledge imparted; it just requires discipline. If such individuals can be disciplined enough to listen, then the knowledge can strike them below the belt, and they will stay humble and listen.

The individual may be going through a lot of difficulties during the knowledge impartation. This is usually the case where the mind is not stable. So it's always advisable to allow such a person to get a stable mindset before the knowledge can sink into the brain. Because knowledge impartation is continued, it will be a waste of time, effort, and resources. A lot of people are distracted in life, which gives them a low level of mindset control. Furthermore, the ability to stay focused is always a problem. They keep thinking of the problems that are bothering them. Buddhism will help you in such circumstances because you will learn how to remain focused. The level of mental concentration in Buddhism is higher compared to any form of religion because the people who do more concentration of the mind through hours of meditation are Buddhists.

There is no way you can defeat a Buddhist who knows his mind because he has a much higher level of mental concentration. He practices more mind development and advancement, enabling him to communicate with a higher source, discover himself the more, and have better enlightenment. How well you know your mind is very important because you meet people on a daily basis and communicate. This leads to the interrelationship between people; their reaction and responses toward you may or may not affect you. And this depends on if you have a mind that can take anything, no matter how bad it is. The question now is, how strong is your mind to receive unfavorable remarks or comments that can be regarded as derogatory? This is one important area where Buddhism will help you. Another aspect I will be talking about knowing your mind is your mindset during the competition, when you compete with others in games, at offices, business, or school. In these environments, there is usually some level of competition. The question is, how prepared is your mind to go through such competition and also win? Even if you win, how would you manage the situation when people try to bring you down? In such circumstances, you will need to know if your mindset can take criticism or attacks akin to those experienced by champions. Do you have the mind of a champion? That is the big question; hence, practicing Buddhism will help you handle such challenges. You don't need to leave your country to visit India or Asia to practice Buddhism. No, you can do this by simply following the laid down pragmatic knowledge as presented in this book.

Again, your mind is who you are. So if you are very timid and fearful, whether you like it or not, people will soon know that you are hiding who you really are and that you have a fearful mind. This can change if you are able to practice

Buddhism because it helps to develop your mind. There is always a need to practice Buddhism because of situations that will require you to have a strong mind. Your mindset will determine if you will be able to handle difficult situations. If you have found yourself in a very difficult situation, knowing the kind of mindset that you have will enable you to determine if you will overcome it or not. Most people in the world today are unable to face difficult situations and often unable to overcome the situations they find themselves in. You can actually get things done or defeat the situation you find yourself in if it is really difficult as a Buddhist, and you learn to have a strong mind. But if you are unable to develop a strong mind, you will find it difficult to beat such situations. The truth is, many people in the world today are affected by adverse situations. They seem unable to deal with it, and that's why they are what they are because of the mindset they have.

If you are poor, you may have been born that way, but that doesn't mean you should remain poor. No, if you have the right mind, you can advance and free yourself from that situation. This will happen if you have the mindset of a successful person. You can become rich with self-determination to make money, and that will only happen if you have a mind that can carry you through the process of becoming rich.

Becoming rich may not come easy, but it is really possible if you are able to learn the power of knowing your mind and developing it.

In the political circle, we have leaders who have spent some years preparing for leadership, while others never really took time to prepare for it. Great leaders like Mahatma Gandhi of India, prepared for leadership. As a leader, he spent years studying and practicing the art of knowing the mind to fight a just cause, which was void of using weapons. All over the world, he remains one of the most talked-about leaders from Asia with a great gift of mind control and human leadership qualities that can change a course of action. Meanwhile, there are other leaders who think that power involves owning a weapon and using it to intimidate others or wage war and win. How wrong they are. If only they could see that they are just weak people with weak minds that cannot influence anyone in their course. They are only able to do this with the barrel of a gun or a weapon.

Preparing yourself for the future also means you have to prepare your mind for the tasks ahead. You can only do that by understanding your mindset. If you don't know your mind, then you cannot start to achieve anything. You will only exist as a normal human being who doesn't know anything other than the fact that he is just like any other person. Understanding and knowing your mind will also help you to connect with your partner, the person who is right for you. Both of you will be able to know and understand each other. This will make you a perfect match for each other when you are in a relationship or seeking to find a life partner. Knowing how being intimate with your partner will lead to bonding is a necessary factor in marriage. It is not just loving a person alone that matters, but when the connection is there, there will be a complete bonding. This cannot take place without knowing the kind of minds that you and your partner have.

Fixed Mindset Vs Growth Mindset

A fixed mindset, as the name implies, means that you are unable to develop your mindset or change it from the present state because of your personality type. You find it difficult to change your mindset, and that is bound to affect you in everything that you do. A fixed mindset remains adamant and unwilling to change. This can be linked to real-life circumstances where we have people who are unable to accept things the way they are or are unyielding because they just don't want to change their mindset about something. One of the major reasons people do not make progress in whatever they do is because they have a fixed mindset. They are unable and unwilling to shift their mind towards something different from what they are used to. There are several factors that are associated with a fixed mindset. It is very important to learn and know when to have a fixed mindset, and when not to have it. Not that a fixed mindset cannot be applied in some circumstances, but it should be understood that a fixed mindset as defined is totally different for a person who has it and can adapt to the use of it.

A fixed mindset can be shifted when the need arises. When the position of a belief system comes to play, one can fix his mind on what he believes in. For example, if you believe in yourself and that you will be successful, that kind of mindset is acceptable because you fixed it on something that has to do with your belief system. It's something that you fixed your mind about yourself. You believe in yourself; it's about you, it's going to work, and you don't doubt yourself. In this case, that becomes a positively fixed mindset. But when you refuse to have a change of mindset, are unwilling to learn, and remain adamant in the face of opportunities that can change your life for the better, then that becomes a negatively fixed mindset. And this is very unhealthy. The reason why several people are poor today is because they have a negatively fixed mindset. One that is unwilling to accept the change or opportunity, and that is why they remain where they are in life.

A fixed mindset, therefore, has different meanings in different circumstances. The more you are able to understand this, the more likely you will become in tune with the practice of Buddhism. The power of the mind cannot be overemphasized. Fixing your mindset on something is what makes you think of it, and place your focus on that thing. Fixing your mindset on something that you know will happen leads to expectation. Expectations can come out positive or negative, depending on what is involved—understanding matters when it comes to the practice of Buddhism. The right mindfulness and understanding in the practice of Buddhism is really important because the practice is based on the mind of the individual, coupled with the ability to understand and read meanings to events and situations of life.

A fixed mindset can be healthy, but it can also be unhealthy. Buddhism teaches happiness and inner spirituality that lead to self-discovery, as well as fixing your mind positively on gaining happiness. Happiness can be obtained through self-suffering. Now, liberating yourself from worldly attachments opens up your mind to become a new human being through rebirth to a new self, leaving your old self to the memories of the past but still remaining fresh. This is a positive way of fixing your mindset on something that is acceptable and practicable.

An unhealthy mindset makes an individual reject the right way of doing things. Always reacting instead of responding to situations based on the conscience of the mind is very different and can constitute a negatively fixed mindset. The individual with a negatively fixed mindset is always a problem in the society. This is because he is always thinking adversely against the acceptable standards, especially when contemporary society is involved. A negatively fixed mindset individual may not bring peace; he may not be open to dialogue and is more aggressive than others. This is the major problem of conflict that we have in the world today.

Many individuals who engage in violence always have these problems, such as the terrorist who has a fixed mindset on carrying out acts of terrorism. These kinds of people have already fixed their minds on such negativity and are not ready to change it. They would rather die as terrorists than convert to responsible human beings. This is not about religion alone, but it's also about the individual's disposition and nature of how he views and accepts the society. As well as how he wants to enforce his beliefs on people and control the society based on his own standards. Fixed mindset individuals don't believe that other peoples' opinions count, and they would do whatever it takes to enforce their beliefs on people. Such a mindset is very unhealthy and is simply fixated on negativity.

A fixed mindset, if wrongfully applied, doesn't guarantee progress in the life of an individual. Mindfulness is a very essential and helpful part of the practice of Buddhism. An aspirant about to enter into the terrain of mind practice and spirituality of one of the largest, most well-recognized religions in the world and one of the renowned religions that have to do with mindfulness and consciousness of self-growth, should be prepared to shoulder a responsible way of life.

Growth Mindset

Despite the fact that the fixed mindset person has difficulty changing as a result of fixing his mind on what is not rewarding or positive, there can always be a shift in his fixated mindset. There can always be a way out, a mindset growth, which comes in different phases. It can be a process of re-birth and rehabilitation. The re-birth process is always associated with Buddhism, while rehabilitation has to do with individuals who have been submerged in circumstances that have gone deep into their minds. Rehabilitation is usually for people with the following problems; drinking, drug-related problems, alcoholism, and insanity, etc. These are some circumstances that influence people through used substances or depression. There is a variance in what it takes for mind growth and rehabilitation. Rehabilitation processes are always handled by professionals. They have been trained and educated extensively in an institution of higher learning in methods of taking care of those with troubled minds such as those mentioned above.

But when it comes to the growth of the mind in Buddhism, we are consciously involved in the development of the mind. This is achieved through set down pragmatic practice that makes use of purely natural processes such as meditation, concentration, self-discovery, and spirituality. The practice of Buddhism is wholesomely to achieve the form of rebirth that changes the individual's conception and orientation to a new human being void of negativity.

The spiritual level of success is a unique way of spiritual growth, which is always associated with the practice. This is coupled with the help of the belief system that connects to a higher source and that the individuals have an inner self-conscious path in life.

Growth of the mind is when your mind gradually develops into a unique state that enables you to see things through it. You come across a problem. You are able to identify it and take measures that can bring about a lasting solution. The development of the mind doesn't stop with you; it radiates and touches lives. Through your mindfulness and understanding, you are able to create solutions that influence people who seem to be lost in problems that overwhelm them. You are special and different from others through the knowledge of the fact that you have a developed mind. You are able to pursue a course and achieve it easily. Buddhism teaches the mind growth phenomena, and this makes it possible for people to see and know the difference between the growth of the mind and a fixed mindset that doesn't yield to any teaching.

The growth of the mind is an essential feature of the teachings of Buddhism because the practice of Buddhism revolves around mind consciousness and development. When considering the factors of Buddhism like meditation, the belief system, the teachings, the re-birth, re-examination, etc., you cannot help but believe in the fact that all these activities help in the advancement of the mind. And this actually brings a permanent mind growth. Many people around the world today are having problems with mental growth. Yes, you might say that education is the key to an individual's development. I agree with you, but at the same time, what is education to a mind that is not ready to accept it? Not everyone who went to school actually completed the education process because they were never prepared to accept education in the first place.

Secondly, many people who went to school started it from the cradle where it is easier to impart knowledge. It's almost certain that a child who is put through school doesn't have a choice than to embrace it. Of course, as the child grows and is developing, his will later settles into what he was meant or made to study. That is the knowledge he or she will have until such an individual decides to learn new things.

However, the Buddhist system creates awareness into a whole new level and dimension. It is practically based on self-determination and awareness that enhances an individual's development, irrespective of the level of education. The educated person, for instance, may not yet discover a link between a deeper understanding of himself with a conscious mind and another individual outside his environment. This is where the Buddhist is at an advantage. The Buddhist understands what true happiness and self-conviction really mean. He works hard to attain a higher level of mindfulness even if he has to go through some restrictions in life. He is always prepared to afflict himself with a great deal of discipline to get greater abilities through self-consciousness in Buddhism.

Learning Buddhism as a beginner means you have to free or liberate yourself from every distraction and make your mind available for the training. Having a good listening and learning attitude will help you have a deeper meaning of what Buddhism has to offer. Without this, you will not succeed. It is when you learn to listen to your inner self that you will become more successful. You have to make sure you attain a higher level of mindfulness by paying attention and feeling. Also, having the willingness to learn new ways of life such that after your conscious learning, you will become physically and spiritually advanced in your mode of understanding. Growth, therefore, will help you go a long way to measure the level of success. However, you need to understand and acquire the ability to listen and learn. Silence is important because you need to stay calm and learn the new re-birth and cleansing that you are actually subjecting yourself to attain during the process.

With a high level of mindfulness, which leads to openness to learning, be rest assured that your rebirth is something that will easily be noticed. It will reflect on virtually all the activities that you do. By the time you become regular in Buddhism, you will attain more heights. You will be able to realize the differences and misconceptions that other religions or belief systems have of Buddhism. That will be something great because you actually practice it, and it changes your life for the better. This will definitely reflect in the teaching and lifestyle that you will be born into.

Best Strategies to Find Your Balance and Inner Peace

Finding inner peace that gives you a total transformation to a new human being is very difficult in a world filled with deceit, untrustworthiness, jealousy, and insincerity. That's what many people go through on a daily basis. Many do not have an inner peace that makes them comfortable and smile in every situation. They are always having problems either with themselves or their neighbor. This is so because there is always an inner-self battle with the outside world, and many have to realize that the problem is actually not from the outside but from the inside. To be able to win the battle, you have to start from the inside to get the innermost insight that transcends more than what is on the outside. The belief system has a little part to play when you believe you can change from the inside to the outside. For instance, if a person doesn't accept you, it doesn't necessarily mean that they are right. Just because they don't accept you, doesn't mean you cannot be accepted by someone else.

There are people who are looking for you, and they need you more than others, it is left for you to make yourself available. Your availability will only come from your innermost conviction and not from the acceptability of others or what others think about you. It is so sad to see how people are becoming discouraged by the disapproval of others or the bad remarks they receive from others about them. Life doesn't teach us that everybody should speak well of us. Even the most outstanding of the prophets never got excellent comments from everyone.

To find inner peace, you must first discover yourself. Discovering yourself in a difficult world that is filled with grudges and unloving people does not change who you are. You are the one who can create the influential nature that is in you and which gives you happiness. Take a look at a person who is not happy. It is obvious when the person is not smiling, and you ask him, "My friend, what is the problem?" Then he replies, "I am not happy because something terrible just happened to me." Within you, you can feel the pain that he is going through because he is having a bad experience. But the question is, what can you do to help him out of that situation if you don't have inner peace yourself? This is why it is necessary to have inner peace before you can help other people get out of their situation. The first thing to note here is how to get inner peace for yourself.

Another discussion is "getting the balance in the inner peace that you have now." Some people think that when there is no war or conflict, there is peace. That is not true; the fact that there is no war doesn't mean that there is peace in a country or among nations. I remember a certain time in the 60s and 70s when there was no threat of war, but in actual fact, there was a different type of war that was going on the "Cold War." The Cold War era was about space dominance, and space technological development. Nations that were unable to explore space or the galaxy became afraid that someday, the western countries will get into space and dominate. And perhaps get better technology that can make them dominate any kind of warfare. Now that was one form of war that was not fought by the barrel of the gun, and it is still the same today, it hasn't changed.

We have seen nations talking about nuclear weapons. There is suspicion about developing nuclear weapons capable of wiping out an entire human race, and this is not a peaceful situation at all. There has to be an agreement, and everybody has to be on the same page. Everybody has to be at peace with one another; no one should be left out in the circumstances. The same goes for an individual. Your entire body must agree to have inner peace. You must be healthy in all parts of your body, not having pain in some parts. If you have pain in some parts, you cannot be peaceful in such circumstances because you will be distracted, thinking about that pain and how you can stop it.

The Buddhist student masters this and understands the entire discussion on finding the best strategies to get the inner balance of peace. The example mentioned earlier is related to how the man who got involved in Buddhism started. He also had a similar experience where there was a lot of tension in his environment. It was as if everybody was against each other. So much anger, misunderstanding, grief, complaining, pain, and people being unhappy and selfish. He wanted something that could give him inner peace since he wasn't finding it among people who were around him. This is the same scenario that an individual living in modern society always faces. There will always be confrontations and challenges coming from people around you. In the face of all these troubles, how will you be able to cope? What are the strategies you need to apply to free yourself from the numerous troubles that accompany this kind of person? Here I will explain some things that you need to do as an individual so you can free yourself from the shackles of backwardness.

Self-conviction is one of the most important things here: You have to be convinced that it is possible to achieve inner peace and balance with the strategy you are going to adopt. Conviction is the self-consciousness, perception, and acceptability that you are definitely on top of the situation. Never believe in what people say or think about you, having the mind that you can always have inner peace, and it doesn't have to come from someone else. Self-conviction is one of the major keys to attaining inner peace because you already know that your peace is within you, and it doesn't have to come from the outside. Despite what you are going through, your inner peace should remain intact. Once you know this, you will be able to create a balance between yourself and the inner peace consciousness. I never doubt myself once whenever it comes to creating a balance between my inner peace and what goes on around me.

I know circumstances will always come to take or draw that inner peace away from me, but I always remain resolute in the face of problems. Why? Because my inner peace is well-balanced. I am the one who has it and not someone else. It doesn't depend on others. Therefore, it becomes impossible for anyone to take it away because it's simply in me.

Knowing your weakness: One of the strategies that will help you have perfect inner peace is to discover your weaknesses, work on improving them, and become a better person. The reason why many people are easily defeated is because they allow people to easily spot their weaknesses. When people know your weakness, they tend to capitalize on that, and they easily use it against you. The victim doesn't often realize it, but that wouldn't stop him from asking himself the question, why is this person doing this to me?

In fact, they often ask such questions, and this tends to disturb their inner peace in the long run. So, the best thing to do in such circumstances is to start working on your weakness. You can only do this when you know or spot your weakness. Having a weakness will always lead to an inner peace imbalance because when you give out peace to others, you will be expecting peace in return. You may not get it if people tend to use your weakness against you or pay you back with a bad attitude simply because they know you are weak. For instance, I have a friend who is very humble and has a gentle-like manner. Each time there is a fight, he tries to settle it. People who know him very well know he is a peace-loving person. But he has some young men who often like to bully him. They know he is a peaceful and gentle person, but they can't help bullying him because they already know that he won't fight back.

The lesson here is that you don't necessarily have to settle every dispute by actions; there are better ways you can pass a message across without having to participate in actions. Words can speak louder than actions sometimes. The Buddhist mindfulness can be accomplished with words to express issues, and mere words, if properly applied, can win the heart. Yes, I know that actions can speak louder than words, and that ideology is action-based. But words can be so powerful that they can bring tears to the eyes of many people, while mere actions can bring tears to the eyes of one person. This can be achieved through Buddhism. Once you are able to influence people with abilities such as these, you can change everything around you.

Happiness: Being happy gives you inner peace, so whatever comes your way, whether it is good or bad, always learn to be happy. If you have a problem that seems to defy every solution, this can cause an imbalance in your inner peace. This is because you will always be thinking about the problems, and your mind will not be at rest. It creates an imbalance in your innermost being. It's okay, everyone has problems, and if that problem is not solved in the present, it will be solved later. Don't let problems bother you. Instead, let your peace of mind take control of the situation. From the beginning of the world, there have always been problems. We came into this world to meet problems; there are so many problems. If we let problems stop us from being humans or concentrate all our efforts thinking about the problems of the world, we would never get anywhere in life.

Therefore, leave the problem or find a solution to it. There is no problem without a solution. When there is no solution, the problems can be kept where they are until you find a solution for them.

Therefore, problems shouldn't steal away your happiness. You did not create the problem. And even if you did, you can always find a solution. But if you can't, let it be, especially if it doesn't affect you directly.

Rest of Mind: If you really want inner peace, always make efforts to have rest of mind, let your mind be at rest. Let your mind be at rest with everyone around you; your neighbors, family members, colleagues at work, friends at school, course mates, people in your political circle, and those in the same or different religion with you. Why give yourself so much pain and trouble with a restless mind? If you have issues or misunderstandings with anyone, settle it. You can always make peace by discussing issues with someone you have a misunderstanding with. You have to allow your mind to be at rest with everyone. That is how to maintain inner peace. You have to be peaceful with yourself and the people around you. So always try to allow your mind to be at rest and don't have any grudges against anyone.

Smile: "Smile" is one of the simplest five-letter words yet so powerful. A smile can change a lot of things about you. No matter the circumstances you find yourself, smile. "Smile" is the most powerful five-letter word that exists. Why? Because when you smile positively, nobody actually knows what you are going through. A smile radiates friendship, it attracts people to you. A person who was keeping words to himself can easily open up to you simply because of the smile on your face. The truth is; a smile always creates something in your spirit that enables you to see through things that others wouldn't see. You need to understand that a simple smile can turn things around for good. For instance, a certain man was embarking on a journey. He had prepared so well; he arranged his luggage, locked his door, and went off to the road. Then something happened, but he wasn't aware. He lost his keys as he was travelling. He checked his pockets when he got to a point, and he wasn't happy that he couldn't find his keys after searching everywhere.

He was so sad; he started tracing his steps and searching through the path he had traveled. He came across a man who was also traveling along the same path with his dog. The dog had discovered a bunch of keys and ran to it and started barking. The owner came close to the dog, picked up the keys, and placed them in his pocket. A little while later, he continued his journey, and he met the owner of the keys on the road. The man and his dog greeted the man, but he was so sad that he didn't reply since he was looking for his keys. However, the dog kept barking at him. The owner of the dog asked after they had passed each other a few steps, "Are you looking for something?" He replied, "I just lost my keys." While the dog was still barking, the man brought out the keys and handed them over to him, and then he smiled.

The lesson you should learn here is, no matter the circumstances, you should always smile. If not for the dog, the man wouldn't have found his keys. Secondly, he refused to answer a greeting, which would have saved him the stress of having to go miles still searching for his keys. At the point of greeting, the problem of the missing keys would have been solved. Always learn to smile. Smiling will bring solutions to problems. You will not get solutions to problems when you are sad or confused; the solution can only come when you are smiling. Most people find it difficult to smile; I wish they could understand that there are so many benefits of smiling. A smile is so powerful that it transcends the ordinary state of life.

It's a natural phenomenon that creates the balance in inner peace when you go through some difficulty, yet you remain stable and unaffected by what you are going through. A smile is the key to a greater inner peace, more than you can ever imagine. Although the problem may be there, you don't have to make the problem your priority. Make smiling your priority and relegate the problem to the background where it should be. Of course, among your list of activities for the day or week, let problems which you cannot solve, they are placed apart from your priorities. This is because problems can sometimes hold you back from making progress. So if problems are stopping you from making progress, keep them away from your daily activities. I am sure you will find a solution to them somehow.

Stop worrying: A lot of people worry about things that happen in their lives, especially if the going is not good. They tend to be sad, and they worry about the things that bother them. Let me tell you something, the moment you begin to worry about the disturbing issues in your life, that is when you begin to develop health issues. When you worry too much about certain matters in your life, you begin to develop depression. It gradually sets in because your mood is changing, and it starts to influence the inner peace that you have. Then you get agitated or anticipate and see things in a different way. When you worry, it affects the mind; remember a mind is a powerful tool that helps your development. Your mind will not function well because you worry too much.

Worrying affects the mind; take, for example, a man who is driving a car, but is worried about his responsibilities. He has to pay school fees; his rent has expired; he doesn't have the money to take care of his family, and so on. Of course, these are issues that are of great concern. They are pressing needs that need to be addressed, but do you have to worry about them all the time? No! The man doesn't have to worry about those problems; all he needs to do is seek solutions to those problems.

There are different ways to take care of your worries. The best way is to prioritize the issues that need to be taken care of in order of their importance. Which one is more important and needs immediate attention? That's how it ought to be done, taking the issues one by one. If your rent is what you need to pay first, find a solution to that first. If it is the children's school fees that need to be taken care of, handle it first before any other problem. That's how to make things work. If you consider these points, you will begin to develop a balanced inner peace. This is because you will have nothing to worry about when you are able to take every issue one after the other. If you cannot find the solution to a problem, then why do you have to worry about such a problem? If worrying doesn't solve it, then why worry?

Good Health: You need to develop a way of staying healthy with regular checks. Health is wealth; the number one thing that is key to a successful innermost peace is to have good and sound health. Don't mistake always having good food to eat to mean having good health. No! To be healthy doesn't necessarily mean you should have money to buy any type of food you want. Staying healthy means you eat the right food and also give yourself mental and spiritual food, not just physical food. Make yourself physically fit so that you will be able to concentrate on the practice of selfdevelopment and advancement. Buddhist student needs to stay healthy. All your physical components need to be working well so that you are able to study, live in the system, and maximize the benefits. Your inner peace is important if you have to create the balance you need to stay healthy. If you are sick, you will not be able to practice some abstinence rules or obligations. When you need to remain focused and concentrate for hours, removing yourself from the physical world and off to the advanced innermost selfworld where you will see beyond the ordinary self, you must stay healthy. Not being healthy may affect your progress, and this will never bring great inner peace.

Anger Management

Anger is a strong annoyance that generates from the inside of a person. Sometimes anger can become a problem, and this often leads to so many setbacks in a person's life. To manage and overcome your anger, you need to learn from the system of the Buddhist who is capable of controlling his anger through a well laid down procedure. Anger is simply unhealthy, especially in the home, among people, at school, a working environment, in the market, in politics, and in any human interaction. Anger is a very bad attribute that can lead to destruction and disharmony. Lots of people in the world today are unable to control their anger, and this has led to many downfalls for them.

I understand that people have different temperaments; your ability to control your anger may be different from the ability of another person. However, anger can be managed if you follow the right steps to guide you to change from being an overly angry person to a whole new person with a reduced temperament. Anger causes bad health for an individual who is always angry. Getting rid of anger may be very difficult, but in most people, it never goes away. They are so used to getting angry at the slightest provocation. Time is needed for some people with anger issues to get healing. For some people, getting angry is not a problem. They hardly get angry, but when they do, it can be dangerous because they will release all the anger in them since they are not used to releasing it immediately. This often leads to transferred aggression, which makes people wonder if this person has been pretending all along. So now the question is, how can you manage your anger? I'm sure you are interested in the Buddhist way of handling anger.

Shift Your Mind towards Something Else: Anger often comes when you get offended by somebody. The person has offended you and perhaps is too arrogant to apologize to you. This might piss you off, and you feel it's not right; not everybody can take an insult and swallow it. But you can get over anger by just shifting your attention towards something else. Taking your mind off the offense that someone committed against you and directing your mind towards something else is one of the major keys to becoming successful in managing your anger. However, this is based on offenses committed against you by another person. On the other hand, if you have an inner problem of anger, there are other ways you can achieve successful anger management.

Showing Love: One of the most potent ways of managing your anger is to show love irrespective of the fact that you have been hurt by somebody. Love cures and heals anger in a way that you may not understand. When you constantly show love to people, you are able to show a better understanding that you have a mature mind. Even if you are young, you can be a better person when you show love in situations that bring about anger. If you are a loving person and are able to show love to every person that comes your way, irrespective of race, color, or gender, you will be better able to manage your anger. This is because anger comes from the heart, and if you have a loving heart, mind, soul, and body, you will show less anger towards people.

Tolerance: A lot of people find it difficult to tolerate other people, especially when it comes to behaviors that are unethical to society's standards. They tend to hate such people and are unable to stand their presence. No matter what people do to you, you need to learn how to tolerate them. The Buddhist student learns this and gains understanding and knowledge on how to deal with people with different characteristics or behavioral dispositions. "To tolerate" means that you are able to accept people the way they are irrespective of their social class. Do not attempt to segregate or make people believe that they are worthless even when they know they have fallen short of normally acceptable standards. If you meet a poor person, always try to understand that the person is poor and needs help. People are poor not because of their own fault, but perhaps they have not gotten the right opportunity to flourish. You can become a leading light and show them the path to success. This can only be achieved if you show tolerance towards them.

Withdrawal Method: The withdrawal method is based on the fact that when you are annoyed by any individual, all you do is walk away. This has been found over the years to be very effective in anger management processes. The Buddhist student understands that there are a lot of benefits when he decides to withdraw himself from the trouble zone, especially when there is a heated argument. You decide to withdraw yourself from that scenario, not because you are a coward or you cannot fight back, but because you want to maintain peace within yourself and with others. And because you don't want anything that will get you angry, you just decide to walk away from the trouble. This is one of the most effective ways of managing your anger. If you can do this often, as many times as possible, you will be able to get over your frequent state of being angry.

Self-Control: Self-control is very useful when you are annoyed. It is the ability to control yourself when you get angry or when someone annoys you. Not many people in the world have self-control. One of the pillars of the Buddhist student to be successful is to have self-control. No matter what the situation is, if it makes you flare up, you can control it by simply refusing to get moved into arguments or fights. Selfcontrol in any situation is very important because, in most cases, it is during anger situations that vital information is released. If you get angry, you won't be able to get it. Self-control enables you to read the mind of your opponent or antagonist. Whatever he says to you, you remain silent, and you'll be able to digest and read his mind through the words that come out from his mouth. The Buddhist understands the teaching concerning anger management and self-control because he remotely absents his human nature from the presence of the chaotic situation. Anger assumes a chaotic position because it starts from an individual's inside to his outside. A Buddhist student is always well aware of this and works towards self-control, which is the hallmark of Buddhist practice. Hardly does a Buddhist react immediately to an angry situation. There is a lot to learn from being still and maintaining self-control during such a situation. As a Buddhist student, this is the point of call where you will need self-control.

Our daily lifestyle in modern society enables us to interact with people. You will need to understand the true meaning of self-control in most situations because as long as you interact with people, the chances that you will get into conflict are high. You need to develop the characteristics to really maintain self-control because it will always be necessary.

Don't Let Fear Control Your Life

Fear is when an individual is afraid of something. That thing can be connected or may not be connected to an individual. That is why there is the fear of the unknown and the fear of whatever is bothering you. Some philosophers have defined "FEAR" as "false evidence appearing real." This is true because what you conceive in your mind is often what you get. If you are afraid of something, that thing will eventually consume you and defeat you. When you are living in fear, it means you have allowed it to control your life. This is not healthy for your senses, mind, soul, as well as your physical and spiritual development. The Buddhist practice is far ahead in defeating fear because Buddhists are not controlled by it. The mind is capable of many things, depending on what it is fed with. When you permit fear to control your life, you have fallen already because fear comes before a downfall. Many people in the world today actually live in fear of what is going to happen to them in the next minute or later in the future.

There are various reasons people live in fear. For instance, if there is no job for a person, he may become afraid of financial security. Where will he get money to buy the necessities of life, and how will he survive? How will he get money to take care of his family? As long as he doesn't have a job, a business to make money, a source of income or livelihood, the fear of financial security will always be an issue. Until he gets a job, that fear will never leave him.

Another instance; the doctors say you have a problem with your liver or kidney, and you may die at any moment. You end up living in fear of death; that is exactly what is happening to some people in the world today. We have seen people, especially rich people, build fences around their homes and houses, and the fences are sometimes even taller than prison yard fences. They are so afraid; they think someone is after them or is coming to hurt them.

This is the fear of the unknown, but if you are living a good life and are not against anyone, you will live peacefully with everyone around you. Why should you be afraid of something happening to you? There is no need to fear. It often leads to unnecessary panic because your mind will be made up of fear. Any alarm, even when it is false, makes you afraid. This shouldn't be your mindset; don't be fearful about whatever you are doing. Fear has never helped anybody and will not help you either. Somehow, fear has a way of connecting with the nature of a man. When a man lives his life in fear, he becomes timid, in every (circumstance) he becomes afraid of what faces him. Don't let fear control your life, and for you to overcome fear, you need the following attributes:

Courage: You need courage whenever you are faced with difficulty in life. Being courageous enough to face difficult situations and overcome them is very important as you live your life daily. Courage is the ability to face whatever situation or circumstances that come your way without fear. The Buddhist is always courageous to overcome that which threatens his mind. Self-encouragement can be attained by lots of Buddhist practice. The inspiration of the Buddhist religion is essential to the Buddhist because he is able to draw comfort, energy, and courage from the innermost gifts that he has. Courage is also essential in facing difficult moments, and you can only be able to achieve it when you are well-prepared through Buddhist religious practices. The higher level of spirituality and tradition goes a long way to help in the mental development of a timid person if he is fearful, making him leave the fearful life behind him.

The motivation of the mind: One thing that is very effective in changing a fearful life is motivation. When you are motivated, you can defeat your fear. What is required is the "Yes, I can" attitude. Always see yourself as capable of defeating any difficult situation.

Anything that comes your way can always be defeated, it is your choice. The Buddhist is always motivated and will make no excuses when it comes to instances of being fearful. The more the challenges come, the more the Buddhist with his understanding will be motivated to face such challenges or difficulty. You can only draw motivation from your inner self if your mind is prepared. But if your mind is not prepared, you will always get negative responses even if you try. Fortunately, the Buddhist practice will help you out in any type of situation. Motivation to defeat fear may not come from the outside, it has to come from within yourself. It may be difficult to achieve it if you have been used to living a fearful life. Hence, you must admit that you need help which can be availed to you through the Buddhist practice. When you get hold of it and practice it successfully, you will overcome your fear. Fear may come from your work, school, or your environment. You may get threats often from people who don't like you, and the external factor, fear, is giving you problems when it comes from the outside. But when fear comes from the inside, it will give you self-defeat. It's better not to allow yourself to be defeated, you are a champion, and that is the kind of mindset that you should always carry.

Fear controls your life like a human will control a robot. You are not a robot, you were created by a higher source of spirituality, and you are a gift to the world. No psychological stance, set of beliefs, or mindset level that fear holds against you can defeat you. That shouldn't be. Another thing that is responsible for fear ruling your life that you should be aware of or get rid of is the "inferiority complex." People have certain levels of inferiority complex, which is based on the belief that they are not better than the other person. It may be because of your skin color, your mindset, or you think others are better than you in certain circumstances of life. Then you begin to fathom some kind of fantasy around their greatness. You see yourself as someone less worthy than they are, but this is a false belief system that you should not be harboring at all. The first thing that you should always have at the back of your mind is that nobody is greater than you. We are all equal but may have different gifts.

To avoid living in fear of being inferior to others, you need to develop what is referred to as "self-identification of a gift." This system of thinking and self-discovery enables you to discover your own special gift and talent and develop it for better improvement of your personality. Nobody can stop you from becoming what you want to become, and that is why your destiny is tied to something that is worth your life. Your life is special, which is why you live among men. The moment you start thinking towards this direction, the better a person you become. Although we are created with different gifts and talents, we can always identify the gifts and talents that we have. This can be achieved by the practice of self-reflection and re-examination, through the Buddhist spirituality and system of religion.

Over 400 million people who practice Buddhism have discovered how useful it is to defeat fear. This is because of the indebtedness of the level of spirituality, which has led to the discovery of self and instant change in the level of mindfulness. In turn, this has led to great transformation among individuals who practice Buddhism. The knowledge and wisdom gained through the practice have made lots of people benefit from the processes of Buddhism.

In this modern society, you definitely need the spiritual tradition of the Buddhist, which tremendously enhances the state of mind of an individual. The moment has come for you to work on your fears. Through the Buddhist religious practice and spirituality, you will overcome your greatest fears and no longer allow fear to control your life anymore.

How to Overcome Serious Hardship & Adversity

Hardship is when a person is going through some difficult and trying moments in life. There are basically three different faces of hardship. Hardship can come; naturally, it can be self-inflicted, or it can be caused by a third party.

People all over the world go through some levels of hardship, which can come in many ways. It usually falls within the three categories aforementioned. Some people tend to give up whenever they face hardship. They find it difficult to deal with life, are usually upset and give up whenever they can no longer bear the hardship. We have people who are capable of enduring hardship for a longer period of time until they finally overcome it. While we also have people who endure hardship and die in that hardship, which may not necessarily be what they wish for themselves but because they have no way out, it leaves them helpless.

Naturally, a person can have difficulty in life as a result of the circumstances of his birth. A person may be born blind, so the hardship that such a person will be facing is the ability to see. Another example is if a person is born with a deformity, he may be unable to walk for the rest of his life. There are so many instances. Serious hardship can come from these circumstances of birth, which usually leave many in a difficult situation in trying to get the best out of life. Yet, we have seen some people with deformity who have decided to claim that there is "ability in disability" and are able to turn their disability into ability with great achievements recorded in the history of the world. You can also have serious hardship getting pregnant as a married woman. Your husband or many people around you will think you are barren. Some may become abusive that you cannot get pregnant, but this is absolutely not true. The fact that they said so doesn't mean you cannot overcome such difficulty.

You may have started a business, and you feel your business is not doing well. After investing so much into it, your business is still not doing as well as you wanted it to. You run into debts, you can't meet the demands of your clients and customers, and you become very sad about the way things are playing out. Your business is not making profit, instead, you are operating at a loss. This is a very serious hardship because you need to pay staff salaries but you are owing them. So in the face of these kinds of hardship, how do you manage to overcome them? Perhaps you are a student, you want to go to school and get an education, but your parents cannot afford a higher education for you. You wanted to become an engineer but you are unable to achieve your dreams. What's going to be your next action? Will you just allow the difficulty to swallow you up, or start something, or figure a way out of the situation? When you learn and practice Buddhism, it will direct you on the path of success, the path of taking you out of problems. Solutions are developed through the inner virtue that radiates from the inside, empowering you to get one step ahead of advancement against anything that will pose hardship in your life.

Adversity is a misfortune that usually brings hardship to people. Misfortune can be a disease. When you are infected with a disease that seems to defy all forms of curative measures taken against it by a doctor or health practitioner, you begin to lose hope. That is a misfortune. You may be involved in an accident and feel very bad about it because you sustained grievous injuries. This is another way in which you can begin to suffer hardship. You can be bedridden in the hospital for months, medical bills keep piling up, and you are unable to pay. This is another thing that brings hardship.

You got out of the university after your years of study, but have been unable to secure a job. You feel life is treating you badly, and you feel like giving up. Your parents want you to get a job and move on with life or even take care of your immediate siblings. You feel like a failure because you don't have money. Now, you need to consider the fact that hardship is there which cannot be ignored. It is real, yet you can actually turn your hardship or adversity into success. This is the only way you are going to get over it.

Identify the Causes of Hardship and Adversity: It is very important to learn and detect the causes of adversity or hardship. The first thing that is necessary for you to get over hardship is to identify the source or causes of it. This is so important because it is based on practical identification of the root causes of hardship. The process can vary from one type of situation to another. What is obtainable in the urban area may be different from what you would get in a rural area. The hardship that has to do with traveling through a longdistance where you don't have a vehicle, for instance, is easily identifiable. This is because you don't have a vehicle and you need to travel a long distance. You know there is a hardship or difficult situation that limits your movement. Hence you identified the hardship. What you can do is figure out how to get a vehicle to take you through the journey.

Look for a Solution: When you have hardship in your life, it usually tends to make you look for a solution or a way out. Allowing hardship to persist will only make you tired. Many people in the world today are tired already because they are unable to get solutions to their hardship or adversity. The first thing you should do in the face of adversity or serious hardship is to look for lasting solutions to the hardship that you are facing. Solutions can start from within you, following the Buddhist system of practice. Every solution to a problem can start from the inner self. When you provide solutions for the inner self, you will get the needed or right solution to the hardship that you are facing. This is because the conviction you have that you can provide the solution to the hardship can lead you to get the solution from the outside. That is if you are able to get the necessary solution from the inside.

Solutions to hardship vary from one individual to another, and using the Buddhist practice on selfspirituality takes you away from it. Like, the pioneers of Buddhist practice usually leave a troubled zone to a safe and quiet atmosphere where they can concentrate on the development of solutions to their hardship or what they were facing. This usually leads them to an advanced realm of knowledge and understanding of how the solution to problems can be attained. And this is through a higher level of spirituality based on a practiced tradition that has proven to bring success.

Taking control and being in control of the situation is always worth it because it means that you are in charge. Not allowing the adversity to dictate the life that you live or dictate what will happen to you next is like fighting a battle. You resist the hardship from affecting you. Sometimes the hardship may take a toll on you, but you are resolute in making sure that you are going to win the battle. This is a form of selfthought. It goes into your subconscious mind through fighting what you are going through, and definitely, when you adopt the Buddhist system of consciousness and inner discipline, you will always conquer.

Resilience: Being resilient in times of hardship is something that you can actually start practicing and achieve. To be resilient means that you refuse to allow your hardship to put you down. You develop a stubborn spirit. Even if the hardship knocks you down several, you keep getting back up.

To be resilient can be seen in a scenario where a very big dog living in a rich man's house is guarding the house. It has rich food, the big dog is well taken care of, but there was this smaller dog who usually comes around from the street. The smaller dog lived in a very small house, and it desired the food and the kind of house the big dog was staying in. Every day, the smaller dog will come to the big dog's compound, and the big dog will try to scare it away. It always involves a fight, and the smaller dog, after being defeated, will just walk away but still return the next day for a fight. It kept on doing this daily until the bigger dog got tired and left the house for the smaller dog.

So you see, when you are resilient, just like the smaller dog, there will always be a final solution. And often, the result will be positive because you kept on working on how to get rid of the hardship. This same thing is what happens in real life. Those who are resilient in the face of hardship always come out victorious.

Persistence: Persistence is when you keep doing things positively that you know or learned will get rid of the hardship. If you want to bring down a tree with an ax, and if it's going to take you 8 hours, it means you have to use 4 hours to sharpen your ax. This means you have to prepare and carry on the course by being persistent. You have to spend and maximize the 8 hours to chop down the tree. But before that can happen, you have to do the necessary things, being persistent is one of them.

Consistent: You have to be consistent when you are trying to solve adversity. Putting an end to particular adversity that is inflicting pain on you means you have to be consistent. The Buddhist system of religion teaches about consistency, especially in its way of life. The Buddhist never changes or compromises his position to lower the standard of his ancient tradition and religion. This is why you need to understand what it means to be consistent. Being consistent in the face of hardship will prove how strong you are both mentally, physically, spiritually, and mindfully.

If you looked around you today in the world, there are people who are not consistent. We have people who are jacks of all trade, but in actual fact, they are masters of none. That's why you may see people in one particular profession, and they seem not to like what they are doing and deviate to another profession. I've seen football stars who, after playing football, got interested in some other sport like basketball or racing, and sometimes we ask, do they really know what they are doing? To be consistent means you are doing things constantly within the same profession, and you attain a level of excellence because you understand and have gathered experience in that profession. The time comes for the experience to pay off and not dabbling into a new profession by starting all over again.

If you are in MMA sports, for instance, and you are doing excellently well without being defeated, why not spend your entire career there and retire? Why divert to boxing where you don't have the experience or longevity in the sport? You will only end up losing at the end of the day, and that is not a wise decision. If you are good at mathematics, you can develop very well in that area. Why abandon it for another thing which is totally different from the calculation? A Buddhist has a high level of concentration and is always consistent with whatever he is doing. That is why Buddhists are known for being unchanged in their performance from time immemorial. Consistency will make you defeat your adversity period.

Turn Your Hardship into Success: The problem with most people is their inability to transform or convert their adversity into success. When you know you have something that is making you not to move on with your life, and it becomes disturbing, you know you have to do something about it to get out of the situation. All you need to do is turn the hardship into success. I will tell you a story about a young boy who was in school; he came from a poor family, and he was a very skinny boy. When he went to school, there was another boy who was bigger, but just a little taller than the skinny boy.

The big boy noticed how skinny the other boy was and always bullied him because he knew he could beat him up. Whenever the skinny boy gets something to eat, the big boy comes around and takes it away from him, and says, "It's mine now, so what are you going to do?" The skinny boy just cries and leaves; he couldn't fight. One day he was passing through a boxing club, and he saw some young lads going in. He walked into the boxing club, and an elderly man who was a veteran and boxing coach noticed him. He was wondering what could have brought the boy into the boxing club. He observed the little skinny boy walk to the gym and sit down, watching other boys in training.

He was sad, but, the elderly man noticed that the skinny boy was staring at how the boys were boxing. When they had left, the skinny boy went and stood close to the punching bag and threw a punch, but the resulting effect made him fall on the floor. And he felt he was never going to learn how to fight. But the elderly man went to him and stretched out his hand. The boy grabbed it, and he pulled him up, then the elderly man said to him, "I think you are going to be a great boxer one day, come on."

The elderly man gave the skinny boy a card and an appointment for free classes. To cut the story short, the skinny boy went on to become a world champion after ten years of graduating from school. He had lost contact with the big boy until one day after his boxing match, which he had won, he was heading back home, and someone stopped him and asked for a favor. Behold, it was the big boy who used to bully the skinnier boy, who is now a world boxing champion. The big boy was asking for money, he had no job after school, and he went into the streets. He didn't recognize the skinny boy anymore. But the skinny boy recognized him, called out his name, and reminded him of how he used to bully him back then in school. So the big boy who had lost his frame was ashamed and knelt down begging. He was thinking the skinny boy would beat him up because he was now a professional boxer and of course the big boy couldn't fight with him. The skinny boy told him to get up, that he wasn't going to hurt him. But he said something which was striking. The skinny boy said, "Thank you for showing me my path to life. Because you bullied me back in school, I began to learn how to fight, and it's because of you I am a world champion now."

This is exactly what should happen to you when you are faced with hardship and adversity. All you need to do is figure out a way of changing your circumstances and making it work for you. Many people find themselves in similar situations; the problem is they don't make the right move in the right direction to solve their problems or adversity.

Turning your obstacles to stepping stones: The Buddhist approach to adversity is simply the fact that if you follow the teachings and apply it in your daily life, you will be able to change your circumstances, especially when you face hardship. Converting your serious hardships into success is what you will do to achieve success as a Buddhist. Because it is based on ancient teachings that have worked for those who practice it, when you feel overwhelmed by your hardships, see it as something that is going to make you greater in the future. You can actually become stronger by the challenges that your hardship present to you because they will push you to become successful. Without hardship, lots of people out there will not be successful or become stronger. But because they have been made to pass through hardship, they learn through the experience. Hardship presents to us a way of learning new things in the face of difficulty. Behind every cloud, there is always a silver lining, and when you believe this adage, you will understand that your suffering or hardship will only propel you to success.

Best Strategies To Healing Yourself

The best strategies to healing yourself is very wide teaching that is basically based on personal experience and relationships with other people. So many people in the world are affected by the activities of other people. There is sadness, unhappiness, greed, pain, jealousy, conflicts, disagreements, unforgiveness, scheming, plotting others' downfall, etc. The list is endless, as many people are not satisfied with what they are getting out of life. There are lots of people suffering around the world. The process of healing the world has been discussed in the last two decades by a notable musician who sang about healing the world. But how can we heal the world when people don't have peace, and every man has not gotten the right enlightenment? Healing the world begins with an individual. It spreads, and until we all begin to develop the mindfulness of healing each other and actually implementing it, the world will still remain the same.

The process of healing has been developed over the years; there are various instances where people need healing. Basically, the question is, who needs healing? What readily comes to mind if you are going to answer such a question is the thought of a person who is sick. But the truth of the matter is that everybody needs healing; the earth needs healing, anything that has life needs healing, and that is the bitter truth. When we talk about healing, it is allencompassing; therefore, I will take you through the various aspects of healing.

Healing the Earth: Following the teaching about what you sow is what you reap; for instance, if you cultivate land and go planting crops during the planting season, during the harvest you will reap the harvest of what you cultivated. If you plant yams, you will reap yams; if you plant potatoes, you will reap potatoes. You cannot plant maize and harvest rice, it's not possible. What am I trying to say here? The interpretation here is that what you feed your mind is what you will get, and this is exactly why people who take drugs will have the side effects of such drugs. Taking hard drugs will lead to drug abuse, and drinking alcohol frequently will make you form the habit. This can equally lead to alcoholism problems and other problems associated with depression. Now that we have established the fact that there are things we do to ourselves that cause us illness let's go further into other instances where we need healing.

Human illnesses: If an individual is sick, definitely such an individual needs healing because an illness is also a way of suffering. Not only will you not be feeling fine, but you can be bedridden in the hospital as a result of suffering.

So, a person who is sick needs healing, and to get the person healed completely, he needs to undergo some therapy or treatment. This may lead to the prescription of medication to aid the recovery of such an individual. In the same way, we all need to get healing through a process. Therefore, to get healing, you will need to submit yourself and allow treatment to take place so you can get the healing that will restore you to good health. The healing process starts with a physician who is well skilled and trained in administering healing on a sick person. The doctor or physician carries out medical examination on such an individual and prescribes the medicine or starts the healing process. This is how the healing process for a sick person is achieved.

In the same way, we need healing in our lives. Every daily activity that we partake in or carry out affects us. But there are other aspects of healing that are meant to give us spiritual cleansing and transformation both mentally, physically, and mindfully. Before we can understand or become open to the process, we must stick to these tenets for the total healing to take place in us, and they are:

Forgive and forget: Forgiveness is the ability to forgive people when they offend you. No matter the number of times a person offends you, you must learn how to forgive such people. It is in forgiving that we can let go of the pain and grudge, and then we will find happiness. We cannot be happy when we have people in mind, people who have hurt us. They may know, or they may not even know, so it bears no pain in them.

They may be unaware that they have hurt us either with their words or actions or omissions. Yet, we feel angry about it, even when they are not aware of the offense they committed against us, so who is in pain? It's you, of course! Because you carry the offense in your mind and you have not learned to let go, you feel pain each time you see the person that offended you. You are not at peace with yourself. You have to forgive that person and forget about the pain he caused you.

Embrace Dialogue: Human interactions are not void of conflicts and misunderstanding. As long as we are living in the world, we will always have situations and circumstances when we will have a disagreement. The best thing to do in such circumstances is to try to have a conversation with the person who offended you. Have a heart-to-heart discussion, talk to the person about what he has done, and see if he is aware or not. Because sometimes, people who offend us may not be aware that they did. Secondly, whether the person apologizes or not, you can end the problem with dialogue and don't allow it to linger. There is no issue that cannot be discussed and resolved, so always make efforts to be the one ready and open to dialogue. This way, you will not allow the problem to spread further and go beyond the resolution. You will be satisfied that you brought the topic up and that the issue has been resolved. This way, it is a healing for both parties.

Show Compassion: Be a compassionate human being. When you are filled with compassion, you will always be noticed. And you can be referred to as a true peaceful human being who has a human face even in the face of difficulty. There are those who need people to reach out to them, but they are not getting people to show compassion to them. Living a life of compassion in itself is a healing that is beyond compare because you are touching lives, and you have the tendency to be a compassionate human being who cares about the suffering of other people.

Show Kindness: Kindness is something that attracts blessings. If you are kind to people, you will, in the end, get help from an unknown source. It happens because you started deeds that draw and attract nature. When you bless people, the universe will connive and bless you too; it is the law of attraction. Kindness will always attract wonderful things to your life. The more you show kindness, the greater the tendency that you become happy with yourself. This is also a form of healing for your mind.

Detaching yourself from Materialism: Materialism is overtly showing love for modern things of the world.

Perhaps you are so attached to living in a mansion; you want to drive the latest cars, you love flashy cars, you want to travel around the world, you want to play for the best clubs, and there are so many desires. Of course, these are wonderful things in life, and it is great to have them, they give us great comfort. But what if you don't have the money to buy them? What if your income is too low to afford a mansion or a flashy car? The chances that you will not be happy are high in such circumstances. This may bring great discomfort, making you feel bad about it, and in this case, you need healing.

You need to understand that sometimes life is not a bed of roses. We are born, and we all have a destiny. Understand that there is suffering in life; there are ends and a path to the end of suffering. If we attach ourselves to these material things, they will give us a bad feeling if we do not have them, which may even affect our health. That's an unhealthy lifestyle; you need to learn how to detach yourself from all things that are capable of taking away your happiness or making you sad if you don't have them. When you start thinking in that direction, you will receive healing.

Love Yourself: We have people in the world who find it difficult to love themselves. But before you can get healing, you need to start by loving yourself. A lack of self-love is unhealthy and will definitely make you unhappy. The best way to start loving yourself is to make efforts to admit that you have weaknesses, and these weaknesses can be corrected. Don't see others as better human beings than you are. Everyone is unique according to their capabilities and gifts. The fact is that all human beings have the same fate i.e., aging, illness, and death. Not seeing yourself as lesser of a human being than any other person will make you free from what can affect your mind when you are tempted to compare yourself with others.

Don't compare yourself with any other person: living a normal life is not competing with people but being yourself. Don't live your life trying to compete with others. True happiness and healing are not achieved when you are competing with other people. Rather, when you live peacefully without involving yourself in any form of competition, this will enable you to get real healing. There are times when there is competition staring you in the face. This happens if we engage in some form of discipline. For instance, if you are a sportsperson, or you are given targets by your employer, or you have contemporaries in the same business. Or when there is a position that opens in the company, you want to apply for such position or post, and you have other candidates who are fighting to get such positions too; these are situations where you will be faced with competition. For the last one, you don't need to get involved in competition with anyone who is trying to outsmart you in getting into positions. Avoid occasions where you will have to compete with others to get something. This is a form of attachment that will always affect your happiness. When you have situations where you are not happy, you gradually get sick, and then you will need healing to get out of that situation.

Contentment: Be content with what you have. When what you have is not much, and others have more than you, there is the temptation to desire what other people have in terms of possession and wealth. Don't always try to have what others have. With that kind of mindset, you will have problems with your mental disposition, and if you can't get what they have, you begin to fall sick both physically, mentally, and emotionally. This will cause a negative impact on your health and your mind, which may make you jealously sick. When you are in such a situation, you really need help and healing. Avoid being so interested in possessing what others have that you don't. Be satisfied with what you have at the moment, work towards a better future, and you will surely get it. Always remember that there is a time for everything.

Your time will come when you will be able to get those things that you really need.

Devote time for quiet Moments: Healing begins with an individual's effort to get well. Healing is not all about outward signs of assistance that can be gotten from a physician; it also has to do with something from the inside of an individual. Many people have ill health not because they have not eaten well, but because they have never once in many years sat down to reflect on the life that they are living. Sometimes you need to go out to an environment where you can be alone and meditate on the things happening around you. And sometimes you need to take your mind off things that are giving you so much trouble. Develop a positive mindset, a mind free of troubles, and worries of this world. You need a quiet moment to yourself, a time you can be alone and reflect on the past, present, and future. This is a great path to a healing process that comes from the inside.

Change your circle of friends: Show me your friends, and I will tell you who you are; this saying is what has long been known to reveal the kind of person an individual is through the types of friends he or she is keeping. Now what this implies is that sometimes in our lives, the kinds of friends we keep may not be true friends but "fair-weather friends." They are with you because of what they are gaining from you. Maybe they are benefiting from what you have. You may have money to spend on your friends, so partying and enjoying the comfort of your house and presence is what they are after. Once you have a problem, they will simply disappear. And you will begin to wonder if you really had them as friends, or they were just interested in what they were gaining from you. You will be surprised to find that you don't have any friends. This can make you feel bad, and when you remember them, you tend to feel angry. The best advice is for you to change your circle of friends. And when you start gaining friends that are responsible and true, you will feel much better. When you have friends who are like-minded, friends who share your dream, and your kind of mindset, you will feel better having them around you. Rather than friends who are just interested in what they can gain from you and not how they can help you achieve your dreams.

Be in a Healthy Relationship: If you want to experience healing, be in a healthy and good relationship with a person whose qualities you are very familiar with. Not everybody can be your perfect match, but you can get someone who is the perfect match for you. All you need to do is study and take your time to find that person. Many people get into relationships that they end up regretting, and this usually causes an emotional breakdown. When the relationship is broken, they find it difficult to move on. For some people, it may be easy, but for some other individuals, it may take time, while some never forget the person who broke their heart, and that is a fact. It is hard to forget the first person, friend, or partner who broke your heart when you were in a relationship with him or her. So this makes us think a lot, and it always comes with many regrets. We begin to think, "How I wish the relationship did not end," "How I wish I could turn back the hands of the clock," and so on. We have people who find it very difficult to recover from the various bad relationships they had, and this has also led to psychological trauma. It's sad to see people suffer from such conditions. The real deal is this; when this happens to you, yes you may be heartbroken, yes I understand that you have been hurt, but it's okay, life goes on. You are worth more than a broken heart, and you should move on with your life. The future is always bigger and greater than what happened in the past because what awaits you is bigger than what happened to you in the past.

Have you ever thought of why life has been developing and improving ever since human beings came into existence? Have you? Definitely, it's a known fact that, at a point in time, there were no airplanes to fly from one continent to the other in just a few hours. There were no ships to move cargoes or goods from one country or seashore to another, and there were no billionaires. But what do we have today? We have the sophistication, high mental development, higher technological advancement, and the best facilities that support human lives. The information age is awesome, to be able to communicate with a person from one continent to another. This is why we believe that the future is always better. There is an opportunity now and in the future. So there is always a need for you to let go of what happened to you in the past and look forward to a better future, which is the real deal. And this should bring healing to your mind.

Learn and get knowledge about new ways of getting healing: There're several ways of getting healing. What you ought to do is be open to these new and better ways. A closed mind is a closed destiny, so learn new ways of receiving healing. There are so many people in the world today who are the cause of their own problems. They have refused to listen and accept new ways of doing things, and this has hindered their progress. For example, Buddhism is one of the most potent religions with a tradition of directly dealing with any individual who intends to gain enlightenment and knowledge about the new ways of mindfulness. Buddhism helps you to receive healing, especially with the teachings and tenets that have been modernized to help the mind develop into a state where it is capable of receiving freedom from pain and suffering. To this extent, the Buddhist has an amazing awakening knowledge about the realities of life, and how life can be lived. We can actually defeat pain and suffering, which is an inevitability in the lives of humans by following a path that will enable us to achieve that successful ending of suffering. This is one of the major causes of pain and suffering in people who actually need healing.

Open-mindedness: For you to receive healing, you need to open up your mind and be ready to receive it. People in today's world have problems not because there are no solutions but because they are unable to open up their minds and accept the healing that they truly deserve. If you are really in need of healing and you want it for yourself, you need to follow the steps explained herein, and you will be healed completely.

Spreading Peace & Loving Kindness: To spread peace and loving-kindness in the world is easy and, at the same time, difficult depending on the mindset of the individual. To preach and deliver peace to others, you need to be peaceful yourself. So the question is, are you at peace with yourself? You cannot give what you do not have, and this forms the basis of giving and receiving. Giving peace to other people has a starting point, and it begins in an individual's willingness to be open and live a peaceful life. Several people in the world today do not have peace and cannot give peace. But peace can be given by an individual, and he is capable of touching and changing lives if he is well enlightened to influence people. Peaceful living is when you are able to become a third party in a conflict situation. You are the peacemaker, you are a lover of peace, and people can trust your judgment on conflicts; that you will be able to deliver a peaceful resolution during the time of crisis or conflict.

Peaceful Protest: Sometimes in governance, there are certain decisions of the government that can be unpleasant for the masses. In these circumstances, there are protests against unpalatable decisions that tend to affect the masses, especially those that have to do with suffering. In some regions of the world, we have seen how people can take to violence if they are

371

unable to accept what the government plans or implements against them in terms of the policy. This can be seen as an anti-people policy. In such circumstances, we usually experience what is referred to as protest or industrial action, which occasions strike. Union leaders can instigate a reasonable cause to embark on strike or industrial actions against policies that affect them. In cases like this, we can see people who understand what it means to embark on a peaceful protest without having to involve violence in the process; it's one of the highlights of living and spreading peace. If you find yourself in any organization that seems dissatisfied with policies that affect them negatively, it is your duty as a peaceloving citizen of such a country to embark to support a peaceful resolution of crises. Or at least, if it seems too likely to become violent, advocate a peaceful process or protest to resolve the crisis. This is one of the ways of spreading peace.

Live a life of Generosity: Living a life of generosity doesn't mean you need to have before you give. Generosity is not only dependent on material gifts. What you can give to people may be something worth more than material gifts. A person may need love. There are so many people who are in need of good advice, and others who need a shoulder to lean on. We have people in the world who really need people they can say hi to, people they can confide in, people they can talk to. You can reach out to that person. It doesn't necessarily mean you have to reach everyone, but the change and giving in generosity can be achieved if you are able to make a move. There are various movements and religions in the world which began with one person. And today, we have millions of people who have been touched by such religions; Buddhism is one of them. The practice started with one man, the Buddha, and today we have over 400 million Buddhist followers. Be generous in your gifts and talents. If you have a talent or are blessed with a special gift that can help you touch and change lives, do it. And in so doing, you will be able to make a change and transformation through your generous gift to mankind.

Share what you have with others: The more you give to others, the more you will receive. This is great teaching which has been on for thousands of years. There is more joy in giving than in receiving. The most successful people in the world are not those who have taken pleasure in stolen wealth or become rich by inflicting pain on other people. Rather, the most successful people in the world today are people who have knowledge of the teaching of the art of giving. A person who gives is the person who gets the blessing. That is just one of the basic teachings of life. Successful people are able to cultivate the habit of giving back to the society what the society has blessed them with. I wouldn't want to mention names, but I know you are aware of many foundations and charity organizations in the world today. Some are very popular, and some are not so popular. Nonetheless, these organizations have been able to touch lives and contributed immensely to the solving of various human problems. Problems such as providing help to the needy, food for orphanages, relief materials during crisis or conflicts, etc. This is how you can perform acts of giving and kindness to people around you. You can partner with or set up NGO's that can work towards spreading love and kindness to people who are in need, or you can just start a personal course which can lead to a great change.

Show tolerance to people irrespective of age, culture, and race: One of the greatest problems the world has ever faced is racism and intolerance for people of different races and origins. When you have the tendency to show preference and segregation among people, and if you have a prejudicial notion about people, it is a sign that you are not creating a better world. Rather, you are simply making non-peaceful coexistence among people. Learn to show tolerance to people and accept them the way they are. Don't ever think you are any better than other people because all people came from one source. So it is not healthy to stigmatize or segregate people based on color, race, or religion.

Be charitable: One of the best ways you can spread kindness to people is to become charitable. Be charitable and contribute to helping people so that they can live a normal life. There are people who need food, children without parents, no education, and no means of livelihood. Some of these children or young persons get exposed to life on the street. Very few usually escape, but so many have lost their lives on the street struggling to survive. You can reach out to these people and help them to become better citizens.

Visit the sick in hospitals: Lots of people are sick in hospitals. You can visit them and do the little you can to give a helping hand. If you chose to pay the medical bill of one person, you would have done very well by touching the life of that person. You don't have to help the whole world, but you can start by helping someone out of a desperate situation in the hospital.

Do free Empowerment: One of the best ways to really show kindness to people is to empower them with skills. This is a fact because; the best way to help a person is not when you are able to give material gifts. If you give a fish to a person, he will come back the next day to ask for another fish. So why not teach a man how to fish, and he will become the fisherman who will learn how to catch fish and also teach others? That is how life ought to be. Life is about learning and empowering people by teaching them the right path to achieve success and survive. Many people in the world today lack the basic skills and knowledge to survive. To feed and live a normal life becomes a problem when there is no basic training. So you can do something about that, especially if you are an expert, and you know how to train people and educate them in a particular skill. You can share it with people who need help, and you would have succeeded in saving their future. Helping people is one of the ways of making them become peaceful, and that way, you have spread love and kindness through your own efforts.

CHAPTER 2

What is Buddhism?

Buddhism is an ancient religion that was started by Buddha, and it is a spiritual tradition that began over two thousand, six hundred years ago in Nepal. It was started by a certain young man who meditated under a Bodhi tree and got enlightenment. This led to the laying of the foundation of the spiritual tradition of Buddhism.

Origins of Buddhism

Basically, Buddhism is a religion that bears its roots in India, a country located on the Asian continent. The religion was founded on the basic teachings of a man who went on meditating. He happens to be a Buddha who is a person that practices the art of teaching people on spirituality. He bears this title "Buddha," which is drawn from the belief that such a person is the "awakened one." This name was coined around the 5th BCE century following the event that took place.

The early description given to Buddha was that his biological name or real name was "Siddhartha Gautama." However, the descriptions of the Buddha's lifestyle, as written by many authors have been inconsistent. Meanwhile, his background as Buddha is difficult to trace. However, the early documentations on his background depicted Gautama Siddhartha to have been born in Lumbini and brought up in Ganges Plain, in Nepal, along the Indian border. The Buddha was said to have spent his life in what is now referred to as the Bihar in modern-day India and in parts of Uttar as well. There are, however, disputes about his royalty status because early writers claimed he came from a royal family. However, scholars claim that rather, he was from a Shakya community.

The Shakya community was one that was ruled by a small, rich family or republic-like council that based its leadership on seniority, but the ranking wasn't supreme. The life and times of Buddha from a historical perspective have been inconsistent because the authors' works gave divergent views about Buddha. This is not to say that everything about Buddha wasn't a fact. In every religion, there is always some truth in its teaching, which Buddha has been able to thrive with over 400 million followers around the world.

The Story of Siddhārtha Gautama

Buddha was a mortal man and not a god. He was referred to as Siddhārtha Gautama by name. He saw the selfishness, violence, and sadness exhibited by a man in his environment. Because this often led to human suffering, he made his determination to find a solution to end the various suffering of human beings. He went on to study great spiritualists, ascetics, gurus, sages, etc. He further went on to exclude himself from the public and sat under a Bodhi tree. And with a deep meditation practice that took place for about 49 days, he gained great enlightenment and was willing to share his knowledge and newly learned spiritual orientation.

Some writers also claimed that Buddha was given birth to and named Siddhartha Gautama around two thousand six hundred years ago; he was said to be a prince of the monastic order in the Sakya clan in Nepal. Because he wrote two hundred and twentyseven rules for the monks and three hundred and eleven rules for monks and nuns respectively, these rules were to be followed and guide their activities. His death was known as parinivana, and he also suggested that there can be changes to the rules he created.

Over the course of time, there was disagreement between the brotherhood of the Buddha. This gave birth to sectionalism and separation, which created different sects that eventually emerged among the monks. It was clear there was a divide. Some sects emerged and referred to themselves as the Mahayana sect and Hinayana sect. These were the two major sects that emerged, and the

Mahayana sect referred to themselves as the greater vehicle while they referred to the Hinayana sect as the lesser sect or conservatives. Among the remaining Hinayana sect in the modern day is the Theravada sect. Many developments have occurred throughout the years thereafter.

For over two thousand six hundred years, Buddhism as a religion has evolved and is the major source of inspiration responsible for successful modern-day civilization. It became the source of inspiration and major breakthrough in achievements in the lives of millions of people around the world. People from different backgrounds and cultures are now students of Buddha teachings and are following and learning from what Buddhism has to offer.

Buddhism 101

Buddhism was founded many years ago and has been able to inspire millions of people around the world with the ability to generate peaceful teachings that emanate, radiate, and touch lives. Buddhism 101 teachings are about the explanation of the central concepts behind the successful practice of Buddhism in modern-day society. These are applicable and practicable in modern times while providing information that is based on mindfulness, karma, the middle way, the four noble truths, and much more. This teaching constitutes what is referred to as Buddhism 101.

They are what guide you to understand the basic operations or principles of the Buddhism religion. Buddhism helps people who are interested in teaching and religion to get to understand what life is all about and how to follow the Buddhist way of getting enlightenment. The philosophy behind the study of Buddhism and becoming a practitioner will help you to live as an enlightened individual in the world. Irrespective of color, tribe, or race, you can explore the Buddhism 101.

The Basics of Buddhism

One of the most interesting things about Buddhism is its basic teachings. These dwell on doctrines that started from the early days, when Buddhism was established, and which are still prevalent in the modern era of Buddhism practice. It is made up of the four noble truths which are very obvious in the world today. The basic teachings referred to as the four noble truths are:

- "Dukkha" meaning the existence of suffering and which further stresses that.

- Suffering has a cause, called craving and attachment, referred to as "Trishna."

- Cessation of suffering is referred to as "nirvana," and there is also a way to the stopping of suffering which is further categorized into.

- The right resolve, right action, right livelihood, right mindfulness, right effort, right concentration, right views, and right speech.

It is basically based on the relationships and realities that Buddhism proposes in its concept and precept. It is not based on substance or deity or an entity that exists somewhere. Its basic teaching is based on what is realistic and obtainable and also can be practiced.

The basics of Buddhism are also propounded into five wholesome teachings, which are purely based on experience constituting the "skandhas." They form the "Rupa" which is known as material existence. The next in the compilation are the four basics, which are sensations known as "Vedana." The other that follows is what is referred to as the concept of perceptions known as "Samina." There are also the psychic constructs commonly referred to as the "samskara," the consciousness aspect is known as the "Vijnana," and all these are summed up as the psychological process.

The most central teaching is based on non-self "anatman" which stipulates in 5 compilations that there is no independent existence, self-immunity, or soul.

The school teaches that every (circumstance) or phenomenon takes place for the purpose of a course and conditions. In so doing, they will definitely be subjected to an ending or cessation.

It also teaches that there is some form of casual occurrence which takes place.

They are summed up in a 12-group chain called "Pratityasamutpada" and are dependent on the origin. This group of 12 chains is known to be responsible for these characteristics exhibited by individuals; predisposition, consciousness, the senses, ignorance, the name form, cravings, contact, birth, gasping, aging old and death, more ignorance.

These teachings revolve around an individual's birth, destiny, and death and returning to life to continue, depending on where such individual had ended. The term "continual circle of an individual" is a common term in Buddhism. Moral precepts were the basic foundation of Buddhism from inception until a deeper study based on meditation and enlightenment was further revealed.

The regulation of monastic life was based on nonparticipation in vices that were alien to monastic life, including stealing and immorality. Non-participation in entertainment, especially secular entertainment, refraining from viewing secular entertainment, avoiding ornaments and bodily adornment, etc. were prioritized in the practice of Buddhism.

5 Steps to Start Buddhist Meditation

There are basically five steps to start meditation. These steps, when carefully followed, will yield results and you will be amazed by the effects viz-a-viz:

Self-Awareness: In the practice of Buddhism, awareness does not refer to the usual awareness that a layman would describe or express according to his knowledge. To people generally, awareness, in ordinary words, is to be informed or know what is going on around you. But in Buddhism, the first thing you need to have to start your meditation is awareness. In the real sense, in a Buddhist expression or in Buddhism, awareness simply means "awakening of oneself." Simply put, it is to be "awake" or being awakened to what you have around you. This includes having the sense of feeling, smell, colors of objects, the material things around you, knowing or being knowledgeable of what is going on around you, but yet refusing to be pulled or distracted by them. The state of mind is always in the present pristine state. When you are able to command the present and don't allow yourself to be distracted by what is going on around you, that means that you have started your first step to meditation in Buddhism. Applying this to your daily life will help you to be less distracted by worries or criticism, and you can make things better if you follow the practice.

A lot of hardship can come from your family, wants, needs, and desires. Friends can cause you problems, enemies may be against you, and they want you to fail. Also, there can be injustice around you; but you need to free yourself from these problems by starting meditation. Buddha started by meditation to change his present and future. You cannot change your past, but you can influence your future to suit yourself if you are suffering today. Buddha started with the awareness of his mind, his body, and the reality about things around him.

Thinking: Thinking here is based on what we experience in relation to just seeing, touching, and tasting. For example, we are staying with the body while doing the job, without thinking about the job, sticking to the process, so that the action is in the body experience. The functioning doesn't have to come from the head, only allowing the action to take place naturally in the body. In this instance, it is void of thoughts or thinking; it is beyond thinking and is usually an unlettered experience. The process is void of any other addition to it. Thinking only makes the mind more confused, so while you experience what goes on around you, do not allow the thinking or feeling or smell, etc. of those things to distract you.

Thinking is actually good for some people, no doubt. Thinking makes them plan or arrange appointments or think of doing things. This is not the type of thinking that works in Buddhism. The successful kind of thinking in Buddhism is the one that has to come from the inner mind. The one that has to do with inspiration, detaching yourself from what is around you and thoughtfulness that radiates inwards is exactly what we are talking about.

Meditation: Meditation that has to do with the awakening of the mind should be void of sleep. Meditation that leads to sleeping off is not Buddhism. Complete enlightenment is derived through meditation from a sitting position void of distraction. Meditation that awakens the reality of the moment suffices as the real act of Buddhism compared to sleeping and dreaming. Meditation cures ignorance; it is great medicine for being ignorant because, through meditation, the individual is awakened. It awakens the reality of life and exposes a person just like an individual standing in front of a mirror exposes himself to the way he is, void of any hidden secret. The mysteries of life can be seen through meditation, which opens up the depth of great awareness in the reality of life that exists in our daily activity.

Meditation by sitting or Sitting Meditation: This process involves finding a quiet place to carry out meditation where you are free from interruption from anyone or anything. It can usually be carried out in a noiseless room; specifically, it can be done in a little corner of the room. This particular activity involves the voiding of every distraction that can come from your spouse or children, including telephone calls or text messages, no matter what they are. Make it clear to members of your family that you should not be disturbed at this point in time. If you allow disturbance, the whole process will not be effective, and you will not get a good result out of it. In modern times, finding a quiet place outside your room may be difficult, especially in the urban city, which is usually noisy. So create a space in your room and make the room sealed from distraction. Take note that your family may see your decision as awkward and selfish, but let them understand that you deserve some level of privacy, which ought to be respected. If others want to learn or participate in the process, it's acceptable to give them the opportunity too. This means meditation can also be done in groups with a full understanding of the teaching.

Sitting Positions: The sitting positions are easy, especially for young people, but maybe difficult for adults. The traditional position is the lotus posture, which requires some effort to start with and it is the most appealing position.

Half Lotus position: The half-lotus position is another positioning that can be difficult for adults to attain and which is also necessary and required in the Buddhist position for meditation.

Crossed Leg Posture: The crossed leg posture helps to make the meditation and adjustment a lot easier; of the three ways of positioning for meditation, crossed leg posture happens to be the choice of most Buddhist practitioners.

Kneeling: Some people may prefer to kneel, this is also acceptable especially if the crossed leg posture happens to be difficult. Kneeling can also be enhanced with the aid of materials like a cushion or stool designed for the purpose of kneeling.

Sitting on a Chair: It is also acceptable for you to sit on a chair if possible because when you meditate, it should be out of being comfortable from any distractions around you. It is advisable to practice the various positions in a sequence so you can find the best position that will fit or that you are comfortable with.

The positioning of Hands and Eyes: Here, you will need to open your eyes and look down at the floor and your feet without placing your attention or focus on any other thing. The position of the arms should be inwards, placing your palm on top of the other palm of your hands, not holding on tight but in a loose manner.

Duration of the Meditation: It is advisable to start with a short duration like ten minutes, which can be gradually increased from ten to fifteen and to twenty minutes in subsequent days. Follow these steps to get the right duration, and do not start thinking about how long it will take you to complete the process. Normally, it is not the duration that really matters but the quality of it. So make sure you get the very best out of your time taken to meditate. The sitting position should be void of the endurance of pain. Rather it should be done with great enthusiasm. Otherwise, it will become worthless when you feel pained, and you seem to be agonizing rather than embracing the situation.

When to Meditate: The best time to meditate may not usually be fixed, but it is advisable to do your meditation when the environment is void of distraction. Some Buddhist practitioners suggest early in the morning, but this depends on the circumstances. It is ideal, however, to do your mediation in the middle of the afternoon when, maybe your kids have gone to school, or late at night when every person around you is asleep. Or anytime there will be silence, you can do your meditation—you will have to figure it out yourself. You can decide to meditate when the time is right and the number of times depends on you. You can decide to meditate more than once or twice a day; it all depends on your preference.

Starting: Once you have started, you can begin taking a position with overlapping palms on your laps. You have prepared your mind towards the course, and there is no looking back and, of course, no distraction.

Counting Your Breaths: Counting your breaths is done gradually, and ten successive breaths are usually counted. If there is a loss of count, you will have to start all over again. Inhaling and exhaling should be done in a gradual process, taking your mind off it during the exercise. If there is wandering away of the mind from the focus, you will need to start all over again. The main purpose of the exercise is to bring you into reality. The process is also to seek the discovery of self and how the mind works. This process will awaken you to the realities. Don't see it as a moment of depression, and do not begin to fill disinterested in what you are doing. Always try to bring your mind back into the exercise even if your concentration is not sufficient, repeated practice will get you going. Exercise patience in carrying on the activity. The secret behind the counting of breaths is that it helps in the concentration of the mind and removing it from all forms of worry and distraction. It enables you to be in the reality and moment of the practice.

Meditation helps to bring you into the real issues and aids the bringing of solutions to problems with the new awakening. It also develops positivism and clears all negative thoughts.

While this takes place, there is the development of a high level of concentration, which varies from one individual to another. In some persons, it may be instant. However, it may take a little while like weeks or months in some people, and this varies. So, yours may be different from another person.

Non-Attachment: Let your mind be focused on the moment, don't get involved in responding to what happens around you. Don't involve yourself in thinking of who is watching or what is passing by. Rather, focus on the fulfillment of the function of what you are doing. If you get distracted, you will not be free, and it will affect your meditation. When you free yourself from the pleasurable things of life, you will get to the realm of happiness, and the freedom of the mind opens up new discoveries.

A Typical Day

Doing your meditation a daily routine or habit is one of the significant processes that lead to the total transformation of the individual. It means, to become successful, you have to create your personal daily mindfulness, and if you do, you are already on the path of Buddhism experience. It has to do with making use of your daily behavioral tendencies in which you will be able to manage a particular set of schedules. This implies that you have to become resolute in taking action. Not just designing a schedule that you will find difficult to follow up, but a mindset of taking action on such a schedule of activities.

Often, human beings tend to take preference for what is easier to do than what is not easy to do. Waking up in the morning and preparing for work may not be easy for some people, but it becomes easy when it becomes a daily routine.

That is the essence of a schedule because you will become used to it. Even if it is difficult, it becomes easy because you do it regularly. Another face to it is that at least when things are easier, we tend to show preference to do it more often and better. So, the six steps to daily meditation are as follows:

- **Make a decision to maintain a particular schedule of meditation that will be consistent:** To put up a meditation session; you should make efforts to schedule a time for meditation. If you don't fix a time, you will keep on procrastinating it and won't be able to stick to a particular time. That's the first step in the right direction; when you schedule a time for your meditation and also stick to it consistently. After your meditation, make sure you keep an appointment for the next day. This way, you will know and have it at the back of your mind. It may not be easy at first, but when you are consistent with it, you will definitely get used to it; your mind will become focused on a schedule that you get accustomed to.

Meditating in the morning when you wake up is very beneficial and can help you start that way before you decide to pick a time. Make sure you don't miss your daily meditation, no excuses. In the event something comes up to interrupt your schedule for a day, you can reschedule the meditation for that day. Make sure you carry it out without allowing a day to pass without doing your meditation.

- **Form a dedicated space for Meditation:** Create a space that will enable you to perform your meditation; this should be a noiseless and less distraction environment which is suited for performing meditation. Get anything that will disrupt your sitting position out of the place of your meditation. Don't allow distraction items like television, radio, computers, windows, and any other items that can cause distraction in the space. The purpose of the least resistance is to make sure we discover our tendencies, not just the distraction. Due to human tendency, it is possible to put on your smartphone, or start browsing on your computer or be tempted to put on your television. These items offer the least resistance, and this is going to take away the main focus of your meditation.

- **Mindfulness of breath:** Start practicing your mindfulness of breath while keeping it simple. I have explained about breathing above. It helps to start your meditation on the right path by calming your mind and gradually building up the mindfulness around your meditation. Secondly, it makes things easy for you, where your mind can move into the moment and reality. Thirdly, it enables the expansion of your Buddhism practice beyond your sitting position and enables you to bring meditation into your daily life.

- **The One-Minute Jump Start technique:** You start by meditating for one minute. While you monitor your progress, visualize if you experience any mental push. Try sitting down for ten seconds and continue for the first week until you get used to it. This process is to enable you to get used to meditation. When this is done in the first week through the second week, you are already on your way to making meditating a daily routine.

- **Mindfulness practice in daily activity aside sitting meditation:** Practicing mindfulness in your daily activities or lifestyle is a way of helping you during meditation; mindfulness doesn't have to be practiced only when you are meditating alone. You can practice mindfulness, as explained in this book earlier throughout your daily life. This will enable you to adjust and improve your meditation. There are various ways you can do daily life practice of meditation, such as when you are driving, walking, or eating. All you do at these moments is to practice mindfulness, and it will help improve your meditation process.

CHAPTER 3

The Teaching of Buddhism

The teaching of Buddhism is to enable the individual, irrespective of class, gender, race, or color, to arrive at a path of perfect enlightenment. This is the ultimate goal, which will be attained when followed with due diligence. The teachings based on the path of arriving at perfect enlightenment are referred to as Dharma, which in ordinary meaning is known as "the nature of all things." Or it can also be known as the "truth in the existence of things." The Buddha teaching can be categorized into seven subtopics which are:

1. **The Noble Eightfold Path**

2. **The path to perfect enlightenment (Dharma)**

3. **Suffering and Neurosis**

4. **Non-self**

5. **Sutras**

6. **Karma and**

7. **Reincarnation**

The Noble Eightfold Path

The Noble eightfold path is teaching that implies the path to end all suffering because it prevents two extremes of sensitive indulgence and mortification of self. It is based on when the body is in a state of comfort and not overindulge. Thereby the mind is at the clarity and has the energy to meditate inwardly and deeply to uncover the truth. The noble eightfold is made of mindful cultivation of virtue, wisdom, and meditation. The Noble Eightfold paths are:

- **The Right Understanding**

- **The Right Thought**

- **The Right Speech**

- **The Right Action**

- **The Right Livelihood**

- **The Right Effort**

- **The Right Mindfulness and**

- **The Right Concentration**

The training in virtue and/or morality comprises "the right speech, the right livelihood, and the right action."

The Buddhism practice is engulfed in the practice of 5 major precepts which the tradition and religion teach as:

- Refraining from deliberate causing of the death of any being that is living and has life.

- Refraining from the deliberate taking for one's own property belonging to another person.

- Sexual immorality or misconduct, especially adultery.

- Breaking promises and lying.

- Drug abuse and alcoholism can cause a lack of mindfulness.

The mindfulness, the right effort, and the right concentration are regarded in the practice of meditation. It is the path that purifies the mind via the experience of a blissful status of internal firmness. It makes provision for the empowerment of the mind to go into the deeper meaning of life via a great moment of enlightened insight.

The Right Thought and the Right Understanding are what make up the revelation of the wisdom of Buddhism, which is always viewed as the ending of all suffering. Also, it is usually said to cause the great transformation of an individual. This is done by producing an unfettered conducive mind and unstirred passion. The person is transformed, and the level of understanding transcends beyond the ordinary man.

The Buddhism practice of this virtue is postulated from the fact that without the perfection of the practice of virtue, it becomes impossible to carry out a perfect meditation. Thus, such an individual will be unable to get the enlightenment and wisdom of Buddhism. The path of Buddhism is a process that brings about gradual development. It is a gradual process comprising the practice of virtue, wisdom, and meditation, as stipulated by the Noble Eightfold Path, which causes or leads to the liberation and happiness in an individual.

Dharma - The Path to Perfect Enlightenment

The word "Dharma" has been used in some religions such as Hinduism, Jainism, etc., and may confer a different meaning in different religions. However, in Buddhism, it means cosmic law and order, which is also applied to the teaching of Buddha. The term is also used in Buddhist philosophy to describe phenomena. The term has evolved to be applied for different usage over the years, such as being postulated as the doctrine that teaches purification and transformation of human beings.

Suffering and Neurosis

The literal meaning of suffering is bearing pain, loss, or inconvenience. When pain is endured, or a distress situation or injury is incurred by an individual, the term suffering applies; or when a person is in sorrow, pain, or grief. But in Buddhism, the Buddhist recognizes the existence of suffering that is based on a cause. And that such suffering for a cause definitely has an ending. Also, there is something that will bring it to an end. Buddhists teach that ignorance and desires are at the root of suffering. Desires in the parlance of Buddhism mean the urge for pleasure in materialism and immorality, which are desires that cannot be satisfied as long as human beings are concerned.

Neurosis is a term that is associated with a person experiencing emotional pain or unconscious distress, which can be seen in some form of illness like mental disorders. The tendencies of neurotic illnesses vary in the degree of affliction, which can

401

be chronic and manifest in the person. Problems like anxiety, obsession, phobia, and disorders are typical examples.

In Buddhism, it is a common phenomenon that you might experience some form of over activeness or noticing changes in behavioral patterns. Note that this is not a Neurotic problem but simply because you're getting deeper into enlightenment.

What Is Non-Self?

Non-self in Buddhism simply means substance-less, and the term is often referred to as Sanskrit Anatman. The teaching on non-self is that in every human, there is no permanent nature or substance that can be referred to as a soul that the human body embodies in an enclave. The teaching is a deviation from the Hindu belief in Atman, which means "the self."

What Are the Sutras?

The meaning of sutras in Buddhism is a set of scriptures (conical) that are known as records of the oral doctrines and teachings or tradition of Gautama Buddha. They are very detailed scriptures that have sometimes been compiled. Found repeatedly in the scripts are words that further emphasize the teachings; it is rooted in spoken words. Other religions, like Hinduism, also recognize and use sutras.

What Is Karma?

Karma in Buddhism simply means 'action.' The term is usually referred and linked to "the law of Karma." The implication of this is that for every action we take, there are consequences of such actions that we cannot escape. The teaching on this is that there are certain deeds, speeches, or mindful actions that lead to the harming of oneself or others. These actions are referred to as bad or unwholesome karma. The teachings identify hatred, greed, and wickedness to be linked to getting returns or consequences as the law of karma demands.

Since harmful acts will end up giving an individual a resultant painful effect, then Buddhism advises individuals to desist from such bad actions. Alternatively, teaching in Buddhism also recognizes positive Karma, which is based on actions of generosity, kindness, wisdom, and compassion. The Buddhist encourages people to perform such actions because they bring good results and are therefore referred to as good or wholesome karma. They bring happy ending results.

When a person is affected in life, when he has a misfortune, the teaching is that you cannot blame someone else for such misfortune. Rather, look inwards, it's probably something bad you did in the past that is affecting you, and you are getting bad results now. But when something good happens to you, it's a result of the good karma you did in the past, and you are getting good results accordingly. The teaching encourages the performance of good deeds so that you will always get good karma in the future. The teaching on Buddhism is that there is no superior or divine being that is responsible for the karma that happens to an individual, either good or bad. And such consequences are never controlled by a divine being. The proposition is also emphasized by reaping what you sow. Hence the Buddhist teaches the performance of good deeds to get good karma and not bad deeds.

However, the teaching on karma also stipulates that bad karma can be mitigated by doing more good karma. If there is pending bad karma, it will be reduced. If there is a lot of bad karma, the more one is required to do more good karma to reduce the painful results. Bad deeds are often seen as bad habits that should be avoided. Moral practices in our contemporary society are the impact that the law of karma has had on the lives of millions of people around the world.

What Is Reincarnation?

The reincarnation teaching in Buddhism is all about bringing to memory the past life an individual lived and bringing it into the realms of meditation. The remembrance of the past life established the rebirths which direct the life of the person in a meaningful or purposeful perspective. This enables a better understanding of the framework of the law of Karma. Normally it takes some time for karma to emerge.

Therefore, reincarnation gives a good exhibition to the notable inequalities of the birth of an individual. Some are born into abject poverty while some are born into wealthy families; some come into the world with deformity while some come into the world with full form void of deformity. These are not, however, proof of bad karma but the understanding that we should be generous to avert bad karma.

The rebirth of an individual is not based only on the present human world. Buddhism teaches that the realms of men or humans are more than just one. There are separate realms that are high, and there are realms that are higher in perspective. There are animal realms, and there are realms belonging to spirits. Buddhism teaches that humans can transcend to any of these realms and can even condescend to human

405

life from any of these realms. The teachings state that many people in the world today came from different realms believed to exist in Buddhism.

The substantive issue involved in this teaching is that there should be regard for living beings because we all came from any of these realms, and we will be going back to any of the realms. That process constitutes the reincarnation in Buddhism, and there is an understanding of a connection with these realms.

What Is the Abhidharma?

Abhidharma is generally referred to in Buddhism as the ancient 3rd century BCE Buddhist scripts that consist of well-informed reworking of the doctrinal materials contained in the Buddhist sutra. It was developed from the scattered teachings of Buddha during this era and was compiled to the scriptures concerning conscious thoughts based on exposing and developing conscious thoughtfulness.

What Is Yoga?

Yoga is a form of body and mind practice that has to do with meditation and combining various methods of positioning. It has been in existence for the past five thousand years, and its philosophy bears its origin from India. Yoga combines the features of meditation, breathing techniques, and physical positioning to enhance relaxation. Yoga has become well known all over the world because it is developed and practiced based on physical exercise. This helps in improving and controlling the body and mind to enhance the wellness of an individual or practitioner of yoga. Yoga, therefore, is a form of meditation and exercise in a general perspective. But in relation to Buddhism, Yoga is aimed towards the enlightenment of the individual through meditation, which is also yoga. The combination of yoga and Buddhist meditation helps to guard the fluctuations of the mind. This helps to keep the oneness of the mind and body which the Buddhist commonly refers to as emptiness.

Postures of Buddha

In Buddhism, there are about four suitable postures that depend and can be practiced by an individual, depending on his preference. They are the standing posture, the sitting posture, the reclining posture, and the walking posture.

5 Zen Buddhism Teachings

The teachings of Zen Buddhism, classified into 5, which can be practiced on a daily basis in modern times, are summarized as follows:

1. **Meditation technique:** It is based on individual preference by finding the right technique that suits you. Also, it will enable you to get the required result and aims of meditation.

2. **Enjoying the Moment:** Each moment of your day should be lived consciously without being afraid or burdened. You should live each moment enjoying it. It's not as if you will not have difficult moments, but just keep it simple and enjoy it.

3. **Being Happy:** Staying happy is finding the need to be happy within yourself. Happiness is not found outside. Your job, your business, or your relationship may give you some level of happiness, but you may not have the power to control happiness from the outside. You can only control happiness from the inside. You stay happy because you are happy and not because you get the influence from outside.

4. **Stay Focused:** To focus means you are following through all the activities such as the routine, ritual, and habits that support the Zen way of Buddhism. You don't

necessarily have to be a Zen monk, but you can stay focused on the habits to get results.

5. **Be Alive:** The Zen way of living means that you should be alive. You are not living in anticipation of what will happen or in panic. Instead, you live a normal simple life, void of a rush to get wants or needs. Living a life helping people and deriving happiness in such is being alive the Zen way.

CHAPTER 4

Buddhism Numbers 3

The use of numbering is a unique system in the history of Buddhism literature. It shows the cultural background in India and some other parts of Asia, where Buddhism gained development. This system of numbering gave taxonomies to different enlightenment.

The 3 Jewels of Refuge

The three jewels of Refuge in the Buddhism tradition are "the completely enlightened one," known as "The Buddha." The second is "the Teachings given by the Buddha," which is known as "the Dharma." The third is "Buddhism," which is the monastic order that practices the Dharma known as the Sangha.

The 3 Higher Trainings

Buddhism recognizes three higher trainings which are:

1. Higher Virtue Training
This aspect has to do with great virtue, which is based on the higher morality standard with awesome simplicity suitable for good behavioral traits. Such that the behavior will conform with the universally accepted standards, which cause no

distress for another person or the person involved. This virtue is contained in the five moral precepts or eight folds of the Buddhism teachings. It is also referenced in the 227 rules. To live out these teachings, one must understand and practice them through conduct by way of body language, speech, and general conduct aimed at bringing peace to all living bodies. It also includes the total showing and practicing of convenience in a relationship. And freedom from unpalatable effects at the simplest level of living in the world. These should transcend selfish interest. It is connected to members of a particular social group with involvements in the properties of a group, which are a very important aspect of human lives.

2. The Higher Mind Training

The higher mind training is one of the three higher trainings that have to do with the concentration level of the mind, otherwise known as the "Samadhi." This comprises the constraining of the mind to maintain the condition that is most convenient to receive success in whatever the person wishes to achieve. You might ask, what is the meaning of concentration in Buddhism? Obviously, people always understand concentration to mean a completely steady mind. As steady and unmoving as an unmovable log of wood. However, these two behaviors, being steady and unmovable, do not really define concentration.

The basis of these words was an utterance of the Buddha. Buddha described a concentrated mind as the mind that is fit for work, referred to as the 'Kammaniya.' This is the best suitable condition for doing a job. A mind that is "fit for work" is the best way to describe what it means to have a concentrated mind.

3. The Higher Wisdom Training

The higher wisdom training (Panna) is teaching that dwells on insight. This is a practice and drilling that gives birth to the full measure of proper knowledge, comprehension, or understanding the true nature of many or all things. Naturally, we are incapable of knowing any living being or anything by its true nature. Often, we only do things or act according to our own ideas. Or we are used to following popular opinion about something, and in so doing, what we normally see is not the truth. Based on this reality, the Buddhist practice includes the insightful training of the mind to attain wisdom, which is the last aspect of the three-fold training of the mind in order to gain understanding and insight into the true nature of all things.

The 3 Universal Truths

In Buddhism, there are basically three universal truths, and they are:

1. Nothing Is Lost to the Universe

The truth and reality are that nothing is lost in the universe. The transformation of matter into energy and from energy into matter is something that takes place in a circle of life according to Buddhist teaching. For instance, a dead leaf returns to the soil. A fruit, when ripe, falls back to the soil. The seed sprouts and it becomes a new plant, and this life cycle continues. The old solar systems disappear and turn into cosmic dust or rays. People are born of their parents, and our children are our offspring, all these continue in life cycles.

All living beings are the same as plants, like other people, as trees, as the rain that falls. All are life cycles; we are part of the system that surrounds us, and we constitute the same things that we see. If we damage anything around us, we are destroying ourselves. If we cheat others or anything, we are equally cheating ourselves. Because of the knowledge and understanding of these basic teachings and truths, the Buddha and his followers do not kill other animals.

2. Everything Changes

This teaching is a universal truth postulated by Buddha that in this world, everything is constantly changing. Life can be compared to a river flowing and always changing. Sometimes the speed of flow may be slow, and sometimes it

413

can be fast. Sometimes it can be smooth and gentle, depending on the location and nature. Sometimes rivers are found within rocky environments. This implies that we can presume or think that we are always safe, but unfortunately, we are not always safe. Such is life and the teachings in Buddhism.

Our ideas about life also continue to change, but the basic truth will always remain. The kind of life that dominated the earth thousands of years ago is not what we have now. Once upon a time, we had bigger or larger animals and beasts such as dinosaurs and others. Archaeology has discovered the debris of these animals, and since they have gone into extinction, does this mean that life did not continue? Of course not, life went on to produce new forms of animals which we have to this day. Things continue to change and take different forms.

3. Law of Cause and Effect

Buddha teaches that there are changes in the world because of the law of cause and effect. This principle is what is also observed in the teaching of modern science. Furthermore, this goes forth to prove that Buddhism and science are somewhat similar in finding out realities about living and non-living things.

The teaching, according to the law of Karma, is also based on the law of cause and effect. It teaches that nothing ever happens to an individual unless the individual deserves it. It teaches that an individual receives exactly what he earns, whether bad or good. We are what we are now because of what we did in the past. Our actions and thoughts will determine the nature of life that we are going to have. If we do bad things, in the future, bad things happen to us. If we do good, the same way good things will happen to us in the future. Likewise, every moment we live our lives, we create karma by the words we say or through the things we do and/or think. If we have knowledge of these teachings, we will not have to be afraid of Karma, but we will be friends of karma. With it, we can create a bright future for ourselves and our generations unborn. This is the teaching of Buddhism.

The 3 Poisons

Buddhism teaches about three forms of poisons. The poisons are thought to be responsible for the keeping of sentient beings locked up in the samsara. They are aversion, attachment, and ignorance. These characteristics take their root in the Kleshas category.

The Different Schools of Buddhism

Theravada is one of the schools reserved for the elders, and it is the oldest school in Buddhism. The school is responsible for the preservation of the traditions of Gautama Buddha (their version) of the teaching, which is availed as the Pali Canon. It is the only surviving full Buddhist teachings in an Indian language that provide the sacred language from which Buddhism originated. The Theravada follows the path of conservatism in monastic discipline and doctrinal matters of Buddhism.

Mahayana

The Mahayana is one of the two main branches of schools in Buddhism and is popularly known as "the Great Vehicle." This school dwells on seeking complete enlightenment for the gratification of all sentient bodies or beings simply referred to as the Bodhisattva vehicle. Any Bodhisattva who completes the school is referred to as the completely enlightened Buddha. It teaches that enlightenment in the school can be achieved by a layperson and that it can also be attained in a lifetime. It has over 54% of membership practitioners in modern times, which is higher than the Theravada.

Vajrayana

The term Vajrayana in Buddhism is referred to as "Diamond Vehicle" or the "Thunderbolt Vehicle." This is linked to a mythical weapon often used as a ritual and called vajra. The teachings of Vajrayana are the practice that utilizes Mantras, Mudras, Dharanis, and Mandalas. They often see the existence of deities and their usage and also follow the Buddha routes to enlightenment as part of their practice. The school was founded by middle age Indian, Mahasiddhas.

Buddhist Philosophy 101

The teaching in Buddhism that has to do with the philosophy and acceptability of certain facts of life is the philosophy of the Buddhist. This includes acceptance of the fact that disease is inevitable, and that emotional pains in the life of a human being and death cannot be prevented from happening. It teaches that human sufferings are the major reasons for attachment to things that are created with form. The solution offers to cure suffering means to detach yourself from these attachments that tend to influence life. Practical means of attaining this have been stipulated in the Noble eight meditations.

417

The 4 Noble Truths

In Buddhism, there are four realities and truces, which are referred to as Noble Truths. These teach about human suffering and are described as:

1. Dukkha: This is a teaching that suffering exists in life; it is a real occurrence and is universal in nature. It teaches that with suffering, there are causes which can be illness, loss, pain, failure, and the non-permanency of the pleasures of life.

2. The Samudaya: The Samudaya teaches that there is a cause of suffering and that suffering is caused by attachment. It stipulated that suffering arises as a result of the desire to control and own things. The forms that this may take are when we crave after sensual pleasure, fame, and the will to avoid unpleasant feelings such as anger, jealousy, and fear.

3. The Nirodha: This teaching talks about the end of suffering. It suggests that attachment can be defeated or overcome, and the mind experiences total liberation, freedom, and non-attachment. The mind becomes void of desires, and suffering ends with the last liberation of Nirvana.

4. The Magga: This teaching emphasizes the following and implementation or practice of the Eight-Fold Path, which is the path to accomplishing the end to suffering.

The 4 Dharma Seals

In Buddhism, Dharma Seals are four, and they can be translated and described in summary as "all compounded things are not permanent." The teachings also emphasize that emotions are suffering pain and that all circumstances are without inheritable existence or do not exist. The teaching is based on the fact that:

1. **Anything that is contaminated is suffering.**

2. **No permanency of substance.**

3. **All phenomenon are devoid of self and are empty.**

4. **True peace is Nirvana.**

The 5 Skandhas

The five skandhas in Buddhism are referred to as Sanskrit, Pali, Bengali, and Sinhala. Each stands for the form or material image, the sensation or feeling got from the form, perceptions, mental activity, and consciousness, respectively.

The 5 Precepts of Buddhism

The teachings are rules that each individual who is truly practicing Buddhism has to live by every day. It is not a commandment, but the followers of the religion are to keep these rules which they should guard against intelligently, and they are:

1) Avoid Killing: This teaching directs every individual to be peaceful, to shun violence and to take the life of another person or living beings, and also to respect life. Hence protecting life is connected to these precepts. To go deeper into the rules or teaching, the Buddhist suggests such an individual to become a vegetarian and never to support or participate in the killing of another.

2) Avoid Stealing: The rule on refraining from stealing teaches non-conversion of other people's property, which does not belong to you. It also teaches to avoid wasting the time of other people by turning it to something else. For example, respect your employer's time he gives you as working hours and don't waste it. It teaches generosity and compassion.

3) Avoid Sexual Misconduct: This teaching talks about avoiding all forms of sexual immorality, especially adultery and rape, which often leads to mental abuse and physical injury.

4) Do not lie: This is a warning not to lie and always tell the truth. No exaggeration, no adding to what is already the truth, and nothing like half-truth will stand as the truth.

5) Avoid Drugs and Alcohol: This rule, if broken, has dishonored every other rule. Buddhism is a meditating religion, and if the mind becomes intoxicated, it will not be able to achieve the aims and objectives of Buddhism. Drugs and alcohol should be avoided at all costs because they are considered harmful to health.

Perfections of Buddhism

There are 10 perfections in the tradition of the Theravada, and they are: generosity known as Dana, morality known as "Sila", insight known as Panna, renunciation known as "Nekhamma", energy known as "Viriya", truthfulness known as "Sacca", patience known as "Khanti", loving-kindness known as Metta, resolution known as "Adhitthana", and equanimity known as "Upekkha".

The 6 Perfections of Mahayana Buddhism

The development of the six perfections in Mahayana Buddhism among the major Buddhist adherence was held as the standard which they ought to abide with. They are categorized as the Mahayana Sutras, which are:

1) **Wisdom**
2) **Generosity**
3) **Morality**
4) **Vigor**
5) **Patience**
6) **Concentration**

CHAPTER 5

Mindfulness Meditation

The teaching of Buddha states that in gaining understanding, all things are not permanent and not capable of giving ultimate satisfaction. Such understanding makes an individual become a Buddha, which means the "awakened one." The final goal for a Buddha is to get to that status of enlightenment. Meditation is a vital technique to get to that state. Mindfulness meditation is the psychological procedure of deliberate attempts through which an individual brings his attention to experience moments void of judgment. This is achievable through the practice of meditation and other mindfulness training. Mindfulness training is a major and essential aspect of Buddhism traditions; the techniques involved in mindfulness meditation are wide. Mindfulness meditation takes an individual to the past, present, and future.

Benefits of Mindfulness

Mindfulness is very good when we are able to develop a habit of it through Buddhism practice. Some benefits are as follows:

- **Having a healthier mind:** Mindfulness enables an individual to have a healthier mind that is detached from depression and all the worries and difficulties associated with an unhealthy mind.

- **Healthy body:** It enables an individual to develop a healthy body that can stand emotional pain and stress, both physical and spiritual. It also helps in the development of psychic energy, which leads to a better immune system.

- **Resilient Mind:** This enables a person to have a very strong mind that can withstand hardship. It is based on being content, having a deeper understanding about suffering, and that there is a cause for it, which will be brought to an end according to the Buddhist way. The individual has contentment when he gains a deeper awakening of himself.

- **Stable Mind:** Mindfulness will help an individual to have a better and more stable mind, unlike a fearfully made mindset. It helps to develop better consciousness and openness to experience.

- **Improved relationship and social life:** With the development of great compassion for friends, neighbors, and strangers, mindfulness enables a person to become a Buddhist practitioner. One who understands the art of showing kindness and relating to people.

- **Improved level of awareness:** Mindfulness helps the development of self-awareness and awakening the deep insight that was hitherto unknown to the individual. The learning process exposes him to a great self-experience.

- **Greater Insight:** Mindfulness helps one discover the individual self in relation to internal peace and happiness, which has eluded many people in the world today; the path to happiness is mindfulness.

Training the Mind

In the Buddhist tradition, mind training is usually carried out based on a set of formulated processes recorded in the Tibet, which is 12th-century literature. It involves the purifying and refining of an individual's motivations, behavior, or attitude.

Freeing your Mind

The teaching of Buddhism is all-round based on mindfulness as the basics to develop the mind. It is a way of life that focuses on nurturing a mind to become very healthy. The Buddhist concept has been applied to develop the mind as a means of therapeutic practice. Freeing your mind can help you to get a better understanding, just like the case of Buddha. By meditating and silently allowing the thoughts to pass by, getting inner meaning is to focus on self even while you are in the midst of the vagaries of life. You are practicing self-reflection and detachment of your thoughts from what goes on around you.

Classic Mindfulness Meditation Step-By-Step

Mantras are sounds or words replicated to aid the concentration of the mind during meditation. This is believed by Buddhists to aid the spiritual and physical mindfulness during the meditation process. The mantra is now viewed in modern times as the "intention." It has now been further split into two forms which are "man" meaning the "mind" and "tra" which means "vehicle." Therefore, the mantra is a spiritual instrument of sound or vibration that you can utilize to enter into a deep state of meditation.

The quality of mindfulness meditation can be achieved by a simple exercise in a step-by-step process, which was adopted over 2,600 years ago by Buddha viz-a-viz:

- Breath Awareness: Pay attention to your breath, concentrate on the sensation of the breaths in your nostrils all through the expansion and contraction in your chest or belly. Avoid controlling your breath, but only observe it and calm naturally. It can be difficult at first but do your best.

- Count Your Breaths: The in and out breaths should be counted, that is, your inhaling and exhaling to about ten times. Don't get distracted, but if you do, repeat the process. It's not a competition; it's about your efforts.

- Acknowledge Your Feelings and Sensations but Do Not Judge: The focus is concentrating on the breath during meditation. It is possible you'll get body sensations or thoughts or feelings, but don't lose focus.

Repeat the process until your meditation sessions end.

Different Buddhist Rituals

There are varying practices and rituals in Buddhism that enable an individual's journey into great enlightenment. These rituals were inspired by already established religions in parts of Asia, especially India, Japan, China, Tibet, etc. In summary, some rituals and practices in Buddhism are:

- Meditation which dwells on concentration and mindfulness.

- Mantras, which is based on sacred sound or phrases.
- Mudras, which is the teaching on symbolic hand gestures.
- The Prayer Wheels, which are the recitation.
- The Monasticism.
- The pilgrimage to sacred locations.
- The veneration or referencing of Deities and Buddhas.

CHAPTER 6

Japanese Buddhism

Buddhism was introduced in Japan in 552 CE; this was when the official introduction was made. Since its introduction in Japan, the impact of Buddhism has led to the development of Japanese culture and society. This has become a great history of Buddhism. In modern day Japan, the famous schools of Buddhism are the Nichiren, Shingon, Zen and Pure Land. About 34% of Japanese people have been practicing Buddhism since 2008 and the number has been increasing since then. About 60% of the people of Japan already have Buddhist shrines in their various homes.

Buddhism In This Era

The study of Buddhism in the modern era has been in demand. If it has to be practiced and gain wider experience, it must be expanded to the scope of evangelism. This can be done using the modern-day media to spread the message, doctrines, and benefits of participating in Buddhism. Buddhism will go a long way to impact greatly on the society in terms of quality of the individuals that we will have in the world, which is going to be a whole new generation of people. There is a need to shift from conservatism that dwells on ritual and prayer only to a much more universal inclusion. The 21st century has also brought in technology advancement. With the information and communication age impacting greatly on the society, Buddhism needs to be reviewed and ways of fashioning out means of communicating to people all around the world.

Creating an environment where Buddhism will fit into the challenges of the 21st century created by the information and internet era is what should be considered by the Buddhist. It's not about preserving the culture and tradition of Buddhism. But it's about posterity, how will Buddhism be transmitted to the next generation? What is the right education for our teaming generation? How are we going to pass the tradition to the modern era? Western education may take over the minds of our next generation without the input of Buddhism. All the history and secret traditions of mindfulness will be gone with history if Buddhism is not revisited with new innovations to the education of Buddhism to the next generation. The new and next-generation really needs enlightenment in an era that is filled with materialism and so much attachment. The best time to take action on Buddhism ideals to be inculcated is now.

Transmission of Buddhism from one generation to another in history has started from one enlightened person the (Buddha) who passed it down through oral teachings. These teachings were repeated by students and disciples until someone decided to put it down in writing. From writing, we have oral tradition and scriptures. So what's going to be the next documentation and teaching in the modern era of the great internet and information age? Certainly, Buddhism needs to upgrade to match with the trend.

Buddha's enlightened words have been written on palms, stones, leaves, walls etc. Just to keep and teach them. It has been translated in different languages and distributed in Asia and other continents for those who would care to listen. People in the modern era have received information via emails and videos. People easily have access to videos and websites that distribute information. Buddhism should not be exempted from exploiting these processes to educate. With schools all over the world now embracing online courses and trainings, the challenge is on Buddhism schools to start something that will make them accessible online. Many of the Buddhism schools would gain more membership all over the world if they are ready to accommodate more converts now and in the future. This can be done by expanding the scope of the knowledge of gaining enlightenment to help the world in solving the problems caused by materialism, attachment, and lack of mindfulness, which are the major causes of several problems in the world.

Creating a Meditation Space in Your Home

To create a space in your room for meditation, there are no specific rules. However, there are standards to follow which will help you in carrying out a good meditation, and they are:

- **Pick a space that you feel good in.**

- **Make your meditation room clean.**

- **Make the room comfortable.**

- **Provide adequate lighting.**

- **Make it natural.**

- **Make it private and personalized.**

- **Make it have a decent fragrance.**

- **Let it be part of you.**

5 Steps to Start Buddhist Meditation

Meditation is basically based on mindfulness. The best way to do it is to take it simply; follow these steps and tips:

1) **Get a good spot for your meditation.**

2) **Choose a comfortable position.**

3) **Free your mind.**

4) **Sit and observe.**

5) **Practice and end your meditation.**

How to Practice Buddhism

If you want to live a peaceful, happy, and mindful life, you can start practicing Buddhism. If you want to discover yourself through a great awakening and want to be more enlightened in the matters of life and beyond, definitely Buddhism can lead you in the right path to achieving them. Unlike other religions that teach about deities and spiritual laws, Buddhism dwells more on personal transformation and essence. There are different sects of Buddhism, irrespective of this. They have foundational understanding that all the Buddhist sects share which arises from a basic teaching and foundational processes that relate to all the traditional practices.

Some of these fundamental basics are suffering, kindness and openness. To start practicing Buddhism, here are some tips:

To start with, there are four vows which are very great Bodhisattva and which you must keep, viz-a-viz:

- **Working to end the suffering of others:** The teaching of the four noble truths can help in this regard. It reminds us that suffering can come to an end. There is a cause and there is a path to the end of that cause. It teaches the cycle of life which is birth, death, and rebirth, hence working towards helping others.
- **Be a disciple of the Eightfold Path:** Emphasizing on the eightfold path and following the teaching is what makes suffering no longer exist—the end of suffering. All the lessons as to speech, action, livelihood, effort meditation, concentration, thought, understanding, mindfulness, etc., and the five precepts, should be practiced.
- **Avoid Desires and Needs:** Remove your desires from wealth, don't pick interest in materialism.

Craving pleasure for these goes against Buddhism.

- **Continuous Learning:** Learn the Dharma and suffering. Learning is a lifelong journey which should not be limited; it will enable you to widen your enlightenment.

- **Practice Buddhism:** Especially the basics of the Buddhist lifestyle, and understanding the rules behind each teaching, especially that of karma.

- **Meditation:** Practice your meditation on a daily basis to increase your mindfulness. The more you practice, the more enlightened you will become. These are the paths to follow to start practicing your Buddhism. Explore the tradition that has impacted on millions of people around the world. It may take you some time but definitely, it is going to greatly help you become awakened or enlightened.

Practicing Mindfulness Meditation for Stress and

Anxiety Relief

The practice of mindfulness meditation for stress and anxiety relief can be done based on focusing your attention on something which starts from yourself — the mindfulness to get stress relief. This process enables you to pay more attention to objects of sound, and the focal point is that these objects come from within. Doing a focus meditation is possible, and you don't need an instructor. However, it should be a personal experience in a quiet environment. A focus meditation is achievable when you fix your mindfulness on the present without wandering off. The elements involved are the sound, the meditation, the breath. Take your mind off the stress you are going through and be more interested in the self breath and practice. For stress relief, more focused meditation is ideal. This is because your attention is taken away from what is causing the stress and put into utilization by taking your mind off the past and on the present.

The most important thing to note is that this meditation can be practiced at home or anywhere that is quiet. Your office may be good, but if it is noisy, it's not a conducive environment. The idea is to relieve yourself of the stress.

Your meditation can start with 5-minute sessions, and you can later develop it by working your way up until it becomes comfortable. You play with it and exercise with it as well. The idea is to start getting used to it as quickly as possible since stress is often caused by working conditions that we are subjected to in our offices. You have to learn to enjoy the moment of meditation.

Focus on your breath because it is the entry point to any form of meditation and will help you remain focused.

Getting into a comfortable position will enable you to relieve stress. Sitting upright can be good, or you can choose the one that best suits you, using a chair or sitting on the ground, whichever is comfortable. Remember, the idea is to relieve stress. Be in a relaxed mode, and make sure you don't fall asleep. Choose any of the meditation positions earlier described in this book.

- **Target your attention on yourself:** Being mindfully present at the moment is important, so pay attention to the sensations you experience as you breathe in and out of your body.

- **Reduce your inner voice:** Don't listen to the inner voice that tends to analyze the stressful situation you have been through. Meditate on the present and the future, turn your mind to the sensation it provides. The goal is to keep a quiet mind void of interaction with stress.

- **Avoid thinking about Failure:** Nobody is perfect; don't let failures begin to run in your mind. It's understandable that a person may be going through difficulty, but when you start your meditation, avoid the temptation of thinking about your failures. The process is to help you overcome it and not stressing yourself even more with thoughts of failure.

Other factors that will help your meditation, as stated earlier, are timing, shorter sessions of meditation to relieve stress, and meditation practice. By the time you start getting the best of the practice, you will notice a stress relief, having more self-awareness and improved memory. The more you practice, the better your chances of getting the right results.

Buddhism for Children

Buddhism was the exclusive preserve of the adult from the beginning. The teachings were for mature minds, and the demands of the commitments could only be carried out by adults. But as the enlightenment began to spread, the teachings, especially of Dharma, were taught to children. Teachings based on kindness, good deeds, respect, etc. were taught to children so that they would connect to their lives. Most children in the early Indian societies were confined to their homes and doing house core activities before the gradual dharma teachings were taught to them.

The Buddha himself was married and before leaving his royal palace, he had a little son.

Western authors have criticized Buddha for leaving his son Rahula Pali behind to go after seeking enlightenment. But Buddhist authors have said it was justifiable because he went out in pursuit of a higher course, which is enlightenment.

Pali Rahula, Buddha's son, however, later became a disciple of his father at age seven. Buddha taught his son the seeds of his teachings and the truthfulness which he saw in them. Teachings like, in your quest to seek the truth about life, you will have to be truthful to yourself. Some teachings he also gave his son included, using his actions as a mirror before doing anything. That actions should be supported with the fact that the end product will be good and not bad. But if the action is bad and harmful, there was no need to embark on doing such actions. After doing good actions, he still has to question his conscience if what he did actually brought well-being to those affected. That action should always be accompanied by a pleasant result—consequence. It should be well thought out and skillfully made in order to achieve the good result. He also taught his young son that if actions brought good results, then it is deserving to stay mentally informed and refreshed, and be joyful.

Having trainings both in the day and in the night in skillful mental development should be of good quality.

The children in our era can also be led in this path of education to really get deeper into the realities of life, to help in their development in life. Buddha continued to teach his son the realities of taking responsibilities for his own actions, and never to repeat the same mistakes twice. He taught him the path of the noble truths.

The teaching of Buddhism for children is seen to be more successful with societies that are used to a higher level of tradition and spirituality. Societies such as some parts of Asia where the religion of Buddhism seems to have taken root and children are also taught on the tenets of Buddhism.

However, there are challenges in the teaching of Buddhism in the modern era. Especially in the information age where the internet and mobile gadgets, especially mobile phones, pads, and computers, are now taking over the world in terms of education, business, and daily life. There is no day a young person is not surfing the internet.

How can Buddhists successfully help this generation of young people to practice the faith?

Schools can set up volunteer centers where we can start with teachers who are able to impart the knowledge. Then students who can participate in gaining enlightenment can begin to enroll in the school. The authorities will have to create an enabling environment for the successful take off of such noble activity. Seminars, articles, and more awareness have to be created to enable this project to expand and reach other parts of the world.

Most youths who would have trained their minds in the paths of Buddhism have been lured into crime. They have constituted public nuisances and developed habits that are unfit or unethical in the society. If only Buddhism would be exposed to these youths to help develop their minds and take them away from drugs, away from the streets and make them venture into the noble life of Buddhism, the world would become a better place.

CHAPTER 7

CONCLUSION

You have had the opportunity to access a great revelation needed for an individual's transformation, as well as impactful teaching that will transform the lives of many people. The era we are now is the stress era because we are exposed to working conditions that take our time. The office, academic activities in school, the internet and media, computers, laptops, mobile phones and devices are taking more energy out of our bodies. We need to get refreshed naturally to enable the recycling of energy or replacement of lost energy through the Buddhism practice of mindfulness meditation.

We now understand that anxiety and stress are some of the enemies of human beings and there will always be a need to end them. The inevitability of our beginning and ending, especially the teaching on the causation of suffering, the fact about life, the cessation of suffering and the path that leads to its cessation, are well understood. We have to grasp the enlightenment that is unknown to many people in the world today. We get the enlightenment by being exposed to the reality of why Buddhism came into existence. How it all began, and how it has transformed the lives of over four hundred million people around the world. What, hitherto, was knowledge that we knew nothing about, has been revealed through this book. Mere knowledge and information without implementation will be useless if we want to get the reality of practicing Buddhism. Until we start, we will not get results by merely reading for the sake of knowledge without implementing it.

Everything in life has karma, and practicing the Dharma will help us to avoid negative karma that will bring unpalatable consequences, as the teaching implies. We have understood why people suffer, and we know how to mitigate or bring the suffering phenomena to a cessation through the practice of Buddhism. The knowledge we have gained is huge, and I am sure several people who have access to this book will be more than happy to start practicing what is in the contents.

True happiness and transformation via set down practicable principles and precepts are what characterize Buddhism. It is not about the promotion of Buddhism. Rather, it is about the benefits you stand to gain when you get enlightenment through the traditions and teachings of Buddhism. You not only become the Buddha yourself, but you will also be able to impact positively on the lives of people. You will do this by taking them through a path that will lead them to the truth of a hidden knowledge. This will help them to develop mentally and spiritually.

Imagine if we have many more Buddhists in the society, how much better our world would be. Take a look at societies like Japan that have exploited Buddhism to develop great minds who are thinking very effectively. The Japanese lifestyle of Buddhism has even helped the country to gain more advancement than other countries that don't have the Buddhist approach to life. The time to get awakened is now. With your ability to read and digest the contents of this book, and the zeal to see to it that you start practicing it, you will absolutely become transformed and enlightened forever. Congratulations on choosing the path to your great awakening! Good luck!

CPSIA information can be obtained
at www.ICGtesting.com
Printed in the USA
BVHW050137140223
658390BV00012B/365